Surviving the International War Zone

Security Lessons Learned and Stories from Police and Military Peacekeeping Forces

Surviving the International War Zone

Security Lessons Learned and Stories from Police and Military Peacekeeping Forces

Robert R. Rail

CRC Press
Taylor & Francis Group
Boca Raton London New York

CRC Press is an imprint of the
Taylor & Francis Group, an **informa** business

CRC Press
Taylor & Francis Group
6000 Broken Sound Parkway NW, Suite 300
Boca Raton, FL 33487-2742

First issued in paperback 2018

ISBN-13: 978-1-4398-2794-9 (hbk)
ISBN-13: 978-1-138-37434-8 (pbk)

Library of Congress Cataloging-in-Publication Data

Rail, Robert R.
    Surviving the international war zone : security lessons learned and stories from police and military peacekeeping forces / [compiled by] Robert R. Rail.
        p. cm.
    ISBN 978-1-4398-2794-9 (hardcover : alk. paper)
    1. Military history, Modern--20th century--Anecdotes. 2. Military history, Modern--21st century--Anecdotes. 3. Military police--Biography. 4. International police--Biography. 5. Peacekeeping forces--Biography. 6. Military biography. 7. Rail, Robert R. 8. War and society--History--20th century--Anecdotes. 9. War and society--History--21st century--Anecdotes. I. Title.

D862.5.R35 2011
355.009′049--dc22
                                                                        2010033151

Visit the Taylor & Francis Web site at
http://www.taylorandfrancis.com

and the CRC Press Web site at
http://www.crcpress.com

This book is dedicated to all warriors of peace who have shed their blood, their sweat, and their tears on the soil of foreign war zones, who in the historic past fought against each other, and who now unite against injustice and inhumanity to bring peace to the world.

CONTENTS

CONTENTS

CONTENTS

FOREWORD

Mohamed Khafagi, Egypt

After working with the United Nations International Police Task Force (IPTF) as a peacekeeper in foreign war zones, as well as being a regular staff officer to the United Nations, it became clearly apparent to me that a book of this nature would be a great help in our efforts to bring peace to the world. I envision that this book will significantly help all of the wide-ranging public, colleagues, future peacekeepers, and the local war zone people of those countries we all served in. It is a book which relates to the ongoing history of all of our efforts and highlights our ideas, experiences, and wisdoms that we should be guided by in our future assignments. It doesn't matter if the experiences are sad, or if they are funny, as long as we can learn from them!

I urge you to consider and understand the significant initiative of this book, and how important it is for of all of us to consider the values, standards, ethics, and traditions all war zone local people possess, regardless of the poverty or the circumstances and conditions that they survive in. They have taught us all so much by sharing with us the desperate conditions of their lives, and we have learned the valuable lessons of survival from them.

It is true that we all went to our different war zones around the world to help, assist, support, and defend, but we received so many things in return, especially in Kosovo where we worked together with all of the local people, hand in hand, not only monitoring their routines and lives, but sharing with them the conditions that they survived within.

The reason I am asking you to read this book is that some of our colleagues, unfortunately, did not realize all of this. They kept ignoring the local people who were in the war zone, accusing them of being unintelligent or being lazy, while if our countries experienced what they did we may be even worse than they, and to a far greater extent! It is a wise man who can learn from the experiences of others.

INTRODUCTION

I hope you are touched by this book and that a pearl of "foreign war zone wisdom" starts to cultivate within your thoughts and experiences. I also sincerely hope, with no malice or sarcasm intended, that your concepts of justice and fairness are challenged and laid exposed in your own mind and heart. Consider this world of ours to be a banquet table that is filled with incidents and situations. You are invited to taste and compare the fare on this table with what is on your own "table of values and truths"— the things that presently govern your actions and concepts. But beware of the war zone table because it is generously seasoned with the spices of hate, sacrifice, love, revenge, compassion, anger, sorrow, abhorrence, and all the other emotions that comprise the thorny existence needed to survive in a war zone. You will notice that along with the array of pictures that are included in some of the stories, there are international sayings in the final chapter of this book that I had the pleasure of culling from all of our brother and sister officers all over this world. Some of these sayings will be familiar to you and some will be quite new. Simply consider how these sayings relate to both you and your growing war zone experience, and the stories of this book. One way to get the most from this book is to become as one with all the contributing writers. The stories you will be reading in this book have not been filtered or selected; you are the filter! There will be stories that could offend or anger you, and other stories that, hopefully, you will embrace with total passion. It will also become very apparent to you as you proceed from chapter to chapter that not all of the writers agree with each other, even on the same topic. There are topics where I don't agree with them. The most important thing that we all do agree on is the ultimate mission of this book—to bring to you the experiences you need—to learn and understand about the war zone environment to save your life or the life of another.

As you read about the conflicts and situations, try to become part of the incident and continually challenge yourself by considering what you would have done if you were involved in that actual story. What would you do if you were a colleague of the officer who is involved in some situation in a war zone somewhere in this world? Would you intercede in some of these situations or would you find yourself going along with the actions of the other officer in the incidents being revealed? As you proceed from incident to situation, challenge the growing and developing experience base you are culling. Perhaps, just perhaps, you will attain a much different outlook by the end of this book than you had at the beginning. Is life in a war zone what you thought it was going to be?

You will probably notice that I don't feel it's important to focus on the specific time, date, or place of the incidents, or the groups of people who were involved as the victims, or as perpetrators to the many horrendous acts I write about in this book. This book is not structured to be a formal report of any incident, or a condemnation of any one group, but rather a wide and diverse range of war zone topics that hopefully will help to shed light on the question of why so many incidents have taken place and will continue to take place in the future. Time is just a date on a calendar and never as valid as your own perspective and its relevance to any future situation. A lesson learned from what happened yesterday is still as valid as the lessons learned from what happened 3000 years ago.

The citizens of this world are neither all good nor all bad. When we base our perception of any group of people from what has happened in the past, we are condemning all future generations to repeat the horrors of our history again and again. We must embrace the lessons of the past but not hold onto the prejudices that so often linger with them.

I did some things right, I did some things wrong, and I could have done a lot of things a whole lot better if I had known a little bit more about this world of ours. If I would have just had more plain experience than I did at the time of the incident I would have reacted totally different. That is the main reason why I, and my colleagues, have undertaken the task of writing this book you are now holding in your hands. My colleagues and I are the past—you, the reader, and all future "warriors for peace" are the future and the hope for this sorely troubled world we are committed to live in.

I have done some things during my war zone experiences that some people might consider legally wrong but I had to also think about what was morally and ethically right at that moment in time. I hope you are the type of person who cannot only see the difference but also feel the difference deep in the passion of your heart. I have always been influenced by the clear division in my own mind between *malum in se* and *malum prohibitum*. *Malum prohibitum* is the Latin term for the violation of the written laws of regulations, codes of travel and commerce, and other laws imposed to maintain an orderly society. These are the rules we find in the chapters of the legal texts that exists in law libraries, gathering dust on a shelf. *Malum in se* are the violations that infuriate and enrage the heart and soul of mankind. These are the laws against another person. They include murder, rape, the slaughter of the innocent, and other heinous crimes that offend those with empathy for the pain and loss of others. The greatest weight on my heart is now, and has always been, the suffering and pain of *malum in se* crimes on those in desperate need of our help. I can and have overlooked the "code violation" side of this Latin coin but I have never overlooked the "blood- and tear-stained" side of this coin. The most important thing to consider is not what I did or didn't do, but what you would have done in the same situation. When the coin is tossed, which side will demand the absolute adherence of your dedication? We are all challenged not only to learn from the past but also to build on it so we can achieve a better future for all who come after us. If you are the kind of person who has a passion for justice and empathy for the weak and victimized, you will find yourself in good company. You will be with dedicated and self-sacrificing colleagues who laugh with others and sometimes at themselves. You will be with fellow officers who endure hunger while giving their food to another without even thinking about it. You will be with colleagues who shed a tear for others and never shed a tear for themselves. Don't criticize my colleagues and me for what you think have been our failures, and don't honor us for what you think we did right. Whatever we did right was because there was someone in our past who taught us a lesson that we were simply acting on. It was one of so many "pearls of wisdom" that were given to us for safekeeping until it was the right time to pass them on. The experiences of this book, hopefully, will pass along some critical and some humorous lessons that can be used to help you build your thoughts, attitudes, perceptions, and even the actions you commit. I can live with what I have done in my war zone life, and I hope that you will also have peace with what you will do in your life. After all the incidents have transpired and the dust has settled, and we are all back home, that's the time when we become our own greatest critics. The aspersions cast by those who judge via distant hindsight and hearsay are best considered to be the contemptible and meaningless condemnations of those who have neither lost nor given anything of themselves. Simply phrased, it's more important what you think of yourself than what others who were never there and have never experienced anything think of you. We are all only one small stone in the foundation of understanding that we must build together if we are to achieve a structure that can withstand the erosion caused by conflict and war. It is this foundation that will serve as the base for peace throughout the world. Do I believe we will ever achieve peace in this troubled world of ours? No, I don't! But I do believe,

FIGURE I.1   Look close—What do you think about when you see this?

and will till the day I die, that the strong and the just can never cease their quest for peace. This gift is to be given to the weakest by the strongest. We will never stand taller than when we bend down to raise up the weak to stand by our side. The time will come when they will be able to stand tall by themselves. This is a quest worth the ultimate price, willingly spent, or willingly sacrificed in the service for others.

Too often, we keep looking forward to a future we can build on until that time has passed. We find ourselves looking back to what was once the future, but now it's a part of time we can no longer change. Our only choice is to live with the remorse of our "failure to act" on an opportunity that was right there in front of us. Don't hesitate to do the right thing while you can still make a difference in this war zone–riddled world of ours.

ABOUT THE CONTRIBUTING AUTHORS

If something is written in this book, it has been written by a person who has actually experienced being in a war zone. Nothing has been written by anyone who has not walked the ground or tasted the air or sensed the feeling of being in the war zone environment.

ABOUT THE AUTHOR

Bob Rail, Ph.D., has been an International Police Officer for the United Nations Police Task Force in Bosnia and Kosovo, who served as a war zone patrol officer and was later responsible for designing curriculums and instructing the elite police officers from 56 nations who were deployed in Bosnia, Kosovo, Iraq, Jordan, Asia, Africa, and numerous other areas of conflict. He was also named as a physical confrontation advisor and resource training provider to select personnel of NATO (North American Treaty Organization) and OSCE (Organization for Security & Co-Operation in Europe). In Iraq, Dr. Rail was a resident instructor at the Specialized Advanced Training Unit of the High Institute of the Baghdad Police College, and was awarded a second doctorate degree for his exceptional abilities as an international instructor.

Dr. Rail has an outstanding background of over a quarter of a century of both martial arts knowledge and "on the street" law enforcement experience. He is an internationally respected and acclaimed master instructor. Through all his classes, lectures, presentations, and even casual contacts, he displays a constant flow of encouragement, enthusiasm, and instructional humor.

Dr. Rail is a contributor to numerous television and radio programs, and periodicals. He conducts both training and consulting services for universities and corporations worldwide. He is the author of four other books: *The Unspoken Dialogue* (Varro Press, 2001), *Defense without Damage* (Diane Publishing, 1995), *Custodial Cuffing & Restraint* (Varro Press, 2002), and *Reactive Handcuffing Tactics* (Varro Press, 2002).

1

My Life's Lessons

GO FETCH, BOY

The story of the fox and the rabbit was told to me long ago in the hard to remember past, at a time in my life when I just didn't fully appreciate its lesson.

I was just a little kid, wearing hand-me-down clothes from my big brother, who gravitated to and greatly treasured the hard and painful lessons of life that an old black man was willing to share with me. He told me about his existence on the sometimes ugly streets of Chicago. He relished telling one and all that paid him the honor of listening, where his wisdom (and the scars he bought it with) came from. I felt lucky to be in the numbers of those who were allowed the gift of hearing what this old man had to say about everything and anything that crossed his knowledgeable mind. For the price of "go fetch," I earned the admission price to hear another great story from someone in this world who had the time to talk to me. He only had to say "go fetch boy" and I was off like the wind. I would get a bag from somewhere and scrounge up 12 clean, empty, glass soda bottles, and return them to the little corner store down the block for the two pennies each deposit. It was a great little neighborhood store and I loved going there for any reason.

At that time in my life the store was a haven because it was so different from the other places in my life where there was little to attract me or catch my interest. I thought it was a huge and wonderful place. After all, to a little kid like me any store that had soda, candy, bakery, and little toys in small plastic containers was the best place on Earth. From the big happy lady behind the counter, to the squeaking old wooden floors, to the dog that was always sleeping in the doorway sunlight, it was a great place to wander up and down its one aisle with my hard-found deposit money tightly held in my hand. I would walk up and down that one aisle, over and over, consuming everything with my eyes until my interest was totally satisfied. With the returned deposit money I got one soda pop from the case on the floor and one soda from the big noisy cooler with the glass door. Sometimes the lady would charge me two cents more for the bottle that came from the cooler but sometimes she didn't. When you're a little kid these big money transactions mean a lot to you. When I brought back our sodas, the old man would always give me a great big smile with his big old yellow teeth, and then give me one approving nod of his old gray head, as he held the cold glass bottle tightly against his forehead. He would always take a moment to rub the refreshingly cold glass bottle from side to side across his forehead while saying to me, "you did good boy, damn good."

Now, he would say that it was time for another "black pearl of wisdom." That was his slant on his stories and on his life. After what he had endured in all his years of life he had earned the right to say it any way he wanted. "Listen up boy!" he would tell me as I sat on the old, cool, cracked concrete floor with a wide smile on my face. "A fox can run faster than a little fuzzy rabbit. A fox can turn a corner in the blink of your eye, faster than any rabbit made by God could. A fox can run all day and all night without so much as takin' a deep breath. So why does that rabbit usually get away? Are you listening to me boy? Well … why? I'll just have to tell you why because you're still young and dumb to the world and haven't learned much of anything useful in your life yet. The fox is just runnin' for its dinner, but the rabbit is runnin' for its life. That's motivation boy. Remember what I'm saying here! The rabbit is motivated to run or it's gunna be eaten. There's going to be times in your life, boy, when you just have to make yourself motivated or you will lose, or get hurt awful bad."

The older I get the more weight his words carry in both my mind and my heart. After the stories, sometimes, if he wasn't too tired he would show me some of his "super punch" boxing tricks. The talk in the neighborhood was that many years ago he used to be such a good boxer that he actually made money and traveled all over the country fighting other men in warehouses and empty buildings in front of big crowds of people who paid to see him fight. When he would walk the streets where we lived I noticed how all the other men on the street would smile timidly at him and give him a lot of room when passing him on the sidewalk. They made sure he had room as he sat in his chair in the shade in front

2

of his building. I was always a little bit confused and even surprised that young men who were bigger and stronger than he was would still give him such respect. He would show me how to punch with my left hand as hard as I could into the face of my opponent and then quickly punch with my right hand, and if I could, to punch again and again with the better power of the right hand. He called this his special one-two punching.

Many of my afternoons passed by quickly between "go fetch," great stories, and the super punch one-two training. One day I came by the building to surprise the old man because I already did the "go fetch," but this time both bottles of soda pop were cold from the cooler at the corner store, and I was going to trick him into asking to choose which hand had the cold soda in it. This was going to be the day I tricked him and tricked him good. He thinks he's going to be ready for me today, but I was going to be ready as a rabbit for him instead. When I got to his room down the hallway there were two men moving out what little furniture he had. As I stood in the doorway I became as cold as the sodas in my hands. One of the men said, "If you're looking for the guy who lived here, kid … I'm sorry, he's dead."

I don't know how long I stood there. Perhaps if I just closed my eyes and pretended that I never heard those words it would all change back to the way it should be with just him and me. But no, I was alone again in a terrible way. I just left the sodas on the old wooden table that was left in the corner of his room. I was hot and sweating, but I didn't feel thirsty anymore. I walked away and kept walking aimlessly for most of that day. My heart was torn, it hurt, and I cried for him and I cried for myself and what I had lost; but that's alright because that's the way little kids think, and I was just a little kid who hadn't grown up yet. I was always just called "boy" and will always deeply regret never knowing his name, but I will always remember his wide smile and the time that we had together, just him and me.

For a brief time I had some success climbing through the ropes by myself and getting into the ring to fight in the amateur boxing world. I can remember how I felt using my skill and aggressive power to "deck" someone who was foolish enough to get into the ring and go against me. I was only a welterweight but I had the huge power advantage against most of my opponents because my upper arms were bigger around than my neck. I could hit really hard so I focused most of my efforts on hitting my opponents and not enough time developing my abilities to not get hit.

Before long I found myself winning fights and moving up in the skill and caliber of who I was fighting. Now my fights were getting much harder to win because my opponents were getting better and the mistakes I was making were resulting in my being "paid back" by getting hit back. I found out that I was actually doing the "one-three super punch" but now I was getting hit with the "two." I was having the unfortunate experience of sitting on my ass in the middle of the ring and looking up at the referee. The worst part of all of this was that getting hit didn't hurt at all. You know that when it doesn't hurt anymore you are really hurt bad. Pain is the warning sensation your body sends to your brain to make you stop doing something. When you stop getting that signal you've gone way too far over the edge. I realized then that what I had been doing to my past opponents was now being done to me. This turnabout was a very sobering and undeniable shot of reality in my young life. This was neither a good nor desirable circumstance. After a couple times of experiencing this novel situation I decided that it was time for me to get motivated "like a little rabbit" and seek out a new future career path.

My life would now go on with the wisdom of the "scars of experience" from a friend that will never be forgotten, lighting my way through many dark moments in a very uncertain future. As the years passed and I served in one war zone after another, I realized that the lesson to be learned is that if you are not motivated to survive you better play rabbit and get motivated!

Every war zone has a name for it. Some call it the red zone. Some call it by code names or sectors, or even by grid reference numbers on a map. No matter how they refer to it, you're walking in harm's way. Once you have gotten into it, you will always remember that the way you look at the world will never be the same again. I remember saying to my old police partners back in the states after happily returning from my first war zone that it's not where you are, but what happens while you're there. You can never fully understand or be able to anticipate your surroundings but you can understand yourself and anticipate your reactions. Be honest with yourself and know your limitations. Plan on how you can work to strengthen them. There are times when you will be in a quiet area, where things are peaceful and calm, and all of a sudden all hell breaks loose around you. The strange thing is that there are times when most of the world will never hear about where you've been or what you've been doing because nobody cares about that small piece of land on the map except you and your partners. There are other times when you cruise through your tour of duty mostly unscathed and when you get back to your own country everyone wants to know what was going on because of all the media reports. News was being made about where you were, pumping up the conflict and putting their own usual twisted spin on what they wanted the rest of the world to think really happened. There were times when you could attribute more of the stories we heard back here at home to it being a slow news day, than it being about the actual truth of what had happened or what action you knew had been taken.

I remember tiredly trudging through the moonless predawn streets of one war zone and suddenly hearing a whizzing sound going past my head—then a pinging sound and something bouncing off the vehicles and the stones under my boots. Getting shot at is not like on the television or in the movies. There it's all drama, special effects, flashing lights, and other strange sounds. Getting motivated and reacting to the attack was an immediate and unconscious response. Returning fire was a training-instilled reaction that fortunately required little to no thought on my part. It was not a conscious choice for me and the other officers to engage the ones who were shooting at us. It was the natural reaction we had to survive and defend the lives of our partners, like we all had been trained to do. You react because there is no time to think about your response to what the hell is going on around you—or at you! And there is no time for you to pause to think about what you have to do.

Between fate and circumstance, and a dimly lit doorway with armed combatants, there was no time or alternatives left. Before I could back off the trigger I had fired off almost an entire magazine of my weapon's ammunition. You can never acquire "enough" conflict experience in your life so these experiences are all crucial trainers. The challenge was surviving long enough to learn the lessons that went with this combative situation. Good training and just plain luck prevailed, and we just mindlessly and automatically fell into the "cover and reload" mode. I had to reload and maintain my ammo magazines as soon as I could because I didn't know if the next street I would walk on would be worse than the last one. Your ammo magazines are a treasured burden; they are your best insurance and lifeline in uncertain surroundings. I fired off too many rounds from my weapon's magazine because I was just so damn charged up—my heart was pounding louder in my head than the sound of the rounds discharging from my weapon.

The ensuing stench from the smoke of burning cars, bodies, warm flesh, and feces that are the aftermath of conflict will be etched in my thoughts forever. I vaguely remember briefly lying down, scrunched under a vehicle for cover and reloading. It wasn't the best spot to pick, but it was cover and safe for the instant it took to load magazines and gather back my train of thought. I often wonder why some memories are so strong while others only come to mind when other thoughts, smells, and sights trigger their remembrance. I just lay there, tucked up with a partner, under the vehicle for a "cover and reload" moment, with a slippery wet ammo magazine. My eyes were wide open as I strained to hear the distant crack of weapons' fire. It didn't sound as close to us so that was a relief.

No paperwork, no report number, no forms to be filled out making sure that all the little boxes were filled in and all the spelling was correct with copies going through all the proper chain of command. Out here it's just magazines in and magazines out, and move on. That's all there was to the incident for now—and later, just random thoughts about little things that remind you from time to time about what took just seconds to occur but will stay with you forever. I couldn't shake the thought that there had to be more to it all, some sort of aftermath to what just happened. But why should there be anything? It was done and it was over. Sometimes you reflect back in your thoughts and think, why me? Why here? Why now? And then you remember, "It is not where you are, but what happens to you while you are there."

As the light of day grew brighter I saw why my ammo magazines were wet and slippery to my touch. They were covered with my blood because my hands were so desensitized by the endorphin rush caused by the conflict that I didn't even feel my broken fingernails or any of the cuts on my hands. The fingertips on my right hand were all cut up from reloading my ammo magazines. We were all quiet as we gathered our thoughts and realized we came through it alright. Needless to say I felt the elbow and knee scrapes later. The side of my head started to hurt and I remembered hitting the bottom of the vehicle when I cleverly tried to stand up under it; but at the time your mind and body switch gears and you just aren't in a mental state to try to think. We were remarkably "motivated" and weren't thinking about the little details that didn't matter at the time.

I think about the lesson of the candle and the flame. When you tell some people that the flame will burn them they still fall victim to their own compulsion and put their hand in the flame. They need to learn by their own experience just what it feels like. Others can learn from the experiences of others and avoid the pain of the candle's flame. I know in my heart that I was spared the pain of many candle flames in my life, and for that I am grateful—for each and every "pearl of wisdom" I was given even when it was a time in my life when I couldn't appreciate what I was given and how well it would serve me my entire life.

Whenever I am back in my country and I'm being thanked for serving in some war zone, I reflect on the sacrifices of the men and women of our nation, now serving, and those who served in our fading memories. I recall Vietnam and the lack of respect and outright animosity toward the soldiers from much of the public and the media as they returned, despite the fact that it was our government and the political elite that chose to send them. I can't imagine the mental anguish and emotional pain they endured being subjected to such scathing and unjust scrutiny.

The fact is that they, as well as our current rank and file deployed throughout the world, responded to a call of duty to serve and protect our country and country's interests in adverse and sometimes unimaginable circumstances. We, as a nation of people, in turn have the responsibility to respectfully listen to them. It is the least we can do for the time and service they have rendered to us. Personally, it is always an honor for me to meet them and learn from some of their experiences and pearls of wisdom they have kindly offered me.

FILLING THE CUP

It was a great day for me, or at least I thought it was. I had fought in a small, local martial arts tournament and won my novice match quite decisively—at least that was my perception of "my outstanding performance" that afternoon. I was going through the classic "winner's syndrome" with all the symptomatic side effects of talking constantly and only about my fantastic techniques. I was talking a bit too loud, talking to everyone, even those who didn't know me, and talking to those who could not have cared less. I soon found myself talking more and more about less and less until I had ranted without taking a breath, about everything that amounted to nothing.

My instructor at that time was a slight but nimble Japanese man with an attitude that never changed. Any time you encountered him he had the appearance of total boredom. He would frequently say that nature made man and whiskey, and that one could not exist without the other. There were times when he would be on the training mat, teaching us something, and he would simply stop the training. He would start muttering something in Japanese while shaking his head in disbelief at all the mistakes we were repeatedly making in our training. He would then go into his office where the salvation of his frustration was a bottle in the bottom drawer of his desk. We all quietly knew about the bottle but never said anything.

On this particular day after the novice tournament my instructor decided to save the ears of all the rest of the students in the training hall and told me that we were going across the street to have a cup of tea. When I tried to explain to him that I didn't drink tea he put his hands over his ears and said, "Quiet your mouth and come with me, not invitation, order." I obediently tagged along behind him as we walked across the street with me yapping like a puppy all the way. As we entered the ornate Chinese restaurant my martial arts mentor said to me and anyone else within hearing range, "Chinese tea fair, but Japanese food better," and then he sat down and ordered a pot of dark tea and two cups. The pot of steaming hot tea with lemon slices arrived at our table and my mentor asked, "What you learn from tournament match young man?" I was elated that he would ask me anything and now I had the opportunity to talk about my favorite subject—me! I started rambling off without even taking a breath about how I was fighting my adversary with all sorts of different techniques because of his size and style, not even realizing that my instructor was trying to add his comments. I went on and on, not even slowing down about how I was countering my opponent and all the while my teacher was trying to counter my incessant comments without success. It was then I learned a simple lesson I would carry with me for the rest of my life.

My frustrated mentor picked up the pot of hot tea and filled his cup. He then proceeded to slowly fill my cup to overflowing, and then to my shock and amazement he continued to casually pour the tea, quite deliberately emptying the entire pot all over the table and all over me. For the first time in literally hours I found myself speechless. The words he then spoke were concise and needed no explanation. "The little cup is like your little brain. It is so full that there is no room for the tea of my words to be held in your cup. If you wish to learn anything you must first empty your cup."

When I was deployed to my first war zone, I went there with "an empty cup" and several very heavy equipment bags. I realized how important it was to immediately start a routine where you utilize what is available around you in that particular war zone to develop good habits for your mind and body. You must fill your cup with good habits right away before you find other situations or persons filling your cup for you with all the bad habits they have that will literally tear you down day by day both mentally and physically. I remember many unfortunate individuals who were actually examples of what not to become. They never knew how closely they were being watched in their day-to-day war zone lifestyle. There was one very likeable gentleman whom we all knew and cared about who got involved in a drinking contest with the locals to see how much *rakya* (local distilled whisky) he could consume at one time. We all just looked at each other with the same sad expression and shook our heads when we learned he had died of alcohol poisoning after consuming 16 shots of *rakya* whisky, drinking one shot after another. Many inexperienced officers would come to the conclusion that they had experienced enough of the war zone and would face whatever consequences necessary to get the hell out of the war zone they were in, even if it meant harming themselves or destroying a reputation they had worked so hard to achieve.

If you're really lucky you will have access to a gym or some other training facility where you can work out. It will have a full array of equipment such as treadmills and weights and perhaps even some gaming areas at your disposal. That's if you're lucky. If you're not as lucky then it's up to you to make yourself lucky by improvising what's around you so you can keep exercising both your mind and body. I remember tying water bottles on a broom stick and using that piece of high-tech equipment for most of my strength training. As time passed I was able to get in some great workouts even though the sight of me and the water bottles was probably quite strange to anyone who saw it. Running can be very difficult for

Figure 1.1 Any place to train is a great place to train.

9

those who like to get out and do roadwork. Most of the deployments do not have a treadmill, and that quickly limits your "safe" choices. Running on ground that was once covered with land mines, even if it's cleared and supposedly safe, is still a bad choice in my book. You could still get blown up because you found the one land mine some mine clearer missed. I have a huge respect for the mine-clearing units but no one is perfect and it's just not worth the risk when you can jump rope with a cable, or do jumping jacks, or deep knee bends, and not have the shadow of losing your leg looming over you. If you do have an outside area that's safe for running make sure you run at a time of day that is the best for your body. An example of this would be running or training in Iraq in the morning before the temperature gets over 100 degrees (or more)! You will learn to love those cool desert mornings.

One of the other things to always consider is the surrounding danger threat from the enemy and the security forces that are there to keep you safe. Make sure you are properly dressed and that the posted guards know who you are and what you are doing so there is no chance of an accidental shooting or even a "stop and challenge" situation happening to you. Also,

Figure 1.2 There is nothing better than a cool morning workout.

you always need to constantly be aware of how much liquid you're consuming. Drink, drink, drink! If you don't hydrate yourself you'll end up waking up in a medical station with a needle in your arm. Remember that dehydration can and will take your life and the life of your partners.

Make it a part of your routine to attend any and all services, meetings, and any other social events that are offered to you; it really helps to keep the good attitude going strong in your mind. Spending time by yourself like a monk is understandable if you are a monk but not if you're a deployed officer in a war zone where you need the interaction of others to help you adjust to the conditions around you. One of the constructive things you can take home from a war zone deployment is the skill of understanding and speaking another language. This isn't just great for the mind exercise. It could also prove useful in saving your life in a combative situation. If problem locals aren't aware of your skill, no matter how limited it may be, it can very helpful in figuring out what trouble they are contemplating. Simply keep a note pad on you all the time and write down one word a day. Don't worry about proper spelling or grammar. Start by writing everything phonetically and then read the entire growing list to yourself once every night. You'll be utterly amazed at how much you can learn in a very short amount of time. Others around you will look on in shock as you grow in your communication skills with the locals and even with your colleagues from other countries.

Keeping the lines of communication open back home is also very critical to maintaining stable mental health. It really helps to have a consistent touch base with loved ones so your existence in the war zone environment doesn't become overwhelming or misunderstood. High stress situations are sure to reach out and touch you now and again and having a solid base at home helps stabilize things. It also helps make your deployment time pass by a lot faster when you are regularly e-mailing and or telephoning family and friends back home. Remember, let your friends and family help you by sending you some of the comfort foods and other good stuff you can't get in the military PX store. They really want to help you and be involved with you in some way. It makes them feel better about you being in a war zone, too. They want to help you, so let them, and share some of your thoughts and thanks with them, but be careful not to give out sensitive mission information or scare the hell out of them with any of the nasty circumstances you're getting into from time to time. Last but never the least on this list is to make plans with your loved ones back home about all the things you plan on doing when you get back into their hugs.

11

Figure 1.3 Train like your life depends on it because it does.

Keep your mind focused on home, because you *are* going to be heading for home with great experiences and lessons learned sooner than you think.

Look for a balance in all the off-duty activities you become involved in. You need to have good consistent workouts but you don't want to push yourself to such an extreme that you're either incurring injuries or you start to shy away from your training program because it has become too difficult to perform on a regular basis. Don't become involved in your mental or physical training or even your social activities to the point where they become a compulsion or an addictive alternative to the stress surrounding you. You need to have time in your day to simply sit on your butt and do absolutely nothing. See a movie or listen to some music you like—whatever it takes for you to relax and let your mind and body recuperate. Things aren't going to be perfect and you will have to change your training and other forms of recreation repeatedly. It's important to remember that the key to doing well in a war zone is to remain flexible and not to become too personally involved in your own life. Take all the negative things you can think of, including some of the low-life jerks that make themselves and everyone around them miserable, and put them in a tightly sealed, psychological box. Then with all of these negative emotional feelings being separated from you, just think outside of the box, … or stuff the box, … or wrap the box, … or mail the damn box back home, but whatever you choose to do, don't just sit there enduring all the frustration and anger that can accumulate inside you in a war zone environment. Don't just sit there thinking about the imaginary box and doing nothing. The very best thing you can do is to get rid of the box, and have a nice cup that is filled to the brim with "good habits." You can have a cup alone or even have a cup with a friend but the main thing to remember is that when your cup is full there will be little room for all the other negative things that can be poured into your cup from the teapot of the war zone you're surviving.

2

Adapting to the War Zone Environment

You can and will become conditioned to even the most severe circumstances and surroundings when you live in that environment for any extended period of time. It is human nature to adapt through any physical and mental adjustment needed to be able to "live to tell the tale."

I think back to one of those Iraqi days where it was so damn hot you had to measure the temperature on a meat thermometer. That's not just a cute little play on words. It was literally so hot that the only way to accurately measure the outside temperature was to get your hands on a thermometer that could withstand the heat of an oven. There were a couple of places on the FOB (forward observation base) where I was stationed where some misguided person had put up a regular thermometer near a door or window. The sight was the same with every regular thermometer we saw that was exposed to the Middle East sun. The little bulb that's in the thermometer that contained the indicator liquid would burst and the red liquid would run down the wall where the thermometer was hung, leaving a permanent red stain to remind one and all of just how hot it gets in that part of the world. Long after the thermometer was replaced the red stain would be there. It kind of played on our minds every time we saw those stains running down the wall. It was a constant reminder of the heat that was ever present. You just couldn't get that out of your mind or forget it for even one second. It reminded me of an old Western movie scene where a desperate stranded cowboy is staggering through the desert sand in search of water and stumbles across the skull of a steer that's been bleached snow white by the blazing sun and he just collapses in a state of total breakdown looking at the skull. Whether we wanted to admit it or not, the red stain that was running down the walls was our skull in the desert, and the reminder was ever present to all who stumbled across it.

It was the state of affairs that you had to walk wherever you wanted to go. Very few of us were fortunate enough to have a set of keys to any type of vehicle to be able to drive to where we needed to be. If you were going to be walking to where you had to be then there were a couple of extremely critical things you needed to do before you started your little trek. Whether it was a short walk to the mess hall or a long trek across the sand and dust to a building across the compound, it was best to think of the precautions needed in this extreme heat in terms of the inside and the outside of your body. As far as the inside of your body is concerned, the key word is hydrate! I know you've been told all the proper things to drink when you're in a roasting environment and the wind in your face feels like a blow dryer set on high, but let me add this to the list—liquids! Anything liquid was the motto I lived by and survived by. Never turn down anything to drink just because you're not thirsty. This is a preemptive effort at hydrating your body so you don't collapse literally a few minutes later under the blistering white hot sun that can and does kill those who don't take heed to the rules nature imposes. I will say this now and I will probably say it later but it bears repeating: There is no such thing as "toughing it out" in extreme heat. It's a very simple formula that you must remember at all times. If you want to function in a desert environment you have to consume enough liquid to keep a balance in your system so the blood that flows through your veins will be able to continue to do so. If you're foolish enough to fight nature you will always lose. I have had the occasion to see more than one officer a hell of a lot tougher than me lying face down in the dust, delirious out of their minds, carrying on a conversation with a nearby disinterested tree. And if you are fortunate enough to have the opportunity to do your cardio workout indoors on a treadmill instead of outdoors, running to show everyone how tough you are, please take the indoor option. The people who will have to carry you over to the medical unit after you collapse in the dust will also thank you. You can tell the senior officers who have been in this scorching shadeless setting by their pockets. There will always be a water bottle in them, and usually more than one. Remember, water means life and no water in your pocket means you're making a very big mistake in judgment. No walk out in the sun is so short that a water bottle in your back pocket is not a good idea (or even a self-imposed requirement). Either you carry a water bottle around with you in your back pocket or someone else is going to be carrying you around later. It doesn't matter how strong or how tough you are—no water, no life. That's why they call it a desert. The desert doesn't forgive or waive the rules. It simply punishes all who fail to be prepared with incredible heat, making it impossible to endure its daily wrath.

It's always best to consider the demeanor of a celebrity of the desert to know how to survive in that world, and that celebrity is our associate the camel. You don't see a camel wearing jogging shorts while running laps around a track, and sipping from a water bottle. If you do then you have other problems that have little to do with what we're discussing here. The lesson to be learned from our friend the camel is that of conservation, the conservation of effort and the conservation of water and energy. Except for the bad breath, be like a camel. Move slowly and with deliberate and calculated effort. Don't expend effort on unnecessary tasks that could be done at night or indoors, or in the shade, if you can find some shade.

Figure 2.1 No matter if you are in the sun or the shade, you must drink constantly!

17

Figure 2.2 Take water with you everywhere.

Now might be the time for some gross but extremely critical information for you to remember. On a constant basis, and when I say "constant" that is exactly what I mean, you will need to monitor your water consumption—morning, noon, and night. When you are living in a blast furnace environment, pay close attention to the color of your urine. This advice is the advantage I had being married to someone with a medical background. Ideally, your urine should be almost clear and light in color. If your urine is dark that means you're running low on water in your system and desperately need to hydrate. That means NOW! If you don't start playing chug-a-lug with a water bottle immediately you will find yourself in a situation where the next choice won't be yours. The next decision will be made by a medical unit when they decide how many intravenous lines they need to run into your semiconscious body to stop your major organs from shutting down before you die. Yes, it is that serious. And it's not just the color of your urine but also the amount that your body is putting out. Let me explain it to you this way: You consume liquids, hopefully in large amounts, and the result is that you then discharge the liquids through your digestive system minus the sweat your body discharges in its effort to help keep you cool via the evaporation process. Remember—when you don't get enough water into your system your major organs can literally shut down from lack of fluid. Your body will be unable to sweat to perform any cool-down function of evaporation on your skin. If you ever notice blood in your urine, that becomes a totally different matter to contend with. Either you have just been too close to a bomb blast and sustained concussion damage to your internal organs or you have some other problem that needs immediate attention from the medical unit. This isn't a situation you can afford to put off until another day. It should be attended to as soon as possible. When I say as soon as possible that does mean now! I remember a couple of real nasty days when I loaded up like a dam ready to burst at morning breakfast at the chow hall. I had downed several cups of my favorite food group—coffee—and then proceeded to consume large amounts of orange juice and water, followed by a Gatorade®. I put one more Gatorade in my back pocket as I walked out of the chow hall and I was ready to start my day. I literally sloshed as I waddled out of the building when I trudged off to teach my police training class that was about a kilometer away. The absolutely amazing thing was that I didn't have to urinate until later that afternoon. My body literally sweated out almost all of the liquid I had consumed that morning. It was so hot on some of the days that I didn't even realize how much I was sweating because the sweat would instantly evaporate off of my body. When it's that incredibly hot and the humidity is extremely low, your sweat will evaporate before you even notice the condition of your clothing being wet.

I'm always asked how the locals have done so well adjusting to the severe conditions of the heat and climate they've been born into. The answer is simple. Unfortunately, they haven't and they suffer like everyone else. There is a limit to how much anyone can do whether you're a local or a stranger to adjust to this oppressive climate. They do suffer less than we do because they have learned to adapt their lifestyle to the harsh conditions of their home territory. The lesson to be learned here is to observe and copy the behavior and lifestyles of the locals you find yourself surrounded by wherever you are deployed or sent.

As far as the outside of your body is concerned, what you choose to put on it is what shields and insulates the inside of your body from the effects of the sun. Just as you wear combative body armor as protection from bullets and shrapnel, you must also wear the appropriate clothing to protect you from the sun and the heat. Start thinking about total exterior body protection that can and will save your life if you are ever left incapacitated by an accident or attack. There is a reason and a purpose all the Middle Eastern and North African people wear white, loose-fitting clothing from head to toe. It's not just for the cameramen and the movies, it's for their survival. Always remember to copy the locals in every way you can. They've learned the necessary lessons through time and the pain of failure so you don't have to. Dress in the lightest colors and also the thinnest, most breathable fabrics you can get your hands on. Hats are not—I repeat, are not—an optional item of clothing. They are not worn as a fashion statement. If you think for one minute that you can skip wearing a hat under the white hot, roasting, blistering sun of the Middle East or North Africa, you are sadly mistaken and will soon find yourself suffering—sunstroke at the very least and at the worst you can die. A couple of times we showed the new people the little trick to teach them how brutal the sun can be. We soaked down all of their cotton cloth hats and walked off to the chow hall. By the time we made our short walk across the compound to the chow hall door, their hats were totally dry. Another major rule is to respect the brightness of the brilliant white hot sun. Even if you are wearing a pair of good quality sunglasses from the military PX, don't look directly at the sun. The result may not be as severe as looking on the face of the Greek god Medusa and being turned into stone, but you can be blinded or suffer severe sight damage and that's bad enough. What is most important is that it is preventable with just a little bit of good judgment. The sun appears to be white for a reason. The air is clear and the humidity is extremely low. The brightness of the sun is beyond radiant and extremely penetrating and strong. It can and will cause damage to your vision. There has been more than one officer who has come in from the outside sunlight and has experienced temporary sun blindness. Wear the best projectile-proof sunglasses you can obtain from the military PX. Your eyesight is well worth any investment you can make.

On those occasions where you have the opportunity to drive or ride in a vehicle you may want to think about walking if you only have a short and safe distance to go. Remember, if the vehicle was parked out in the sun for any period of time it may have all of the similarities of a preheated kitchen oven. When the outside temperature is anywhere from 120 degrees to 130 degrees or even greater, the inside temperature of the vehicle you are considering riding in is just about perfect for baking a nice batch of biscuits. Or perhaps you would rather enjoy having a grilled steak or burger off the hood of the vehicle, with a side order of sun-fried eggs and bacon. As humorous as all of this may sound, the reality is there has been more than one officer severely burned getting into a vehicle parked outside in the sun in that part of the world. If you are going to be riding in a vehicle, open the doors and let it air out with that nice cool air of the 120s or 130s. If you just jump in and go for a ride you may have more in common with a baked ham than you ever dreamed or wanted to. Another important thing to consider is how practical it would be taking a brief ride somewhere just to escape from the sun and get some much wanted relief from the dusty streets and paths. In most cases, the air conditioning is not going to even start to cool down the vehicle's interior until you arrive at your destination. In the case of driving a "thick skin" or armored vehicle, it will take quite a few very uncomfortable minutes to cool down. And remember, the thick-skin vehicles do not have the ability to allow the windows to roll down or open. The only method of ventilation is by opening the doors. That's the price to be paid for the safety these vehicles provide. With all the steel plates welded into the doors and the body frame and extra thick bulletproof glass in all the windows, the option of cooling down from any outside breeze is severely limited, if not impossible. Also, consider the color of the vehicle. If all things are equal and you do have a choice in traveling in a dark-colored vehicle as opposed to traveling in a light-colored vehicle, it is always a better idea to choose the lighter-colored vehicle. This is because the lighter-colored vehicle will stay much cooler by virtue of retaining less of the sun's heat. Also, a dark vehicle stands out more as a target, whereas a light-colored vehicle tends to blend in with the surrounding ground cover much better. Relentlessly keep a frame of mind that allows you to take advantage of every little thing that makes your mission safer, easier, and more comfortable.

One afternoon my stomach was telling me it was hungry so I had very little choice in the matter but to tolerate the heat and trudge over to the chow hall to fill up my growling friend. Sitting down with a tray of hot food at a table across from a very young Army ranger, I was greeted by the young ranger with a brief and respectful "Sir." I am always amazed at how the older I get the younger these outstanding representatives of our country appear to be. I replied with the customary "Where you from?" We quickly finished our polite verbal exchange and then settled down to do what we were both there to do in the first place—eat hot food. It was always strange to me how it could be as hot as a blast furnace outside and we all still looked forward to the hot food that was prepared in the assembly line of the chow hall. Perhaps it was because the only alternative to eating at the chow hall was consuming an MRE (meal ready to eat). MREs were the several courses of "food" that were in the "indestructible" brown plastic pouches. If a chow hall was nonexistent or shut down or if you were away on a tour of duty, many times it was the only safe alternative you had to going hungry. The first few times I had the pleasure of "dining" on an MRE while I was in other war zones around the world, it was a novelty to carefully cut open a plastic bag with your knife and then squeeze your main course out of a plastic tube. It was kind of a neat, toy-like experience but that wears quite thin quite fast. You can easily spot the veteran officers as they "gut open" the bag and grab the cookie and other important stuff out of the container and offer the rest of the contents to one of the new people.

While we were all sitting at the table, engaged in our favorite pastime of eating, we came under a brief rocket attack—a common flyover interruption. I should explain a little so you have some background on the different sounds you're exposed to and get used to hearing and reacting to. Weapons-fired bullets are like a bumble bee going by you and then pinging or cracking off of whatever is around you. Mortars make a flipping sound with their fins as they fly spinning through the air. The rockets however are as loud as hell and if they are close by, you can literally feel the vibration they cause. It's like feeling the shockwave of a nearby bomb blast as it passes through you. My reaction to the sound of the rocket going over our chow hall was a slight pause in my eating and watching my industrial-strength Jell-O® shake on my plate. Of great interest to me was the overall demeanor of that very young ranger sitting across from me. He was operating under a rhythmic cadence of fork to mouth, without hesitation or interruption from the "annoyance" of the rocket flying over the chow hall. I knew his concentration wasn't because the spaghetti tasted so great. After all, it wasn't old neighborhood, Chicago-style spaghetti so it had to be something inside of him. It was apparent to me from his bearing that he was as fit as an individual warrior could be. He was battle ready and prepared to meet any challenges that confronted him. As we neared the end of our eating with our food trays now considerably lighter, the casual conversation resumed. It turned out that this very young ranger had been serving in this war zone for over eight months and had no intention of going home to South Carolina or the next deployment "until this job's done." He was a clear and excellent example of adapting to the war zone environment, both psychologically and physically. This young man was easy to respect, and it was comforting to know that there were so many other outstanding men and women who were also such exceptional examples of discipline and dedication. It is always comforting to know these people serve our country now, as they have done in the past, and hopefully will be there to do so in the future.

When we could put together a day off with a morning cell phone call home to our loved ones on the rare occasion when we could get through, that made the entire world seem to be a lot better place in our eyes. We would then relax by sitting around in the cool morning air of less than 90 degrees, talking about what we would be doing if we were smart enough to have stayed home. These were great times and they gave us all a chance to verbally blow off some steam and to complain about whatever we could never change anyway. It was during some of these semicool mornings that the new people arrived and we did what we could to help them adjust to the conditions we had to contend with while living there. The new arrivals spanned the spectrum from the long-term, those serving over a year; to those who arrived for the short-term operations of just a couple of weeks or so. They were mixed in their experience levels, some being veterans of other war zones or conflicts and others being away from home for the first time.

I will always remember one new instructor who got deployed to our FOB from one of our government agencies back stateside. He was there for a short-term mission to work with and train the local police. As he strutted up to several of us sitting in a circle, enjoying the cool morning, I had a feeling this was no longer going to be one of our kickback, relaxed mornings. He unfortunately stood out like he was new and that was not a good way to start off in a place like this. When you want to fit into any group of people it's just common sense and good manners to move into the group slowly, easily, and quietly. But obviously that was just not this person's manner. He was noticeably a trendsetter, and unfortunately I mean that in a bad way for him. In a loud and interrupting voice he exclaimed, "Hot enough for you?" Out of the seven of us sitting there in a circle slowly drinking coffee and water, there were seven of us who just looked down at the dusty ground and shook our heads at this awfully lame and brainless remark. This was the perfect example of how not to ease into a group. A proper way of working into any group under those conditions and environment would have been to simply say "good morning," introduce yourself (by name only, not rank or title), wish everyone well, and then shut up and sit there and wait for a little polite ribbing. The show was not over by any means, and we all knew it because we had seen it so many times before. The more insecure or anxious some people are, the more they try to make up for their "self-perceived" shortcomings by covering themselves with all of the macho weapons' crap and assorted toys they can carry or hang on their body. Along with being dressed like a walking tank, they then engage in blowing a verbal smoke screen out of their mouth to cloud the main issue of just who they really are and what they really know, and where their experience comes from. This government agent needed to understand that there were no Rambos here—just a lot of great regular people with diverse talents doing the best job they could in a very difficult place. Our uninvited guest waddled over to an available chair and with obvious effort wiggled and wedged his overequipped carcass into the seat. When I say overequipped I mean that he looked like he was selling "war zone warehouse" inventory door to door. We were all sitting around in our shorts and T-shirts while our guest was decked out in his full body armor, combat boots with attached knife on one boot and a handgun on the other boot, and a waist belt that had everything on it, from another pistol to knives and special lighting to an extensive array of clips and ammo. The only things he was lacking on his equipment array were a roll of laser-guided toilet paper and a Superman decoder ring. One of my colleagues sitting in our circle asked him if he had any spare foot warmers, but he was so busy talking about himself that he didn't even hear the remark that the rest of us were chuckling about. He then decided to inform all within range of his loud obnoxious voice of his worldwide experience and extensive special operations credentials. It was rather difficult for us to continue our own conversations with each other because of the distraction of his loud voice proudly ranting away in the background. He was boasting about his stateside experience and all the special missions he had engaged in while stationed in South America and also his excellent ability to speak Spanish. He was never aware of the looks he got when he made that statement. One of the people sitting there in the circle made a crude comment about how great it would be to have him speak Spanish to the local Arabic speakers. His voice, however, did become a little quieter when he abruptly realized that no one sitting there that morning was listening to him. It was an interesting moment when one of our colleagues tried to talk to our unwelcomed guest about a very common special operations technical issue. The only response from our guest was a blank stare. He had no idea in hell what the proper technical answer to the comment was. Neither did I, but the difference between our guest and myself was that I never pretended to know anything about the topic. I know what I know and also know enough to know what I don't know. Like the old saying goes, his mouth wrote a check that he didn't have the ability to cash. What I have long believed and tell others is that you never get a second chance to make a first impression. In the case of our morning friend he was now labeled, marked, and graded for the rest of his time in the mission. Butting into a circle that contained that much experience and hyping yourself up was not the smartest thing for anyone to do. It's okay to be a legend in your own mind if all you do is talk to yourself. If this person was trying to make an impression on one and all that morning he did achieve his goal but he really finalized his image with us later that day when we had a rocket flyover.

Because of our location it was not at all uncommon to have rockets flying overhead at the FOB. If the rockets were low or when they got closer to our position they became louder. We would pause our conversation until we could hear each other again and then resume talking. That, however, wasn't the reaction of our combat-hardened, highly experienced, Spanish-speaking veteran guest. All of our mouths dropped open in total surprise when we watched our uninvited visitor react to the threatening roar of the rocket flying over our position. His startled response was to hurl his water bottle up in the air, scramble out of his overturned chair, leap the three steps to the safety of the nearby building doorway in one stride, and then literally tear the door knob to the entry door off the door as he frantically charged out of the building. Just for the record, in a past first mission I do remember launching a cup of coffee about a meter into the air when a nearby armored personnel carrier set off a huge nasty land mine close to my location. After I made a self-disparaging comment about still having clean underwear, we all had a good laugh out of the moment and we all bonded a little bit closer than we were before That's the way it should be.

It was nice to be back to just talking again with our new guest temporally gone from our morning circle, keeping a rather low profile over the course of the next few days. It would be several more days before he quietly and rather sheepishly returned to sit outside with any of us again. Rumor has it that as soon as our guest finished his time with us, someone mailed the torn off, twisted door knob to the main office of our friend's federal agency as a memento of his time spent in a war zone. I think it could have made a great paperweight to put on top of a book like *How to Win Friends and Influence People*. There are a lot of lessons to be learned from how this person conducted himself and how much better it would have been for him to just adjust to the environment slowly and quietly with his eyes and ears open and his mouth shut.

3

War Zone Experiences

MY FIRST MISSION

Wolfgang Schmitz, Germany

I was 49 when I started my first international mission. Before that I had made some official trips to Hungary, Estonia, Lithuania, and Czechoslovakia. It was shortly after the breakdown of the former Warsaw Pact and these countries were looking for support to come closer to Western Europe.

All these trips were very well organized by the visited countries and we didn't have to take care of anything. But now I was going to an unknown country for one year where the war had ended only a few years before.

I am a German police officer with the rank of captain. I worked in different jobs in my organization, the Federal Police, former German Border Police. I worked for most of this time as an instructor in the field of law, for example, criminal law and criminal procedure law.

I have two children; in 2004, they were 6 and 12 years old. My wife had agreed to the mission after many long discussions. From the beginning this was one of the most important points—that the family agree to the decision to go abroad for a long time.

In missions like UNMIK (United Nations Mission in Kosovo) my ministry had decided to send only active police officers. You must be physically fit and you have to pass a selection process; most important is your knowledge of English. After having passed this process I had a general-information course about peacekeeping operations from the UN (United Nations) and EU (European Union) and a special course about the country I would be sent to.

This is where you get your first information about the situation in the country, about work in the UN, and especially living conditions in the country: security, accommodations, traffic, jobs, shops. If you don't have colleagues who have been in the country, this is where you will get information about everything you are interested in.

So, theoretically, I felt like I was well prepared for the mission in Kosovo but many doubts were left. What would happen to me? And I must confess: The day before I left for Pristina, the capital of Kosovo, I thought about canceling the mission.

We were about 40 police officers, a mixture between experienced officers and newcomers, who left via Düsseldorf Airport to Pristina. At that time I didn't know that the airport in Pristina would become my first place to work.

We arrived three months after the last big riots between the Albanian majority and the Serbian minority had taken place. On our way to the center of Pristina we could see the traces of this clash: burned houses and cars, a destroyed hospital. This became my daily view from my accommodation at the airport for the next weeks. Here I got my first hints of the brutality of the conflict.

After we had moved to the hotel, we went out to visit the city. I had never been to the Balkans, but it felt similar to being in Turkey— lot of small shops with cigarettes, mobile phones, music, and so on. And in the center of the city, more relics of the conflict: ruins of buildings and burned churches. In the beginning I felt like a tourist but later on I had some closer contacts with the people and got different views of the conflict. You have to stay neutral in this conflict, but sometimes it's very difficult. You are not allowed to be influenced by your own opinion and you try to do your best to stay neutral. In a lot of discussions it was very difficult not to support one party's view of the conflict. I had a lot of these discussions and I could see the hate and intolerance of both sides. A lot of these people I spoke to had lived during the war in the western European states and I was astonished how good they had learned the language of their host countries. It was very easy to find people who spoke quite good German. A lot of these people who lived abroad for some years had problems trying to reintegrate in their own country. Most of them wanted to go back.

But let's go back to work. The UN starts most of the police officers with one week basic training. Here you get your first contacts with international officers and I got a first impression about the different view of police work in varying countries. There is a wide scale from "my words are the law" to "a servant of the society." The training week includes an English test, shooting and driving tests, and a lot of information about the UN, their regulations and expectations, the history of the country, and some basic law information. If you pass this week you will go to your new unit to start working there.

For me, work started in the airport of Pristina. I must confess it was the most boring job I ever had in my career as a police officer. On our daily way to the airport we passed some remnants of the last conflict between the ethnic Albanians and Serbs. I will never forget the burned hospital, houses, and cars along our way. In the airport I had some closer first-hand contact with people from Africa and Asia. I remember an Indian officer who told me that in his family palm-reading was a long tradition and he offered to read my palms. I don't believe in arts like this, but I was really astonished about the results of his readings. I swear, I gave him no information about my past life and tried to avoid reactions to his statements. I left having many doubts about my original opinion.

A lot of Kosovarians also worked in the airport. A lot of them had been in Western Europe during the war and some of them spoke good German. I liked to discuss this with them, but every conversation ended with the question of where the reason for this conflict lay. It's a discussion that goes back hundreds of years: Who was the first tribe that settled in that region? We as Germans have a long tradition in conflicts with our western neighbor, France. Some regions belonged sometimes to Germany and sometimes to France. Today I don't know anybody who says that these regions must come back to my country. In my following missions in Sudan and Georgia the reasons for the conflicts reminded me of this first experience. Peace is possible, but we must first learn to accept others.

After a few weeks I got the chance to work for the Police Training Centre (PTC) in Pristina. It is now the capital of independent Kosovo.

In PTC all incoming contingents from the contributing countries will make their induction training. That means they get information about history, the UN and their regulations, and basic information about the system of law. Here I worked for about 11 months and I liked it very much. I am still in contact with many of the officers.

It was funny to see Africans sitting in our classrooms together with Danish officers. The Africans, not used to the low temperatures, were in thick jackets; the Danish were in short sleeves; I am still angry that I didn't have the chance to take a picture.

I had a flat about one mile away from the office. Especially in the summertime, you could see a lot of people watering the sidewalk on your way back to your home. Most important for you, this meant there was a high risk that you would not have enough water for a shower in the evening. This disaster happened many times in a week. Sometimes you could see people watering the sidewalk only minutes after a heavy rain shower. I asked some locals but nobody could explain this strange behavior to me.

Compared with other missions living was easy in Kosovo. With different shops and a few good restaurants, the security situation was calm and quiet most of the time. In Darfur, for example, we lived in small containers. We had restrictions in movement after dusk and the safety situation was often very close. A few UN members were killed during my time in Sudan.

The very best in all these missions are the colleagues. Every time I found people whom I formed a close connection to. With a lot of these people I am still in contact after all these years and I hope to see them again at home or somewhere in the world in another mission. We can share a lot of experiences from the missions and from police work over the whole world. We all can learn a lot from others wherever they may come from.

FIRST MISSION: CAMBODIA

Pascal Cuffaut, France

I'm Pascal Cuffaut, 45 years old, serving in the French Gendarmerie (French police with military status) for over 26 years, including more than 7 years in international missions abroad with the UN and the EU, in Cambodia (UNTAC), Bosnia and Herzegovina (UNPROFOR, UNMIBH), and Kosovo (UNMIK, EULEX).

My first international experience was in Cambodia in 1992, when I was 27, and freshly promoted to staff sergeant in my police force. On very short notice, it was requested that the French government send volunteers for service in the unarmed, UN police monitoring mission in Cambodia (United Nations Transitional Authority in Cambodia, UNTAC). I applied for this mission because I was attracted to this unusual adventure in a country far away from mine, and in less than 15 days, after a quick medical check, a quick succession of injections, a collection of overseas equipment, and at last a basic briefing about this faraway country and the mission, I was ready and on the way to this exotic place that sounded like a journey into French history—as Cambodia was a former French protectorate

Figure 3.1   Pascal Cuffaut.

(1863–1953). French gendarmes were already serving there a century ago. Now I was going to be a part of history.

So, in April 1992, I was on the way to this both familiar and unknown land with 65 of my colleagues. I knew only very few of them. When we arrived in Phnom Penh airport it was 40 (105°F) degrees. At that time in Paris it was only 7 (43°F) degrees. We disembarked in plain clothes as we were traveling the first part of our trip with a civilian, commercial flight (Paris/Bangkok), but the TV was there as we were the very first French police contingent for this mission. We were told to put on our police uniforms and return to the plane and pretend that we were disembarking again. So, as soon as all of us got our luggage (approximately three similar green military bags per officer) in the room used for arriving passengers that quickly transformed into a sauna, we tried to rush and collect our stuff and get dressed in our uniforms for the TV. After the "show" we all (65) got into a 55-seat local, outdated bus, while our luggage was loaded into a flat bed truck. We all were suffocating in that wheeled oven, but we all kept our eyes wide open in order to have an idea of the place where we would stay for maybe the next six months. After half an hour we arrived at a midrange hotel in Phnom Penh where we would stay for the next week. We checked in, then went into our air-conditioned bedrooms, but where oddly the electrical control panel was in the bathroom! And of course a few days later one of my colleagues got an electric shock, fortunately without serious injury.

At 18:00 hours it was already dark outside and curiously this city of hundreds of thousands of inhabitants was with no street lighting. It was my task to take our guys to the White Rose Restaurant at the opposite side of the city where we should take our dinner and where the French Headquarters were settled on a temporary basis. A UN minibus with a local driver arrived at our hotel, and he just mentioned in poor English that he was at our disposal for this evening. I ask him if he knew this White Rose Restaurant and I showed him on the city map (with only a few pieces of information on it) the approximate place. It seemed that he didn't know the place but as a polite Cambodian that can't lose face he just smiled and invited us to get into this minibus and I was on the way to our headquarters in this unknown, dark city, without any bearings, trying to find my way with this little detailed map. We succeeded after 30 minutes (later on I learned that we could have reached this place in 10 minutes) and I had to go back to the hotel and repeat this operation several times because we were 65 officers. It was the very beginning of the UN mission deployment and we couldn't have more than one minibus for the contingent. The day after we all managed to get to the place by our own means: taxi, motorcycle, rickshaw. It was fun, not only for us but also for the locals because they weren't used to seeing foreigners using local means of transportation. Usually, the foreigners were only traveling inside air-conditioned 4x4 vehicles. (Later on when I was deployed, I bought a little motorcycle and I used it to go to the office. I was in uniform and the locals were happy to see me sharing the permanent and usual traffic jam that we see in the Asian countries with them—where nobody is respecting the traffic rules, and everybody was driving with only one motto, "Never stop your vehicle. Just keep going even if you should risk your life." And this is what happened more than once, especially when more and more UN and other NGO (nongovernmental organization) vehicles were on Cambodia's roads. You could see a local bicyclist cutting his way through the huge 4x4 vehicles, risking his life, and just smiling.

We got our blue UN equipment: blue beret and badges. I needed an armband in order to sew my UN patch on it so I removed the green hood I had on one of my battle dress uniforms and asked one of the local cleaning ladies of the hotel if she could make an armband with the template I showed her. Again, with a large smile she said "yes." The next day she came with the exact copy of the armband I was looking for. I asked her how much money she wanted for her service, and as I understood it, I should give her whatever money I thought she deserved. As I was freshly arrived in this country I didn't have a clue about the prices of things, services, or salaries. I gave her $5 U.S., and later on I learned that it was one month's salary for her. So immediately everybody in the hotel was ready to help us in all ways. We went to Cambodia with green battle dress uniforms that we used for tropical missions and only one "blue uniform" in case of an official ceremony. But shortly after our arrival we noticed that the local people were a little bit reluctant to talk to somebody who was wearing a battle dress uniform as they were used to seeing green uniforms all the time during the war periods. So our contingent commander asked us to work in a blue uniform—the uniform we used to wear in France—but we took only one with us. So we went to a local tailor and he copied our uniform to the best of his knowledge and means. There were no washing machines and our laundry was hand washed in untreated brown water. After the mission everything was just good to be thrown away.

For the first few days in Cambodia, and because this huge UN system was starting slowly, we were not really employed yet on official UN duties. We were on standby, waiting for orders. As we were the very first Civilian Police contingent, one day the UN decided to send French police officers to a village about 10 km from Phnom Penh in order to get more information about a recent incident involving a villager who was killed during a demonstration. I was appointed with two others colleagues to conduct this task. We were the first UN officers involved in UN duties for this new mission! We got in a UN-marked pickup truck with one language assistant and we drove toward this mentioned place. As we arrived, we rapidly became the focus point of the village. We had to meet the "council of the wise," share coconut milk and fruits ... and we started to discuss the matter of our presence only after all these traditional customs were observed. But shortly after we mentioned the case a local police vehicle arrived like a whirlwind, full of armed officers. As soon as they got out of their vehicle they pointed their weapons (AK-47, RG7) at us, and they immediately stated that they were the police and that we (the UN) didn't have anything to do here. We started to explain that we were the UN police and that

Figure 3.2 Local laundry.

there is an agreement between their country and the UN, justifying our presence and explaining our mandate. They started requesting an official document regarding the mission and so on. Obviously, not everybody in Cambodia was clearly informed about the UN mission. Perhaps they were only pretending, as later on when we could conduct this investigation under better conditions, it was obvious that the villager killed during the demonstration was shot by the police, but we never could bring any evidence of it due to the fact that no one wanted to give us any testimony. It was our first contact with the local police. The force we should work with … and we had to step back under the threat of their weapons and their determination. A couple of days later we received a strange, new instruction regarding the French contingent. The "new policy" would be to deploy French gendarmes (two French officers and one Australian signal operator) all along the Cambodian/Vietnamese border! This was in order to prevent a new invasion of the Vietnamese army (the Vietnamese army invaded Cambodia from 1979 to 1989). How could two unarmed French gendarmes avoid having the Vietnamese army from entering Cambodia again? We prepared a list of pairs of gendarmes ready for this strange mission. One afternoon we got a message that the first two gendarmes should be ready to take the UN helicopter in order to go on reconnaissance in the zone where they would be deployed soon. Two names were picked and they went to fly over the spot where they would be deployed after their situation report and the request of their logistic needs were complete. When they came back they mentioned that the spot where they should be deployed, according to just the grid references given by UN, was in the middle of the rice fields with a few wooden houses and no other real man-made features around. The UN was ready to supply them with any transportation means they wished (four-wheel drive vehicle, motorcycle, boat) according to the season. (During the rainy season, Cambodia is only a vast lake and most of the places can be reached only by boat. There is not even enough hard surface in some villages to land a helicopter.) They got a generator and a few other pieces of equipment that they would need to be ready for their deployment. They went to the local market in order to complete their settlement needs, then were deployed to the spot named C/V 1 (Cambodia/Vietnam 1st post). Day after day new similar deployments were allocated to our contingent along the border. So after a couple of weeks, half of our contingent was deployed along the Vietnamese border. Due to the toughness of these positions, our contingent commander tried to reassure our guys and informed them that every three weeks we would relieve them. But every day the UN mission was getting bigger and new positions were allocated to our contingent all over Cambodia and in all mission pillars. After one month of presence everybody got a position and there was no chance for our officers to be relieved from their position. They were slowly reinforced by newcomers from other contingents but most of them spent their tour of duty on their initial deployment along the border. Despite the roughness of the life, they adapted themselves to this situation and by the end of their deployment they enjoyed it. As of my arrival I worked several times with the UN Human Rights cell, I was appointed to this unit in Phnom Penh. UNTAC was a monitoring mission. In the UN mandate, we were supposed to advise and mentor the local police on their daily duties. We were not to conduct any investigation. But every morning as we were arriving at our office, maybe 20 people were already there squatting, waiting to complain about whatever problem they had. We tried to explain to them that it was not our mission here and that they should go to the local police. They couldn't understand that we were there and we couldn't do anything for them. One part of our mission was to pay attention to police bribes and be sure that the police did not extort money from somebody during their duties. But we learned that the police officers had not received any salary for the last six months as the "chief" of the police "escaped" with all the money! So everything needed to be changed in the local police system, and this was only the beginning of the UN mission. Every day we would see new UN police officers coming from all over the world, arriving in the mission, with almost the same number of contradictory orders about the way we should conduct our duties.

It was the beginning of a great unforgettable seven-month international experience. We were in a postwar zone, with people who knew only conflict for the last 50 years, including the massacre of their people by other Khmer people, "the Khmer Rouge." Everybody had weapons, and behind their permanent smiles were ready to shoot you or booby trap your place in order to protect their houses or their village. Every evening they used to plant mines around their place in order to protect themselves. Every morning they cleaned the place with all the tricks you can imagine. After all these years of war, mines were everywhere—8 to 10 million mines for a surface of 181,035 square kilometers and a population of 10 million. We could find all kinds of dangerous diseases there: malaria, hepatitis A, hepatitis B, Japanese encephalitis, dengue fever, typhoid fever, rabies. The country was poorly supplied in power so no refrigeration, no hygiene in the food we had to eat. Despite all these negative points and the roughness of our life there, there was an indescribable fascination for these people, and a good feeling to be there and to help these people. It was exactly like it was in the ancient stories of the gendarmes who were living there one century ago. It is a strange and difficult feeling to share with people who have never been there. The few things they had they were ready to share without thinking about what would be left for them the next day. This was especially the case when we were in the countryside and it was time to find ourselves food. We had money, but there was nothing to buy. I remember once we arrived in a small village, and we asked where we could buy something to eat. The villager replied that there was no restaurant, no shops, but that he would be happy to share his lunch with us. He boiled water in a pot and added bindweed to it and our soup was ready. In some villages they had not seen "white faces" for decades, as the country was locked to foreigners, and it was the big event every time we arrived somewhere. We were surrounded by hundreds of friendly, curious people who were surprised to see a UN police officer, especially a French one, because for most of them the last one they had seen was 50 years ago during the protectorate time. Old people could speak French, but they told me that they had to force themselves to forget this language because during the era of the Khmer Rouge, all signs of education or wealth (like speaking a foreign language, wearing glasses, being a doctor or teacher) resulted in that person being killed or tortured.

I spent seven months in Cambodia and it changed my life forever. When I came back to France, there was not a single day during maybe more than one year that I didn't think about the people there, living in that beautiful country, but always facing conflict. I had the chance to visit Angkor with its 12th century temples before it was a massive tourist attraction.

In 1995, I was designated to serve in Bosnia and Herzegovina during the war as UN Military Police for six months. It was very tough and so far away from the feeling and my memories of my Cambodian experience. Then in 1998, 1999, and 2000, I returned several times to Bosnia to serve in others missions. Kosovo became the focus of the Balkans the last time

Figure 3.3 Cuffaut and the local Cambodians.

I volunteered to serve on this new UN mission. In total, I spent four years split in several missions in Kosovo until their independence.

MERRY CHRISTMAS, PEACEKEEPERS!

Alexander Gridchin, Russian Federation

My Dear Friend, Robert! My Dear Friends!

It is early morning the 25th of December. Yesterday I received your Christmas card! It is always such a pleasure. Despite the recent years that have brought us all of those new technologies, such as e-mail, cell phones, etc., it is always a great pleasure to open the old door of your post box and find an envelope with your friend's handwriting.

When you find it you see and understand that some of your friends are safe and sound in their home countries but some ... Yes, I am in calm France now, but some of my friends are still in the places where people can only dream about calm mornings, calm days, or a calm life. Some of them are in Iraq, Georgia, Haiti, and Kosovo. My thoughts are with them today! My first peacekeeping Christmas found me in Croatia where I was serving my first UN mission in 1994–1995. (I just realized it was 15 years ago and I was 23 years old. I cannot believe that the time flies so fast!) I came to Eastern Slavonia in June 1994 and my first assignment was to Tenja station. When I arrived there the situation in the area was still tense. A lot of people in that area were wearing some strange paramilitary uniforms. Our station was located in the Zone of Separation in a partly damaged building (some of the local population had shot a grenade into it during the night just a few weeks before).

Before I came to Croatia my international police knowledge was rather limited. In fact I had never worked with any international police officer shoulder-to-shoulder. Of course, we passed a lot of different training courses about international policing, working in the international environment, etc., but practice is practice. I came to a war zone where some 25 brave guys from all over the world were doing their daily, risky job. Our station commander was from Portugal. His deputy was from Denmark. There were also police officers from the Netherlands, Nepal, France, Bangladesh, Jordan, Nigeria, and some other countries. We also had five interpreters who came from Belgrade and Novi Sad.

I do not really wish to list all of what we were doing daily. Surely, most of you are aware that we were going for patrols to the Zone of Separation,

Figure 3.4   Duty officer in Tenja Station, Sector East, UNPROFOR—1994.

monitoring activities of the local police, delivering the humanitarian assistance, distributing medicine from NGOs, but what was most important was that we were living together as a team in a dangerous environment but we were full of optimism, joy, and happiness.

Most of our patrols were in the areas where people did not live anymore because it was in the Zone of Separation. The majority of the areas were mined and we could only use special roads made by UN engineers through the minefields. The previously cultivated fields were full of mines and you could not even think about stepping off this road. At the ends of the roads there were UN military checkpoints, created to make sure that both military and local personnel could not enter the protected zone. In our sector we had Belgian and Russian military components and we used to visit them often. For me it was a special pleasure because I could speak my native language with the Russians. Of course they also liked our visits because it was a change in their routine duties of monitoring the zone.

But that was only one part of our life. Obviously, being separated from our families and friends back home we had to find something to replace it

Figure 3.5 Patrol in the Zone of Separation, Tenja Station, Sector East, UNPROFOR—1994.

while being on the mission. We could not spend time watching TV, for example, because electricity would be on a very irregular basis. There was only one place where the electricity was always on and that was the restaurant "Romanca," where you could eat, play snooker, and socialize after duties.

I will also never forget those happy hours at our station when we used to tell each other about our countries, colleagues, friends, or our football match with the first UN engineers' team from the nearest compound in Klisa Airport (UN Russian Battalion HQ) and after that with the team of local police. I will never forget our visits to the local school where we were giving English lessons because they did not have an English teacher at the time. I will never forget our Christmas together.

It happened that because of a dangerous situation in the area we had to be evacuated to the Sector East United Nations compound located in Erdut. Unfortunately we had to leave the village unexpectedly and everyone only had their documents and evacuation kits with them. Only a few of us had sleeping bags, for example, or even some blankets. We could not leave the compound surrounded by local paramilitaries even to go to the nearest local post office to make a phone call or to send a card to our loved

Figure 3.6 Liaison mission to the UN Russian battalion military checkpoint in the zone of separation, Tenja Station, Sector East, UNPROFOR—1994.

ones. We were all living in the container which served as a cafeteria during the day and "Tenja Station sleeping room" during the night. It was our only facility to celebrate Christmas as well!

If you ask me where we got that Santa I would have no idea how to answer to this day, but it was the only thing that reminded us that we all had families, homes, and loved ones who were thinking about us and missing us lots. Our souls were with them and their souls were with us! We were together in the team of friends, coming from different continents and different courtiers, different traditions and different religions, but with the same spirit. The spirit of peacekeepers! And despite the 15 years that have passed, nothing can change my thoughts and feeling. I am absolutely sure we all feel the same!

I will also never forget the next morning when our friend Ben (he is the one in the photo wearing the Russian military hat) said, "I do not wake up that early because I am on my Annual Leave for today!" These simple words made a lot of fun, because being evacuated in the container the difference between days "on duty" and those "on leave" was really minimal.

41

Figure 3.7 Christmas night in evacuation, Tenja Station, Sector East HQ, UNPROFOR—1994.

Figure 3.8 Ben, on annual leave, UNPROFOR—1994.

Despite all of those difficulties everyone was dreaming of going back to Tenja. We even wrote a song "When will I go to Tenja?" but unfortunately it has never happened. We were, at one point in time, allowed to patrol that area, but because of the security assessment we never went back to the village as a station. Because of that most of the guys were transferred to some other places, including myself, when I got my new assignment to Split International Airport in Croatia in 1995. It was a completely different world. There was electricity, water, shops, even the telephone. Our task was to make sure that air traffic to/from Sarajevo would not carry any military equipment or weapons. We were also a kind of base for UN aircrafts and helicopters as well as Zagreb.

On my second UN mission in 1997–1998, I was first assigned to Gorazde and Visegrad Stations in UNMIBH (United Nations Mission in Bosnia and Herzegovina). It was again different from the first mission because since that time Dayton peace agreement had been signed and the war stopped. You could still feel the tension, but it was already a postwar feeling. Most of the difficulties we were facing were that people tried in any manner to prevent the refugees and displaced persons of the other entities from coming back. They were doing everything possible including blowing up their former houses to make sure that the refugees would not be back.

Figure 3.9 Split International Airport Station, Sector BiH, UNPROFOR—1995.

Considering that the area was still full of those who were wanted by ICTY (International Criminal Tribunal for Former Yugoslavia) for committing war crimes there was still a lot of danger. On a regular basis we were under threat if we were to leave the station or even our accommodation because they would place an explosive that could kill us. We knew it had happened in several places already so the threats had to be taken seriously, but still we could not stop our normal daily work because of it. And we were doing it. If we were not served in the shops in one entity (as they were saying "We do not serve aggressors!"), we used to go across IEBL (Inter-Entity Boundary Line) to buy food and water. But again what was important was that we were one team. In Visegrad, for example, we were only six officers from Germany, Portugal, and Russia and we were all volunteers to come to that area in June 1997. Those who were in Bosnia and Herzegovina, in the Republika Srpska part of the country after the first arrests of the war criminals in June 1997, will understand me perfectly.

After Visegrad Station, I had the honor to be transferred to the International Training Support Section (ITSS) in Sarajevo in 1998 where I was an instructor for the newcomers. Every police officer arriving at the mission had to pass English and driving tests and then we introduced

Figure 3.10 Patrol in the demilitarized zone, Visegrad Station, District Gorazde, UNMIBH—1997.

Figure 3.11 Selection assistance visit to Nepal, ITSS, UNMIBH—1998.

them to different subjects so they would be prepared to work in the mission. Those subjects covered SOP (Standard Operation Procedure), Mission Rules and Regulations, Human Rights, Community Policing, Report Writing, Local Language, Winter Driving, and many others.

Some of us were selected to go to some other countries to assist in selection and preparation of their staff to be sent to the peacekeeping missions. Because of that I went to India, Nepal, Bangladesh, Jordan, and Indonesia through my work in the unit. It was a great experience and there are still times when I travel to different countries for my new job when I meet people who say, "I remember you! You were my instructor in Sarajevo!"

I also remember UNPREDEP (United Nations Preventive Deployment Mission in Former Yugoslav Republic of Macedonia) in 1998–1999, UNMIBH again in 1999–2000 and 2001–2002; but today I do not want to speak about the duties much. I think it is widely recognized that the peacekeepers' great job in war areas saved hundreds of lives and helped millions of people! Today, I want to thank you all, with whom I had the pleasure and honor to serve, as well as all other peacekeepers, and wish to spend this day with your loved ones being safe! If you are in the mission now, please be sure that we think of you today!

MY EXPERIENCE IN LIBERIA

Jan Leif Soerensen, Norway

My name is Jan Leif Soerensen. I have been a member of the police force in Norway for 35 years, until I retired in February 2009. I have worked in different units, but I completed my police work in the Crime Scene Investigation section after serving for 15 years. I served with the UN in five different missions for five years; one year as a military police officer in Lebanon from May 1983 to May 1984, in Eastern Slavonia from February 1997 to March 1998, in Bosnia from September 1999 to September 2000, in Kosovo from February 2002 to February 2003, and finally in Liberia from January 2006 to January 2007. It is my duty in Liberia that I am going to tell you about.

When I applied for duty in Liberia, the civil war had ended about a year earlier. I applied as a Crime Scene Investigation Officer, and I thought I would be used in the Police School, training the Liberian police in these techniques. I was told in Norway that they needed to be taught these skills along with all the other police knowledge.

However, when I arrived in Monrovia after finishing the introduction course, I was attached to a big investigation unit, covering all aspects concerning investigation. Police officers from many countries were present, and I was assigned to a group of crime scene investigators.

My chief was from the Philippines. He was a police officer, but he was also a doctor. He was a coroner (his profession was doing autopsies), and this was going to be my work in Liberia, together with Dr. Servillano Ritualo. This was not what I had expected before I left for Liberia, but it became a very interesting assignment.

We lived in houses in Liberia that we had to arrange ourselves. I lived in a big house with 10 different rooms and three small bathrooms. Sometimes we found crabs in the shower and sometimes we were visited by rats. Electricity was on from 5 P.M. until 7 A.M. We were two Norwegians and eight Swedes in the house, so it was called the Swedish house.

Our office for my first 10 months was in a big building containing all the UN organization. After 10 months we were moved to the Liberia Police Force (LPF) building. We got an office in the cellar. The building was fixed up but it had a very basic standard.

Well, back to work. The doctor and I went to the hospital in Monrovia to do an autopsy. It was a man shot with a shotgun in a village two months earlier. He had been kept in a freezer at the hospital, so that was okay. But

I have to admit that I was shocked when I saw the facilities. It was a small, dirty office. A local doctor was attending the autopsy as a student because he was supposed to be doing this thing himself in the future.

There were a lot of killings in Liberia during my time there. I thought I was going to teach the local police officers something, but instead of doing that I ended up as a driver on a pickup to collect dead bodies.

The doctor and I picked up an average of one man every second day. It was men mostly, killed by machetes. They were stripped naked, tied with their arms behind their backs, and tied on the feet. Then they were stabbed with machetes until they were almost unrecognizable. When we arrived at the crime scene we were always surrounded by a lot of people, and very often nobody recognized the victim. We had to put them on the back of the pickup and bring them to the hospital. These transports had never been done before I arrived, and the hospital had only room for two dead persons in the freezer, so after a short while this became a problem. They simply refused to accept any more dead bodies because of no space.

The dead bodies became a problem because nobody would claim them since they had to pay some money. Sometimes, when we picked up dead persons from the street in Monrovia and they had no relatives, we simply drove them to the graveyard and handed the local gravediggers some dollars to bury them. No one ever asked for missing persons, not to my knowledge.

Sometimes we left Monrovia for investigations in other parts of the country as well. If we did go out we left in teams with four officers and two jeeps. In one of these cases, a young woman had been raped and killed, and then buried in the jungle. So we left for a small village called Zwedru. We got rooms in a small hotel called Muna. And it was some hotel! They cut out electricity at 1 A.M., and we were sleeping in a mosquito tent. I can assure you this, it was very hot! We had, of course, no AC, only a small fan, and at 1 o'clock even the fan stopped working. It was hot! They had showers and water closets, but no water.

When I went to bed the first night, the girl, Wendy, a 24-year-old local who worked at the hotel, knocked at my door and asked if I wanted some massage. I said, "No thank you very much, I am a married man." She answered, "It does not matter. We have boxes of condoms." The next night she knocked again. I said, "I do not need a massage." Then she answered from outside the door, "Do you want me to come in and sing for you?" Funny girl. I went to sleep with no song.

47

From Zwedru we went into the jungle, guided by some locals to find the grave where the raped girl was buried. Our task was to perform an autopsy to find out what killed the girl. She was taken out from the grave. We washed the body and found out that she was killed by a stroke to her head.

This was one of the cases I worked on. It was a lesson of a lifetime, and I developed many good friendships during my year in Liberia. Dr. Ritualo and I crossed Liberia several times and I learned a lot from him. We went places where the children cried when they saw a white man because they had never seen that before.

It was a very difficult task to teach the Liberian police to be proper police officers. They didn't have anything, starting with pen and paper. Transport was also a big problem. We got cases in the jungle that would have taken four days of walking, so it was not possible to go to them. We had to consider our personal security in the jungle.

Figure 3.12   Homicide investigation.

Figure 3.13 The local doctor, myself, and Dr. Ritualo.

Figure 3.14 One of our groups—police nurse Susan from the Philippines; myself; a Turkish police officer; and Dr. Ritualo from Zwedru.

A PEACEKEEPING EXPERIENCE IN KOSOVO

Jasper Moyana, Zimbabwe

I have been retired from the Zimbabwe Republic Police (ZRP) for just over a year now after 28 years and 33 days of service. I have agonized for a long time on what to write about my peacekeeping experiences with the United Nations Mission in Kosovo (UNMIK) after a request from a fine gentleman, Robert Rail, whom I worked with at the PTC in Pristina.

Background

I have always had a fascination about peacekeeping since the ZRP's first deployment to Angola in the early 1990s for UNAVEM II (United Nations Angola Verification Mission II). I could not go on this mission, but the experiences of those who went left me in no doubt that such an experience would be good for my adventurous spirit and love of meeting new people and experiencing new cultures.

My chance came in 2002 when I successfully met the requirements to undergo training for selection for peacekeeping. At this time I was a senior officer, stationed at Police General Headquarters as Information and Communications Technology (ICT) Training Manager in the ICT Directorate. The training was conducted in the Eastern Highlands of Zimbabwe, rugged mountainous terrain and very cold at night.

Preselection Training

The training program is designed to be challenging both physically and mentally and to prepare potential candidates to withstand stressful situations. Candidates were dropped about 10 kilometers from the training base with full kit and were expected to arrive at the base in time for supper. The only way to make it in time was to run most of the way, with about 6 kilometers of the distance being a steep ascent. Very few made it in time and even fewer wanted to eat!

The group was put into teams and I was one of the team leaders. The training was for two weeks and involved road runs every morning, physical fitness exercises, weapon handling and training, long marches, map reading, history of peacekeeping, team building, and mock selection testing. The routines had no fixed time and could be done during the night for hours on end. I believe the purpose was for members to experience stressful situations which they could come across in the mission.

50

Figure 3.15 Jasper Moyana.

Next came the medical examination, which candidates pay for themselves. This is a full medical examination and more than a third of the candidates fail to make it to the next stage for various medical conditions, which are not disclosed to the unsuccessful candidates. Candidates who pass the medical then undergo training in preparation for the SAT. In this instance we trained in mock tests, driving and shooting for the Selection Assistance Team (SAT), administering qualification tests.

SAT Training and Testing

Training in preparation for the SAT is very intensive and officers with previous mission experience usually assist, including sharing their experiences with candidates for the SAT. This took about a month for our group and the SAT was finally conducted in October 2002.

This was a testing time for candidates as all dreams and hopes of serving in a peacekeeping mission can come to a sudden end. I had confidence in doing well and I was one of the successful candidates at the end. Out of over a hundred candidates there were 62 of us left, with 50 qualifying for armed missions. At this time Zimbabwean officers were being deployed to Kosovo, Liberia, and Sierra Leone. I did not exactly mind where I was to be deployed.

Deployment

Some officers we had trained and completed the SAT with were deployed in December 2002 to Kosovo, with another contingent going in August 2003. Ten of us remained, and the stress was unbearable as I was not sure if we were going to be deployed at all. Our chance came over a year later when we finally left on a chartered flight for Kosovo on the 16th of December 2003. This was a defining moment for the 35 (30 male and 5 female officers) of us and we left Harare International Airport in the late afternoon with a group from a demining company who were going to Iraq. The group broke into song as we lifted into the skies, doing a rendition of a popular road run song, *Pfumo raMungwembe.* We had a refueling stop in Dar e Salam, Tanzania, and then had another stop in Cairo where the demining group disembarked. Midmorning the journey resumed and I recall the beautiful sight of flying over the Mediterranean below us with ships of various sizes dotted all over the surface. About halfway across, the sea was replaced by cloud cover and a gradual drop in temperature and the once jovial group became apprehensive about what lay ahead. Farther on the cloud cover broke and below us was a white expanse of snow and there were jokes about the conditions we were going to face.

Around 1600 hours we touched down at Pristina Airport, with the runway snow covered and trucks doing their best to clear it. The formalities did not take long and we were quickly in the comfort of an air-conditioned UN bus.

Kosovo

As we drove to Beni's Motel, it was getting dark but I had glimpses of broken-down buildings, vehicles, and a generally decayed infrastructure.

We arrived to a hearty welcome from colleagues who were waiting for us at the motel and after checking in we had a few drinks and a briefing on the prevailing situation while waiting for supper. Getting to eat was a hassle due to language problems, but we overcame this through a combination of gestures, sign language, and patience. We were in a different world indeed. Because of the long flight everyone went to bed early to prepare for the next day's activities at the Police Training Centre (PTC).

Our mentor, Yitvah Penga from Cameroon, immediately made us feel at ease with his wit. However, for the 10 of us who had done SAT in October 2002, we were told that we had to undergo the whole process again, which we did successfully, enabling us to join the other group members. The following days were hectic, involving training, ID cards, advance payouts, and shopping for the right gear because being from the tropics we had no cold weather attire. During the first week I also noticed something that I remember up to now; during the winter season, Kosovo is muddy—very muddy—and the black birds.

Posting

After training, three of us, Simon M. (a good friend from training and throughout the mission), Wilbert M., and I were posted to Podujevo Station in Pristina region. We survived the icy road to arrive at Podujevo Station in the late afternoon and after briefing immediately went about to look for accommodations, which we found quickly within walking distance of the station. This was it; all that we had been preparing for had finally come.

We spent the next few days getting provisions, housekeeping, and familiarizing ourselves with the area. I also had a trip to Pristina with an Indian officer who was checking out and had a hair-raising driving experience which nearly resulted in an accident. The three of us were posted to shifts. I was posted to a shift where the other internationals were a Ghanaian officer, later to be tragically killed, and a Bulgarian who was in charge. For me this was going to be tough because I had not done shift work for over 15 years.

I managed to carry out my work without any major problems but at times it was difficult to keep awake especially when doing desk work. We would pass time sharing experiences with those officers who had a limited knowledge of English. There were a few exciting incidents though. One time I assisted in carrying out a raid on a wanted criminal but he had bolted by the time we got there and there was suspicion that he had been tipped off about the impending raid. The guy was wanted for several counts of car theft and robbery. Another time while on vehicular patrol,

FIGURE 3.16 Jasper Moyana at Podujevo Station.

I dropped my beret at a spot where we had stopped for a rest and we had to drive back over 30 kilometers to get it. The most interesting was when we drove up a mountain to check on an outpost that was no longer in use. As we were there, I noticed that the KPS (Kosovo Police Service) officers were getting very nervous until the language assistant pointed out that we were very close to the border with Serbia and they were worried about their safety. There was a lot of snow on the road and going back downhill everyone was very quiet until we were in familiar surroundings. I also noticed that I had forgotten to engage four-wheel drive on the way down but I managed to control the vehicle to safe ground.

One peculiar thing I noticed and wondered about both in Podujevo and Pristina was that the males especially would be spitting every now and then while walking. I really took offense to this initially because I thought they were spitting as a sign of disgust at foreigners, but I later realized that it was their custom maybe as a result of too much smoking. At one time I took some days off and visited friends in Prizren and Dragash and got very drunk and had a lot of fun. I also had an opportunity to see a lot of villages in Dragash.

Podujevo was good to work in, but I needed something more challenging. When an opportunity arose for general instructors at PTC I had no second thoughts and jumped at it because I believed it would offer me more experience in my work as ICT Training Manager back home. I moved to PTC after successfully going through the selection process and went to stay with friends in Kosovo Polje or Fushe Kosovo.

Police Training Center

When I arrived at PTC there were three of us who had been recruited and there was a multinational mix of instructional staff, headed by an Italian female officer, and included American, Russian, British, Canadian, Swedish, Norwegian, French, Ukrainian, Egyptian, Romanian, Indian, German, Cameroonian, and Portuguese members.

My initial work involved observing senior instructors in lesson delivery, English language tests, shooting tests, and driving. After about a week, I delivered my first lesson, Human Rights. I must have taken less than 30 minutes to do the 45-minute lesson. As time went on and through feedback from colleagues, I managed to pace myself and really had some good deliveries on the topics of History and Culture of Kosovo, Media and Radio Procedure, Prevention of Sexual Harassment, General Information, Officer Survival, Monitoring Report Writing (of which I later revised the topic), Transition Plan and Monitoring, Code of Conduct, and HIV/AIDS Awareness. I delivered most of my lessons on Human Rights, Media and Radio Procedure, and Monitoring Report Writing.

I had a most enjoyable time at PTC due to the camaraderie and professionalism that existed among the members of staff. Everyone was focused on achieving the best for the unit and this made it easy for the Chief of PTC, Claudia F., to manage and get the best out of the instructors. As time went on I managed to qualify to conduct SAT for police in contributing countries. My only regret during this time was that I did not manage to go SAT, although there were opportunities where I could have been considered, and I also missed out on a course, Trainer's Development, as I had to go back home to get a replacement passport after the one I had was burnt when the house we stayed in was burnt down.

Disaster

Saturday the 17th of March 2004 began like any other day and we had the Swedish contingent undergoing their tests. Midmorning, I was part of the team that went with them for their shooting test at the range some 15 to 20 kilometers on the outskirts of Pristina. Two days before there had been a drive-by shooting of a Serb youth in Caglavica, a Serb enclave on the outskirts of Pristina, followed by demonstrations, but these had mainly occurred in Mitrovica. One thing I noticed, however, while going to the range was the heavy traffic and people coming into town. We passed by our residence and I thought about my passport which I had left when I went to work in the morning and decided I would collect it later. The shooting exercise went well and I was happy because it was part of my learning process in conducting the shooting test.

We came back around 1400 hours and again the thought of my passport worried me as it was UN policy for peacekeepers to have their passports with them at all times. Back at the office, all was well until just after 1600 hours when I received a call from a female colleague who stayed near us that our house was on fire and the police had prevented her from going to see what was wrong. My initial reaction was to rush there to retrieve my passport and books. I was talked out of it and felt much gutted inside as I knew it would be impossible to replace some of the books. I contacted the other guys I lived with and advised them of the situation. As disturbances spread we were summoned to proceed to an area near the house to secure a field hospital and church that were under attack from rioters.

56

We arrived at the scene where some officers, both KPS and international, were already there. I could see that the house was gutted with the roof already down.

I wanted to venture nearer to see if anything could be recovered but it was pointless and I walked away hurting inside. I later learnt that the landlord and his dog had been beaten to death by an iron bar. Later I was to accompany an Indian colleague, Ajithkumar, to try and rescue his wife who had been trapped in a block of flats that was under attack. As we approached the flats there was a heavy presence of rioters and we knew it was impossible to go any farther. The vehicle was being stoned and I was hit by a stone on my hand while sitting in the back seat. We knew it was necessary to vacate the area as soon as possible. The driver, Terry, displayed exceptional driving skills and courage to take us to safety at the main station. If it were not for him, the situation might have become fatal for us.

At the main station, I sat in an office with a Serbian police officer who kept repeating how he had lost everything he had worked for. He was about my age and I tried to comfort him and advise him to look forward but my words did not have much effect as he kept mumbling to himself over and over again. Outside there was a heavy presence of

Figure 3.17 Houses destroyed by the riot.

Figure 3.18 Homes were looted and burned.

KFOR (UN Kosovo Force) soldiers after information was received that the rioters were heading to the main station. This did not happen and I later went to my office at PTC for a nap. The following day was just as busy, but the situation was coming under control. Most of us from PTC went to perform checkpoint duty at a road going to Gracanica, a Serb enclave, to prevent an attack on them. The hectic schedule took my mind off my own loss, but inside I was hurting. For about a week all who had nowhere to stay were accommodated at the UNMIK administration complex between the city and Kosovo Polje. We were required to move after that and my colleagues who I had been staying with, found a place very close to our previous lodgings.

The support from the PTC staff after the disturbances was tremendous and helped me to adjust well to my loss. About a month after the disturbances, I moved to a new house and went to stay in Caglavica and later my friend Simon moved in with me from Podujevo after he had joined the Missing Persons Unit. In June, I flew back home to get a replacement passport. The rest of the year went by quickly as I was involved in lessons, firing exercises with the PTC team, and visiting various police establishments in Gjilane, Prizren, and Mitrovica. I was involved in arranging for the shipping of our contingent's personal effects and served as treasurer/secretary of the group's welfare fund. An enjoyable occasion was when our deputy police commissioner flew in for our contingent's medal parade.

Despite the relative quiet that existed for the remainder of the year, two incidents occurred that touched me personally and reminded everyone of how fragile a peacekeeping environment can be. The first occurred in Podujevo when a Ghanaian officer I had worked with in the same shift was gunned down together with a local KPS officer in an ambush. This was very sad, because from my interactions with him I knew he was to write his final examinations in accounting and marry his childhood sweetheart after the end of his assignment. The second occurred when a group of Americans were fired at while leaving a prison complex in Mitrovica where they were undergoing training as prison officers. One of the ladies who was killed, an Afro-American, was part of the group. I had become friends with her after their initial training at PTC. After their training, I asked where they had been posted, and she said they were going to Mitrovica. I jokingly told her not to go to Mitrovica because it was dangerous. About a week later, she was dead and I felt devastated.

Returning Home

The last few days prior to our return were bad, as we had little running water and no electricity because of rising tensions among the locals. It was winter, and we had shipped most of our things out. We left Kosovo by road for Skopje for a flight to Zurich, where we spent about 14 hours before flying to Harare via Johannesburg. I was glad to be home, in familiar surroundings and thankful that I had survived the bad times of Kosovo. All in all it was an interesting experience and I would not mind doing it again. I made great friends and am currently still in contact with the majority of them.

THE STRUGGLE CONTINUES IN EAST TIMOR

Marcos M. Quintana, Spain

First, let me introduce myself. My name is Marcos M. Quintana. I belong to the Spanish Guardia Civil Police force and I've had both the honor and the pleasure to serve beside the author in Pristina (Kosovo) between the summer of 2003 and 2004, as we were both part of the UNMIK Civilian Police forces thereon deployed. We were, at the time, part of the staff of what was known as the "Police Training Centre," that is, work mates, but soon thereafter we became friends. It's actually easy to become a friend of Bob. He's the kind of man who will be there, ready to assist you, eager to help you, always willing to share his knowledge; and believe me, there are quite a few things you can learn from Bob Rail, and he'll show them to you in a kind and pleasant way. Our friend Bob is not the patronizing type.

As time and my tour of duty in Kosovo went by and I was starting to foresee the end of it, a cheerful happening occurred. Bob and I had been selected for the SAT trip to Russia. The purpose of the SAT is meant so as to preselect candidate officers to join the UN's CivPol mission. We had an incredible time and that gave me the chance to learn yet a few things more from him. As I said then, "He was the dog, and I was the puppy."

I've been in the policing "business" for 17 years and 4 months, right now. Not too bad for a 36 year old, perhaps. I'm currently posted in the Maritime Police as an engineer and operative officer. My job consists of operating and maintaining the various systems aboard and taking care of the actual policing jobs when the need comes, such as boarding and inspecting yachts and fishing boats aboard semirigid crafts, etc. Previously, I've been in regular patrol duties and as a Customs Patrol specialist. My international experience includes four missions so far. The first one was a four-month tour in Sarajevo (BiH) from January to April 2000, as part of the IMP (International Military Police) forces under SFOR-NATO command. As a note, our police force (Guardia Civil) has some military assignments and, when attached to a military unit sent abroad, acts as the military police for those expeditionary forces. We can also be sent as military police as part of international contingents, as was the case. Similar cases happen with other European forces such as the Carabinieri o Gendarmerie Nationale in Italy or France.

I served in East Timor (2001–2002), then became the subject of this chapter, Kosovo, between 2003 and 2004. After that I took a break until December 2008, when I was sent for three months to Banjul, Gambia, Africa, as a part of a team of technical advisors for what we will call the "Gambian Navy," so as to help them patrolling their own sea and shores, as the problem with illegal immigration was becoming serious in the Canary Islands, and a lot of them were departing from the beaches of Senegal, Mauritaine, and Gambia.

From then on there haven't been any further trips, since according to my girlfriend, Gambia was my last one. But let's cut off the chatter and start with the real thing, the experience a 27 year old goes through in a small island he hadn't even heard of.

Preface: A Few Comments on East Timor

Perhaps a small introduction on East Timor is not a bad idea, given that not all of you might be familiar with it. East Timor is a small island within the Indonesian archipelago. The first time I heard of it and asked its whereabouts, I was told something like "go to Australia and turn left." It's pretty much like that. It's roughly 700 kilometers away, northbound, from Darwin (Northern Territory), Australia. The island was colonized by both the Portuguese and the Dutch, the western part by the former, the eastern one by the latter.

In 1975, Portugal was undergoing a convulsed internal situation, with a right-wing dictatorship in the process of falling apart and a military that was fighting several colonial wars in Africa (Angola, Mozambique) and East Timor. The society was paying a huge toll in these wars, losing their sons, brothers, and relatives in senseless wars. The discontent of the military was so evident that the so-called "carnation revolution," a blood-less coup d'etat carried out by the military, put an end to the dictatorship of Oliveira Salazar, and started the Portuguese withdrawal from their former possessions. In August 1975, Portugal withdrew from East Timor, and in November, the same year, the FRETILIN (Liberation Front of East Timor) declared the independence of the country.

However, the happiness of the Timorese lasted for just nine days. Indonesia, already ruling the western part of the island, invaded East Timor and 24 years of terror ensued, during which time between 60,000 and 200,000 are estimated to have been lost, upon a total population of 600,000 at the moment of the invasion. Nevertheless, the FRETILIN, a left-wing guerrilla movement led by Xanana Gusmao (the current prime minister), continued fighting the invaders.

In 1999, following international pressure led mainly by Portugal, the Indonesian government agreed to hold a referendum in order to let the East Timorese decide their future by themselves, whether to continue as a part of Indonesia, with the status of an autonomous province, or be completely independent and become a new country. The outcome of the referendum gave a 78 percent in favor of the independence, and a terror campaign carried out by irregular, pro-Indonesian militia forces (most

61

of them local population on the payroll of the Indonesian administration) and regular TNI (Tenara Nasional Indonesia) (army) forces ensued. The aftermath left 1400 dead and more than 300,000 displaced people. Neighboring Australia's population demanded a direct action in order to stop the bloodshed, and the Aussie government took direct action by sending their SAS-R (Special Air Services Regiment) as a spearhead for the international peacekeeping force known as INTERFET (International Force East Timor), with an aproximate strenght of 9900, 4400 of which were Australian troops, out of a total of 17 contributing countries, that would be led by Australian Major General Peter Cosgrove. These international forces, and very particularly the SAS-R, engaged the militias in several occasions (including the "Battle of Aidabasalala"), and eventually forced them to retreat into West Timor.

A UN transitional civilian administration was thereafter established, and on the 20th of May 2002, the country became independent, although the UN remained present in the country, providing advisors and support to the newly independent country, and remains there to the present day.

And ... Where's That Place You're Going to This Time?

That's what I heard at home when I explained that I was going abroad again. My Bosnian experience had been relatively recent, but this time it was different. It was a UN mission in a country in which the situation was supposed to be, at the time, relatively stable, but it had provided the TV news bulletins with more-than-graphic footages of the savage killings that had occurred there. The videos of the machete killings (as horrible as this would be) were still fresh in the minds of many, and so they were in the case of my family. It's true that we, the ones who go, tend not to worry too much about these things, but those who stay home waiting for us—they do.

Then the medical checks, the needles ... and you start gathering information about what you might expect. Living and working conditions, health hazards ... and there was no good news. Malaria, dengue fever, Japanese encephalitis, power shortages, and difficulties finding decent accomodations were the answer to my queries. No surprise, though. It was, and is, one of the poorest countries on Earth.

Then, a flight to Madrid and meeting those who were to be my contingent mates: 15 people in total, 14 men and just a single woman. The next day we were summoned by the Main HQ's senior staff, got all of our gear and plane tickets, a pat in the shoulder, and off we went.

A "Warm Welcome" on Arrival

For all those who haven't gone through a flight to Australia, I guess it's difficult to figure out how sore your muscles and the "end of your back" become after 14 hours inside one of those flying cigar cases. That was the longest flight of a total of four we took to get to Timor, but when we eventually got there, we were all struck by the same thing—heat!

Well, yes, it's tropical and you might expect it. But if you are a young southern European who comes from a fairly mild climate, once the door of that airplane opens, it's like a slap in the face. Wearing jeans didn't help, either. Then, after clearing ourselves through customs came the struggle with the mob of taxi drivers who are relentless in trying to grab your suitcases and drag them to their vehicles, but, fortunately, you soon find out that someone's dispatched a driver and a UN vehicle to pick you up and drop you off at your accommodation for the next week. It is something that someone has called a "hotel," but it's actually a set of huts put together in a row, whose furniture consists of a bed, a small locker, and an air conditioner. Soon, you learn that those are luxuries you won't find anywhere outside Dili, the capital.

The following day, with no time to get rid of your jet lag, your "training" starts. Different trainers will train you in different matters, as it always happens during your first week in any UN mission. The newly arrived officer has to get acquainted with the mission, the legal system, procedures, traffic, hazards, local culture and customs, etc., and only once that training is completed and according to your CV (resume), you will be deployed to a station or position in which you are thought to be useful—or so they say.

Wherever It's a Bit Cooler Than Here

That was my thought and my query to the mission veterans when I had a list of possible districts where I could be deployed in front of me. *Lautem* was the answer. "But it's the farthest one," was my answer. But, you know, more than 35°C and 90 percent humidity in Dili and its surroundings helped me make the decision. I eventually decided to trade comfort for distance to the airport and the rest of my colleagues. Later on that decision proved to be the right one.

The day of my deployment, a couple of Nissan pickups driven by Jim, a retired NYPD (New York Police Department) officer and a Bangladeshi colleague whose name I can't remember, picked up the five of us who were supposed to be part of Los Palos (Lautem District) UN CivPol Police Station. That was exciting enough, or at least it was for me.

The outskirts of Dili gave us a few impressions of what was to be expected in the countryside, far from the capital. There were no more brick and concrete buildings. Instead, houses made of wood, cane, and corrugated steel sheets as a roofs replaced them. People seemed to be poorer, although apparently well fed. Vegetable gardens, rice fields, live-stock (buffalos, chicken, pigs) could be seen, so, at least apparently, there were no feeding problems.

The road was bad, twisting like a World Rally Championship special stage. I soon realized that, put aside the fact of driving on the wrong (left) side, there were many other things to pay attention to when driving in Timor. Potholes were big enough for one to be able to fill them up with water and take a bath inside them. Wild and domestic animals would run across the road and it's best if you don't run over them: in the case of the wild ones because in a lot of cases they're big enough to damage your car, and in the case of the domestic ones, because it was a local custom (supported by UN policy) that every driver who runs over an animal has to stop and pay for it to its owner. I guess you're thinking that it's the other way around in the rest of the world, and it actually is, but this was East Timor and that was the UN, so disregard every sensible thought and just follow the rules if you don't want to have any problems.

Sightseeing, though, is good. One has to admit that it is a rather beautiful country. It's quite mountainous, but the green everywhere is so intense and beautiful that it makes the traveling experience worth it. Our Bangladeshi driver tried his best to avoid shaking us too much, but seemed to have good fun whenever he was able to run over a snake on the road, and the bigger the snake, the funnier it was. Later on, we learned how big reticulated pythons were in the lush countryside.

After more than five hours of driving to cover a distance of approximately 250 kilometers, we arrived at Los Palos. There, we had a different kind of "warm welcome"—a truly warm one by our CivPol colleagues. We were all different nationalities, but who cares if you are Portuguese, Australian, Gambian, American, Canadian, British, or Egyptian (and this is just to mention a few different ones). The fact is that I soon realized that I had made the correct decision. It felt like a family, so far away from my own.

As for the traffic, I even thought about dedicating a full page to it, but then I changed my mind in thinking that, perhaps, it would make this whole story too long to read, and it's actually easy to summarize the mess in a couple of sentences: The one with the bigger trucks goes first, and keep your eyes wide open. There were lots of exciting experiences, ranging from finding a local man fast asleep in the middle of the road at somewhere around 11:00 P.M., dodging every imaginable animal, or finding out that the dark thing that is coming straight at you, head-on, with no lights is a truck. More precisely, it would be what in Europe and in British English is called a *lorry*—a big truck! Once recovered from such a scare, and having made sure that you don't need a change of underpants, you keep going just to find out, a few kilometers ahead, that there is no longer a road in the place it used to be. It's the rainy season and the thunderstorm of the previous night has taken away part of the road. There you are, in the middle of nowhere, unable to keep going and unable to reach anyone on the radio (mountain area) to report the situation, so it's best if you turn around and get back home. If you are lucky, you will be able to reach your house and the power station won't be down tonight, so you can drink a cold beer and relax a little bit. Needless to say, pedestrians don't wear any kind of reflective equipment at night, so it's always best if you drive carefully and keep that in mind.

My first five months in Los Palos were as a patrol officer. It was, in fact, my first experience in UN operations, so it made sense that the "newbies" would be sent to the lower, but not less important, level. In my case, no complaints about it, since patrolling was what I was used to doing at home. The differences, though, came in who you have to patrol with. You have fellows from a range of countries with different, let's put it this way, "policing standards." Then, you need an interpreter (or "language assistant" as the UN calls them). Believe me, it feels weird when you are not the one who is addressing the person you need, for one reason or another, to talk to. And if the situation goes tricky, believe me, it becomes really difficult. My advantage in this matter was that as a northern Spaniard, I can speak the Galician dialect which is relatively close to Portuguese, and that proved quite useful. As a former Portuguese colony, there were still people who spoke Portuguese in East Timor. Those who were around 40 years of age or older were, quite often, able to communicate in this language. This included the local East Timorese police officers who were, at the time, starting to patrol along with us. In fact, these people who had had the Portuguese influence kept the polite, extremely formal, respectful, and hard-working attitude of our Portuguese neighbors. Yes, I won't hide it—I have a particular affection toward the Portuguese because they have been so nice to me wherever I've found them.

Living conditions in Los Palos were decent, by East Timorese standards. The five of us, four men and the single woman of the contingent, were lodged in a house in which we had three bedrooms, a decent living-dining room, and a "bathroom" with a useless bath and a hole in the ground (guess what for) instead of a toilet. The bath was useless because there was no running water. A big barrel of water was always present and each of us had a scoop, so the way you washed yourself every day was using the scoop to get wet, soaping up, and then rinsing the soap away the same way. Hot showers were a thing of the past.

Los Palos was just a bit cooler than Dili, but not that much. Long pants and jungle boots were mandatory in a place where hungry mosquitoes and nasty critters were always around. The typical wet season's thunderstorms cooled down the environment sometimes, but if you were caught out in one of those (as it happened once to me), your housemates would have quite a laugh watching you show up soaking wet, cursing, and needing a full change of clothes, underpants included.

Living conditions were quite basic, as I said, and working conditions were not much better. We were always running short on resources, fuel, and manpower. Communications went down whenever they felt like it, including, of course, the sluggish Internet connection that kept us in touch with the outside world. Actually, it was the people I lived and worked with that made it an unforgettable experience. Workmates, civilian UN staff and even non-UN personnel from various NGOs–Los Palos surprised us for having a quite active social life!

The district and its people were mostly peaceful, and arrests were most unusual. The bad part was that we arrived in the middle of the process of preparation for the Legislative Assembly elections, and all leaves had been canceled until further notice. For us, that meant working for more than four months straight on, with no weekly leave. That was hard, but it was what we got paid to do, wasn't it? Even though the district was mostly peaceful, cases of domestic violence, burglary, theft, or missing persons were reported, with a single murder case in those five months. Caution, however, was to be taken in a country in which carrying a machete was as common as carrying a pen in our countries, so you'd better be wary about that. There were a couple of times I was on the fringe of having to use my handgun on upset subjects who wouldn't comply with the instructions of throwing away their machetes. And you can bet they are good at handling them, and that a machete wound is something serious everywhere, not to mention in a tropical environment.

Something to mention about East Timor and its legal system is that there were two parallel ways of making justice. On one hand there was the usual penal code and courts, but on the other, a "traditional" system of justice was also present. Every village had a head of village, and every few villages (say, a "county") had another head. These people were, in most cases, elderly people who were very much respected by the population and who had the authority to mediate in disputes and establish compensations or punishments. During our training, we were instructed to keep a close relationship with these persons and to appreciate their opinions, since they were the ones who closely knew the persons involved in whatever situation we had to face. We did just that, and it proved quite useful when dealing with minor offenses.

Tutuala, Final Deployment, the Loss of a Friend, and the Human Aspect of It

After those five months working with no leave, I eventually got three weeks off and decided I needed to get home. In the beginning of the mission I was very eager to visit Australia, but by the end of those five months I had changed my mind and decided that what I needed was to see my loved ones and have a meal prepared at home by Mom, a hot shower at home, my own bed, and so on.

Right after the second week at home I got an e-mail from Miguel, one of my housemates. He said something like, "Man, bring everything you can that we can read. I don't care if it's the owner's manual of your fridge, an Agatha Christie novel, or the telephone listing, but we two have just been transferred to Tutuala and we might need that ...." That was Miguel, one of my contingent mates, with that typical southern Spanish sense of humor. But I have to say he made me worry about going there. Later on we laughed about it. He had already had a look at Tutuala prior to knowing that we were being transferred there and he knew that the place was simply gorgeous. All you had to do is look at "our" beach.

Tutuala was the most remote place in the whole country. There was nowhere to go if you wanted to go farther away, and there was no "civilization" in a radius of 45 kilometers, but it was so peaceful, people were so kind, and we were so integrated with the local population and authorities that we soon were quite happy having been transferred. We had the privilege of a car to go to Los Palos whenever we needed supplies and to attend to our duties. Our car was a Tata, an Indian-made car with quite unique handling and a specially particular gearbox, but she took us everywhere and proved reliable enough on those roads. Our diet, although a bit more varied than the local population's diet, consisted mainly of rice, pasta, fresh fish whenever we could get it from the local fishermen, and eggs and chicken from the "Dom Bosco" (Salesian Brothers) Missionary School in Los Palos. Not too bad.

I've intentionally left this part for the last "chapter" of my contribution to Bob's book, since I believe it the most important. Up to the present moment, all I've tried to do is to give you, the readers, a picture of what the country and its people were like. Now, I'll try to get you through what it felt like to live in East Timor for a young man who, until then, had never lived without all the comforts we are used to in the so-called "Western World." If something, put aside the fact of people walking around with machetes, shocked me at the beginning, it was the living conditions. As I said, East Timor is really poor, and to be honest, as the international and well-paid staff that we were, we had the privilege to have the best accommodation money could buy. The problem is that the "best accommodation" in villages had a power supply, in the luckiest of cases, that was reduced to a few (four to six) hours per day, and where you were very lucky if you could hire a house equipped with a generator. Then you had the fuel problem—perhaps you had the generator, but fuel was not always available.

I slept in a sort of camping tent made of plastic and mosquito net. It had taken a month for us to find a mattress to fit inside it, and in the meantime an inflatable mattress was all I had to sleep on. Needless to say, the inflatable mattress ended up thoroughly patched. I would wake up on the floor almost every night. Something else I should mention is that we were advised during our training to check our boots and clothes for unfriendly visitors on a daily basis. This proved to be a very good idea. There were a couple of times I spotted and killed a scorpion inside my bedroom. And this might sound funny, but one of the Portuguese officers failed to do this one morning and got stung in a very sensitive place. His contingent mates said that for a few days, "he had the biggest one in the whole island."

There was no running water in either Los Palos or Tutuala, but at least in Tutuala the situation was slightly better. We had a working toilet (the only one in the whole village), a small sink (with a mirror!), a small fridge, and a generator that provided power to our police station. The station had an adjacent building we used as a kitchen and "mess" or dining facility. As I said, we could afford the "best" accommodation in town, and whoever had a decent house tried to rent it to internationals. We were lodged in a house made of concrete blocks up to a height of approximately 3 feet, and then bamboo canes cut in half and fitted together one after another, with a wooden frame supporting the whole thing finishing the walls. The roof of corrugated iron made temperatures inside the house during daylight hours simply unbearable.

We got bottled drinking water from the UN, but the water for the toilet and the "bathroom" had to be transported from a reservoir about a mile or so away, in the middle of the forest. We would fill big plastic bins and bottles (25/50 liters) that were then loaded on the car. The reservoir could only be reached by following a very rough, steeply sloped track in the middle of the forest. We were lucky enough to have a car so ferrying the water from the reservoir was not a big deal, but the local population wasn't so lucky. Whoever was at the reservoir when we got there in the mornings could get a lift, but the sight of women transporting heavy loads of water with nothing more than a piece of cloth on their heads between them and their fully loaded water containers was very normal. And that was just the beginning of the day for them!

When I first got to the mission I met a British veteran from several UN missions. He was on his second year in Timor at the time, and told us that "a UN mission is always an experience, but East Timor is a life-changing experience." Indeed, it was. The young man that came back from that tiny island a year after having departed from his comfortable and civilized Spain had understood how many live on so little, and how lucky we are for having been born where we were. In Timor there were no famines, but health problems, including tropical diseases like malaria and dengue fever, were a real concern. In our little village of Tutuala, our only car served as an ambulance on several occasions, rushing sick children and adults with serious malaria cases to the local hospital in Los Palos. It really pleased us to have always arrived in time and to never have any fatality. Nevertheless, loss of life to diseases curable in the first world was relatively common. To complicate matters, traditional medicine played a major role in that society. We even knew of a case where a seven-year-old girl died as a result of a snake bite because she was treated with traditional remedies first, and was only taken to see a doctor when it was already too late. In any case, antivenoms were only available in Dili, a five-hour drive from Los Palos, or one hour away when a helicopter MEDEVAC was activated.

Health care was provided mainly by NGOs such as *Medicos do Mundo, Medecins sans frontiers,* USAID (U.S. Agency for International Development), and so on. There were a few hospitals run by locals, nurses and doctors, packed with patients and running really low on resources.

With the subsistence economy that East Timor is, people live on the few livestock they keep, their vegetable gardens, and trading their surplus at the local markets. As I said, there were no feeding problems for the population since whoever needed it got help from either the NGOs or the UN directly. Poverty is something that will strike whoever has a heart, and in my case, it really caused me to appreciate how lucky we are, and to honestly learn that it is possible to live and to be happy in such a simple life. Even in our case, being the "privileged" internationals, we got used to that: living with no television, no running water, no hot showers, no radio, no newspapers (a stock of books was the boredom-killing solution), no electricity, no restaurants or bars—actually, nothing of the life we had been used to, but the people were happy! They were aware that there was a better world outside, but they focused their attention on enjoying what they had, not complaining about what they didn't have. That was something that really changed my mind and my personality. And that is what made it child's play for me to adapt to a much easier mission like Kosovo.

Next time you complain about your house, your car, your job, your boss, your wife, or the town you live in, just keep this in mind: There are so many living on so little that would wish to have what you complain about. We are privileged people on this Earth and it is, in my humble opinion, something about which to be grateful. At least I am, and spending a year in East Timor and sharing my life with those people played a major role in changing my mind about that.

So as to finish my little contribution, I would like to dedicate a few lines to the memory of Miguel Mancilla, my partner during my seven months in Tutuala. During our last CTO (leave), I took a couple of weeks off and headed for Sydney, Australia, a city I had always wished to visit. Miguel and an Egyptian friend chose the island of Java. Miguel tragically passed away when the hotel he was lodged in caught fire. Our Egyptian friend was able to make it to the street, but Miguel's room was on the top floor and there was no chance for him. We had a couple of weeks left and we would have been done in East Timor, but Miguel didn't make it. Perhaps, the photos that our ETPO (East Timorese Police Officers) hung from the walls at our station are still there, as his memory is still in our hearts.

East Timor is still, and always will be, in my heart. God bless them and give them the chance they deserve.

INTERNATIONAL COLLEAGUES

Volker Laib, Germany

I served in the United Nations Mission in Bosnia and Herzegovina (UNMIBH) from 1998 until 1999. I was a young officer at this time and did apply for this mission. My motivation was to get the chance to work together will police officers from all over the world.

When I arrived in Sarajevo in summer 1998, we had to spend our first week doing training for the mission. After I had finished my English test I applied to get the certification to become an investigator in my mission time, but it all ended totally different than I had thought. I had to do my oral interview with an American police officer to get the certificate. After we had finished it, he asked me if I wanted to stay in the training center, working with him in the so-called "Research and Assessment Unit." I agreed to do that and it was, with no doubt, the best decision I could have made.

In our training center, we had all the incoming contingents and I had the chance to meet officers from all over the world. I, for example, worked together with people from Chile, from the Fiji Islands, from Iceland, from Portugal, from Canada, and of course from the United States. Plus, we had all the trainees for a week, such as officers from Jordan, Argentina, Nepal, India, Bangladesh, Ghana, Nigeria, and Thailand. I learned a lot about foreign cultures, habits, and ways of living. And the most important and valuable asset I made was building up friendships with a lot of people. Some of those still exist; of course, still the friendship with my testing officer, Jimmy. He and his wife visited us in Germany, and my family and I went to Texas and spent some days with him and his wife.

We had a daily morning briefing at 9 A.M. and at that time all officers came together in one room and we talked about the work during the day, about the incoming contingents, and all necessary matters. You should have seen how good and close we all worked together, the good mood and the high motivation we all had. You should have seen all the officers from around the world following the same goal, which was helping the people in the country, ending the problems, and trying to make a better life for them. Almost every morning I thought that we had something like our own small world there and we had no problems at all. Some politicians should have seen our group, proving that different origins, colors, genders, religions, beliefs, habits, and cultures are no reasons for war and hate.

71

There are so many great memories of my mission time in Bosnia. It was definitely an experience of a lifetime and I am very happy to contribute to this book.

TALES FROM CAMBODIA

Hesham Youssef, Egypt

Background

Cambodia has suffered over a quarter century of civil war, including four years beginning in 1975 of mass genocide (resulting in the deaths of two million people according to recent estimates) and economic ruin under a Khmer Rouge government. Vietnamese troops drove out the Khmer Rouge in early 1979 to establish a communist government of the Cambodian People's Party (CPP) led by Hun Sen. Resistance forces made up of the Khmer Rouge and noncommunist forces under former Cambodian leader Prince Sihanouk and his son Prince Ranariddh fought the Vietnamese-backed government until the Paris Peace Accords of 1991.

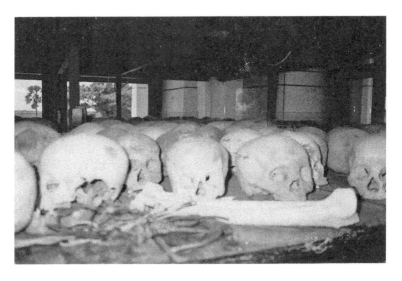

Figure 3.19   Killing field display.

Figure 3.20 One of the killing field memorial displays. (There were more than 15 around Phnom Penh.)

Figure 3.21 The map of Cambodia made of the skulls of the Khmer Rouge regime victims.

Paris Agreements Signed

The Agreements on a Comprehensive Political Settlement of the Cambodia Conflict were signed in Paris on October 23, 1991 at the final meeting of the Paris Conference on Cambodia. They were the culmination of more than a decade of negotiations in which the UN had been closely involved from the outset. The Agreements, also known as the Paris Agreements, invited the Security Council to establish the United Nations Transitional Authority in Cambodia (UNTAC) and to provide it with the mandate set out in the Agreements. The Council fully supported the Paris Agreements in its resolution 718 (1991) of 31 October 1991 and requested the Secretary-General to prepare a detailed plan of implementation.

The final session of the Paris Conference on Cambodia met from October 1st to the 23rd in 1991. Cambodia was represented by the Supreme National Council (SNC), with Prince Sihanouk as its chairman. Also present were the five permanent members of the Security Council, the six members of the Association of Southeast Asian Nations (ASEAN), Australia, Canada, India, Japan, Laos, and Vietnam. Yugoslavia attended in its capacity as Chairman of the Non-Aligned Movement. The peace plan that emerged from the Paris Conference became known as the Agreements on a Comprehensive Political Settlement of the Cambodia Conflict. The Agreements consisted of a Final Act and three instruments: the Agreement on a Comprehensive Political Settlement of the Cambodia Conflict; the Agreement concerning the Sovereignty, Independence, Territorial Integrity and Inviolability, Neutrality and National Unity of Cambodia; and the Declaration on the Rehabilitation and Reconstruction of Cambodia.

Culture and Religious Awareness in Peacekeeping Missions

One of the most important and critical matters for any mission planning is to recognize the culture and religious beliefs in the mission area. All peacekeepers must know and respect the diversity and differences between their beliefs and the host country's beliefs, as negligence of this matter could lead to serious repercussions. This knowledge could be done through the advanced peacekeeping mission, which is usually sent before the main mission components are on the ground, or it could even be done through the personal readings of the peacekeeper.

In Cambodia, the common religion was Buddhist, with little minorities of Christians and Muslims. Some of my colleagues inadvertently made some mistakes concerning this matter. Here are two funny stories about them.

Never Eat the Avatars' Food

When we arrived in Phnom Penh, and while we were discovering the surroundings, we noticed in almost all the shops around our residence that the owners put small wooden niche or a temple in front of the shop. In the morning we saw them put, with great humility, a big tray filled with food, drinks, and sometimes a lighted cigarette. One of my Egyptian police officers thought that these fruits and drinks were for hospitality. Every time he got inside any shop he would eat some of the bananas and a can of juice from the tray and swallow them while bargaining with the seller. I noticed that the people were not comfortable with this behavior and in one case the face of the lady seller went pale.

I asked our interpreter Chan-Tuo about this matter. He told me that this food is an offering for the gods. I asked him how they know when the gods got enough and it is time to remove the tray. He said that it is when the flies fall into the plants!

I immediately told my group of officers about this matter and emphasized the importance of respecting this ritual.

The Ride of the Granny Souls

After being deployed to Kampot province, about 150 kilometers from the capital, we were redeployed into a police station, Chum-kiri, 45 kilometers inside the jungle where everything was stopped in the 18th century.

No water, no electricity, no roads, no houses, and so forth. We found a wooden house without a toilet as they were using the rice fields as a big toilet. When it was dark, we started to hear a variety of sounds that were coming from the nearby jungle. Suddenly, we heard a very strong, strange sound but this time it was inside the house. We felt also something was moving up and down on the wall. With a torch light, we saw a big lizard was chasing insects inside the house. One of my colleagues started to chase it and swore not to sleep before catching it. It took two hours to kill this clever creature. As a mark of victory, the man tied the lizard from the tail and hanged it on the wooden balcony! The next morning I heard some loud voices under the house and the tone of them was not friendly at all. When I looked from the window I noticed some people under the house who were shouting and looking angrily on the hanged lizard. Once again I called the interpreter who was very worried. when he saw the situation. First, he removed the animal and said, *"Som-toi, som-toi!"* which means "sorry."

Figure 3.22 The common sight of a street-side offering.

When we asked him about all this, he said that according to the Khmer beliefs, the souls of the dead grandmothers used to visit their families from time to time and when they would come from the other world they used to ride the bodies of the lizards. So they respect this animal and consider it hallowed. Once again, it was a lesson learned by us, to respect the lizard in Cambodia although we chase them in our own country!

FIGURE 3.23 The number of accident victims in peacekeeping missions is more than minefields. The driver tried to avoid a big cow who survived, but the driver did not!

AN UNEXPECTED TURN OF LUCK

Evgeny Omelchenko, Russian Federation

I received an e-mail from my old friend Robert Rail (United States), with whom I have worked in United Nations' Missions in Bosnia and Kosovo for almost four years. He asked me to write a few stories about my experiences of serving in the war zones of Bosnia, Kosovo, and Liberia. I had no hesitations whether to write. Of course I agreed. The problem was where to start from and I decided to write a few words first about myself.

One of the main differences between a loser and a lucky man is that the loser does not fight for the space under the sun. He is floating in the life stream like a piece of wood in the rushing waters, hitting shores and different obstacles. Like a normal human being, he hopes for a better life, waits for positive changes in his life, but receives no gifts from the destiny, because he is not looking and fighting for them.

A lucky man may not realize that he is really lucky. He is always on the run, moving forward, planning his next day, week, month ... doing, or at least trying to do, his job well, and sometimes feeling a slight touch of an unexpected turn of luck.

77

FIGURE 3.24   Evgeny Omelchenko in Kosovo.

In April 1993, I realized that the unexpected turn of luck touched my shoulder, which sent me on a UN Mission to Zagreb, capital of Croatia, one of the six republics of Yugoslavia. What did I know about Yugoslavia? Frankly speaking, I did not know very much. I knew that Yugoslavia was a friendly country to Russia, located on the Balkan Peninsula. The Yugoslavs actively fought under the leadership of Joseph Brose Tito against Fascist Germany. Many of the Russian people in their 80s and 90s preferred the Yugoslav furniture and shoes.

After being selected for the UN Mission in Former Yugoslavia I was 1 among 13 other lucky Russian police officers flying from Moscow to Zagreb. What was waiting for me there I did not know. I was thinking how it would be, and what follows is how it was.

During the breakup of Yugoslavia, located almost in the center of Europe, washed by the warm and clean Adriatic Sea, this country was suffering from civil wars: the War in Slovenia (1991); Croatian War of Independence (1991–1995); Bosnian War (1992–1995). Slovines, Croats, Serbs, Bosnians, Christians, Catholics, Orthodox, and Muslims fought against each other for the land and independence.

The United Nations Protection Force (UNPROFOR) was the first UN peacekeeping force in Croatia and in Bosnia and Herzegovina during the Yugoslav wars. It existed between the beginning of the UN involvement in February 1992, and it restructured into other forces in March 1995. UNPROFOR was created by the UN Security Council. The initial mandate of the UNPROFOR was to ensure conditions for peace talks and security in three demilitarized "safe-haven" enclaves designated as United Nations Protected Areas (UNPAs) located in the former Yugoslav republic of Croatia: Eastern Slavonia, Western Slavonia, and Krajina. They were places with strong Serb populations that had organized into the self-styled Republic of Serbian Krajina, which had led to tension and fighting.

In 1992, the mandate was extended to so-called "pink zones," controlling access to the UNPAs, some border control and monitoring of civilian access to the pink zones, and control of the demilitarization of the Prevlaka peninsula near Dubrovnik.

Other extensions of the mandate included protection for Sarajevo Airport from June 1992, and from September 1992, protection for humanitarian aid in the whole of Bosnia and Herzegovina, and protection of civilian refugees when required by the International Committee of the Red Cross (ICRC).

Zagreb is the capital and the largest city of Croatia. Zagreb is the cultural, scientific, economic, and governmental center of Croatia. According to the city government, the population of Zagreb in the beginning of the 1990s was approximately 700,000. It is situated between the southern slopes of the Medvednica Mountains and both the northern and southern banks of the Sava River. Zagreb lived its own life, looked nice and clean. Nothing displayed evidence of war in this city.

UN Headquarters was located in Zagreb and was part of its busy life. From here, in the beginning of May 1993, I was sent to the south of Croatia to work at the Split Airport as a police monitor. At the very beginning there were six of us, one Canadian officer, four Colombians, and one Russian—that was me. We were working together with United Nations Human Rights Council (UNHCR), ICRC, and the Split Airport police. We were responsible for the safe transportation of humanitarian aid and passengers between Split and Sarajevo by air.

The first days of work were the most difficult in terms of communication. We all spoke English, but the spoken English was Canadian, Columbian, and Russian, then it was French, English, Dutch, Norwegian, American, Kenyan, Nigerian, Polish, and Jordanian. The longer I worked in the mission the easier it was for me to be able to understand different pronunciations and accents.

One of my first friends was an English sergeant, Shaun. He had been working in the office next to our unit, located on the first floor of the Split Airport building. When we had time we spoke about English and Russian culture, literature, people, habits, traditions, songs, meals, and beverages. He gave me a book about the history of the British Grenadier guards. When I was reading this book I found much resemblance between the history of the British and Russian armies during the 18th and 19th centuries. We started exchanging jokes and found that many of them had the same story with little differences.

When working in a "family" of the UN officers every day I discovered many interesting things, for example, the exclusive sense of humor of the French UN police officer, Andre. Looking serious at first sight, Colombian UN police monitor Miguel appeared to be a very interesting person and personality. They all became my friends for years to come.

When I was living in Croatia I spoke with Croats. At first sight it looks like the Croatian language is very similar to Russian. I would *not* say so. The character, the tempo, and the stresses used in words sound similar but are not clear in terms of understanding. Besides the Croatian language, most of the Croats used to speak the German language, because traditionally Germans loved to spend vacation on the Croatian shore of the Adriatic Sea.

Private hotels and restaurants were traditional coastal businesses. The new generation of Croats also spoke good English. Living among Croats I saw how proud the Croats were to be Croats. The Split Airport photographer prepared ID cards for us for easy entry into the airport area. He and I talked about the beauty of the Croatian land, the present situation, and the local people. We spoke English and understood each other very well. The only word which the photographer disliked was the word "local" when it referred to himself. "If you are not a local, who are you?" I asked him. He answered that he was a citizen of Croatia. This reply surprised me, but after these words I began treating Croats with sympathy and respect.

In the beginning of February 1994, I worked at the Sarajevo Airport. The regional UN Headquarters was located in the Post and Telecommunications (PTT) building. The road from the airport to PTT was not safe as we could expect cannon or mortar shelling or snipers shooting at us.

The city of Sarajevo was famous for its traditional religious diversity, with adherents of Islam, Orthodoxy, Catholicism, and Judaism coexisting there for centuries. Due to this long and rich history of religious diversity and coexistence, Sarajevo has often been called the "Jerusalem of Europe."

Sarajevo was in ruins but not defeated. The city itself was divided into sectors in accordance with the ethnic group living there.

Day to day, hundreds and thousands of shells were continuously demolishing houses and streets, killing people. Water, food, and medical supplies were getting into the city with humanitarian convoys by road and by the air bridge. Those who lived in Sarajevo and those who saw Sarajevo through binoculars as a target knew that the airport needed to remain in working condition, so every day UN police monitors working at the airport were counting new holes in the walls of the police office in the airport building, writing the date when the hole appeared next to it.

On February 5, 1994, it was reported that a mortar shell landed in a crowded, open-air market in Sarajevo, killing at least 66 people and wounding more than 200. Horribly mangled bodies and severed limbs lay scattered amid bloodstained market stalls in the bloodiest single attack on Sarajevo's civilians since the war began. "There were trucks of dead, there were legs, arms, heads—as many as you want," said a wounded young man while waiting for care at Koshevo Hospital.

It was not immediately known who fired the shell into the Bosnian capital, which was under siege by Bosnian Serbs fighting the Muslim-led government. But President Alija Izetbegovic's spokesman, Kemal Muftic, declared that the 120-millimeter mortar shell was fired from a Serb-held position north of Sarajevo. Bosnian Serb leader Radovan Karadzic, however, suggested that government soldiers had fired on their own people to persuade NATO to go ahead with threatened air strikes on Serb positions. But there was no evidence to support his charge, which was dismissed by the Bosnian government.

A UN international military group was sent to analyze the crater in an attempt to determine the shell's origin. When this analyzing group was leaving Sarajevo for Zagreb after finishing their work, I approached one of them when they were at the Sarajevo Airport and asked what kind of explosive caused these dramatic casualties? Experts reviewing evidence had concluded the following:

No shell could have caused such devastation.
The nature of the injuries indicated that they were caused by a cone-shaped explosive device placed among the crates in the market.
The device contained a propelling charge (which accounts for the high percentage of internal injuries), a phosphorous bomb (which caused the burns), and some shell heads of hand grenades.

The device was probably detonated by remote control. The number
of killed was 34 persons and about 200 wounded.
It probably weighed no more than 15 kilograms.

Having military experience, I had concluded to myself that it was difficult to contemplate that a 120-millimeter mortar could cause this number
of casualties, even in a confined space like the market. I was not aware of
such a high number being killed by a single shell in any other occurrence.

All UN police officers (five or six of us) working at the Sarajevo Airport
with Antonio, a Portuguese officer as head of the UN police team, including myself, worked those days and nights in close contact with ICRC
and UNHCR, sending wounded people on medical evacuation aircrafts
(MEDEVACs) to Denmark, Switzerland, and Sweden for shelter and medical care.

It is a usual thing for confronting sides to have prisoners of war
(POWs). Once or twice I participated in POW exchanges. The French
Foreign Legion was protecting Sarajevo Airport and Dobrinja (a town
on the outskirts of Sarajevo). A platoon from the French Foreign Legion
that was located close to the airport was sent to Dobrinja, in three
APCs (armored personnel carriers) where the said POW exchange was

Figure 3.25 Sarajevo, UN Airport, Omelchenko with UNPROFOR Commissioner
M. Orally—1994.

scheduled to take place. I sat in an APC; the daylight could hardly come into the vehicle through the armored windows. Some five to six French armed soldiers in helmets were sitting there. At first glance all their faces were much alike. I was trying to look at the road through the window to shorten the waiting time. I was thinking and drawing in my mind how the exchange would be. When we drove for some time one of the soldiers spoke to me in my language, surprising me very much. I asked him where he was from. He spoke Russian with a little accent and I could not recognize his nationality. Then he said that he was from one of the former Soviet Pre-Baltic Sea states. Maybe because the road was not flat or the route was short, the talk with this soldier stopped as unexpectedly as it started. When we arrived at the spot the exchange failed this day due to some unknown reasons. On my way back I was sitting in another APC and did not see that soldier anymore.

As we live, we walk, we breathe, we speak, we meet with different people, and we see many faces. When working with the UN, we travel, we speak foreign languages, we see hundreds and thousands of faces, and the next day you may not remember those faces or their voices. Sometimes we meet people once and make friends forever. At the end of summer 1998, I was working in Sarajevo in the UN Induction Training Unit. I was supposed to go to Bulgaria on UN business to select Bulgarian police officers for UN police service in one of the UN missions. American police officer Robert Rail from our unit was sent to Bulgaria together with me.

What did I know about Bob? I knew that he was a unique specialist on body sign language, on defense without damage, and a karate instructor. When I first saw him I concluded to myself that this professor-looking man could be a good lecturer on body signs language, teaching people to read other people's intentions by their way of looking at something or somebody and by their gestures. I could not imagine that he was a karate instructor and trainer on contact with offender without damage until I attended his lecture. After the lecture he put two chairs approximately 4 to 5 feet apart and then he put one foot on one chair and another foot on the other chair and stretched his legs. The trainees burst out applauding, whistling, and screaming "wow" and "cool!"

Our route to Bulgaria was Sarajevo–Zagreb–Sofia–Istanbul–Zagreb. We worked for about five days in Sofia, enjoyed views of the Bulgarian capital, took hundreds of pictures, and were ready to return back to Sarajevo. After working hours Bulgarian liaison officer Dimitar Christov would take us to different memorial places explaining the history of his country and displaying heartfelt hospitality. It was not easy for Bob and

Figure 3.26   Robert Rail demonstrating his fantastic stretch.

me to leave a newly made friend. When working in the UN, meetings and departures are usual things that we mentally understand, but it was always difficult for us to accept this.

We arrived at the Sofia airport. The Turkish airlines plane to Istanbul was one hour late and this situation brought me into a pessimistic mood because we had only one hour in Istanbul to catch our connecting Croatian Air flight to Zagreb. When we landed in Istanbul my pessimism became more realistic when we saw the tail of the airplane decorated with white and red quadrangles (Croatian Air) leaving the tarmac. We immediately reported to the airport authorities that we were on UN business in Bulgaria and lost our flight because of the delay with Turkish Airlines. We got invitation cards to stay overnight at a five-star hotel and were promised that all our problems would be resolved the next morning as soon as we appeared back at the Istanbul airport.

The next morning Bob and I appeared at the airport with the hope that everything would be alright, but in reality it appeared to be that nobody was able to help us. Moreover, Turkish Airlines authorities advised us that our stay at the five-star hotel was given to us by mistake. We were short on money and now we were on our own. We had to find a cheap hotel and a Croatian Airlines agency. So we decided to split our efforts into two routes: Bob would try to find a cheap hotel and from my side I went to the police office located in the airport to find Croatian Airlines.

Three times I told my story to the police authorities, but they did not speak English. Finally they found one low-ranking officer who took me to the booking office. So I returned back to the starting point having made a big circle. I approached a booking office with the sign "British Airways" and learned the location and phone number of the Croatian Airlines office. Bob in his turn found the only cheap hotels to be in the narrow, dangerous "backstreets" of the city.

The next morning we approached the hotel reception and luckily the clerk spoke Russian. I asked him to hire a taxi for us and explain to the taxi driver to take us to the Croatian Airlines office, located downtown in Istanbul. After 30 to 40 minutes of driving our taxi stopped at the office for which we had been looking for the past three days. In the office Bob displayed his best ability to charm the women working in the office and finally we got free tickets to fly to Zagreb. During the flight we finally felt that all our troubles were already behind us. We were glad to return back to be ready to fly to another country, to do our work, and to face new adventures.

Why Did I Go to Africa?

Why did I go to Africa? Many times I used to ask myself that question. The last time I thought that it was really the last time, but I am once again on my way to Senegal. Why? First of all I was heading to Senegal on UN business and second, simply, it was interesting.

Early one October morning we drove from Pristina (Kosovo) to Skopje (capital of Former Republic of Macedonia). The airplane to Zurich takes off at 0700 hours. The boring sound of windshield scrapers cleaning windshield from drops of the rain and rolling tires were making us fall asleep. A heavyweight, athletic-looking, African American police officer, Damon, was sleeping on the rear seat. As we arrived we had to run a few meters from the car to the terminal in the rain so we walked into the departure hall absolutely wet. Despite the early hour there were quite a few passengers. I thought to myself how different looking they all were. For example, there was a young man dressed in a cream-colored suit with the same color hair speaking loudly on the cell phone, drawing everybody's attention to the fact that he was standing alone in the center of the hall and putting a belt into his pants.

Traditionally, while waiting, passengers begin smoking, sending clouds of smoke into the air of the small departure hall. Somebody sat next to me and lit a cigarette. Neither Damon nor I were smokers, so we had to smell the blue smoke of the cheap and not very cheap cigarettes, regretting that the ventilation was not working or not switched on. A familiar song was playing in Bulgarian and in the same language, which Macedonians refer to as the Macedonian language, we were invited aboard the plane.

Neat and clean, the Zurich airport was living its life like a Swiss watch, once being switched on, working endlessly. A second hand overtakes the minute hand, a minute hand overtakes the hour hand, and only the hour hand does not overtake anything. I was having cappuccino at the airport café, looking at the clock, and waiting for Damon to finish his breakfast. After a two-hour flight we arrived at the French airport Charles de Gaulle—another check-in and six more hours in the plane. We flew over the northern coast of Spain, along the Gaskin Gulf. Little by little the clouds covered the mountains and I continued reading a book, which I always take with me on any journey.

Senegal

Senegal (French: *le Sénégal*), officially the Republic of Senegal, is a country south of the Sénégal River in western Africa. Its size is almost 197,000 square kilometers with an estimated population of about 12.5 million. Senegal's local language is called *Wolof* which means "our boat." Dakar is the capital city of Senegal, located on the Cape Verde Peninsula on the country's Atlantic coast. The name of the capital comes from the name of the *dakar* tree. Senegalese use the leaves of the *dakar* tree to heal people. There are only two seasons in Senegal: dry and wet. October is a dry month, one out of six dry months counting from September. A Senegalese police officer, Luis Mbae, met us in the airport and drove us to the hotel Independence in the center of Dakar. On our way to the hotel I asked Luis what the Wolof phrase was for "how are you doing." He replied, *"bebenen."* Through the open window of the car I was looking on the streets and buildings of the Senegalese capital and questioning myself, *Bebenen Senegal?*

First, we drove along the Atlantic Bay, and then turned into the city. There is two hours difference with London time. It was 1900 hours so it was already dark. Luis said that the sun always rises and sets at the same time—in the morning at 0700 hours and in the evening at 1900 hours. Adverts in the business houses and restaurants give a little more light to the poorly lit streets.

86

Figure 3.27   Luis Mbae and Omelchenko.

An old hotel air conditioner, slightly freshening air, woke me early in the morning with a clattering noise. By 0800 hours we were in a main Senegalese Police HQ. High-ranking police officers enthusiastically met us in the office where we explained how exams on English, driving, and shooting would be held.

About 200 candidates arrived from different corners of Senegal for testing and for being certified for the UN police service. The center for testing appeared to be a group of military barracks. All candidates were divided into two more or less equal groups. When I walked into a barrack the room was full of people. Friendly smiles displayed the white teeth of the candidates sitting very close to each other; flashes of photo cameras from different sides gave more light. I asked candidates whether they were ready for the test. Did they have pens and enough ink in their pens to write? They nodded their heads. When I smiled in return and wished them success, little by little the tension went down and then disappeared.

During the break, Damon and I were invited for a cup of coffee. Groups of 8 to 10 commanding police officers were already sitting in the canteen. As we entered they waved and welcomed us to join them. A

Figure 3.28 Students being tested.

waiter in white was serving us coffee and kept stepping into the path of the person talking, so we were all turning our heads to the left and right in order to keep eye contact with the speaker. Everybody was talking. One of the officers was talking on a mobile phone, gesticulating with his free hand and laughing loudly. In this friendly, relaxed, and chatting atmosphere, I could not recognize who was the chief of the center. Every one was equal and free to talk despite the number of stars on their epaulets. Then I saw one of the officers with a serious face slowly sipping hot coffee and asking Damon about how the testing procedure was going. This must have been a chief of the center I concluded to myself during this democratic coffee break.

The day of testing came to the end and in the evening Damon and I decided to take a walk in Dakar. As we left the lit hall of the hotel we entered the warm and dark street. Some people were appearing from the darkness and inviting us to take a taxi to buy something on special discount for foreigners and to visit their night club. It did not take us much time to make a decision and we returned back to the hotel.

Figure 3.29   Coffee break with colleagues.

Three days of testing passed quickly, like it was one day. What did we know about Africa? We saw only megapolis—the capital of Senegal. What was Africa like in our imagination? Usually, we got information about the black continent from TV, newspapers, and journals. I asked Luis to show us what Africa is really like and he took us to the National Park of Living Nature. Hundreds of hectares of bushes, baobab trees, giraffes, crocodiles, birds, turtles, monkeys, ostriches, and other different animals were in this park. We spent a full day with the guide seeing all the nature.

The following morning during breakfast at the restaurant of the hotel Independence, Luis Mbae took me to the window and pointed to an island in the Atlantic Bay, which could easily be seen from the 14th floor of the hotel, and said that he was going to take us to Gorée Island, made famous by its part in the *Atlantic slave trade*. This island looked like a giant footprint.

After a few minutes we arrived at the Dakar seaport. Every hour a rather big boat takes passengers to Gorée Island and back, carrying tourists and local merchants to and from the island. While waiting for the

Figure 3.30 National park in Senegal.

boat's departure we were looking at the ocean. A big oceanic boat under the flag of the Netherlands stayed not too far away from us. Hundreds of seagulls flying around, the smell of diesel, and the African sun made the picture complete. In reality, this picture was not complete because suddenly from behind me I heard a woman's whisper, in English, with a mild French accent, "My name is Brigit Bardo. I am the owner of one of the shops on Gorée Island. Please, come and visit my shop." I turned back and saw a pretty, dark brown-colored woman's face, two lines of snow white teeth, a big colorful red and yellow scarf tied on the head in a special manner, the same color skirt, and a big necklace composed of cheap stones. She said one more time, "Please, do not forget. My name is Brigit Bardo." As I saw later I was not the only one to whom Brigit was advertising her shops. During this short sea trip, I noticed this owner of the island shop walking on the boat, chewing a long white toothpick, and attracting the attention of tourists with her statuesque figure.

As we got closer to the island we saw buildings, built in a way that was modern two centuries ago. A group of children dressed in white and black ran to the mall to watch the boat coming to the island.

Figure 3.31 The view from the hotel of Gorée Island.

As we walked on the island we saw many shops selling Senegalese souvenirs and improvised exhibitions of slavery made with African painting.

Gorée is known as the location of the House of Slaves (French: *Maison des Esclaves*), built by the Afro-French Métis family about 1780–1784. The House of Slaves is one of the oldest houses on the island. It is now used as a tourist destination to show the horrors of the slave trade throughout the Atlantic world.

On one of the squares we found a Catholic Church with a tablet saying that the head of the Catholic Church, Pope John-Paul II visited the island in February 1992, and pronounced a prayer of sorrow for the people who were sold into slavery.

The day was coming to an end. It was time to return back to the continent. This day brought us closer to the end of our mission in Senegal. We boarded the boat and went toward the port. I was looking at the water, watching the shore of Gorée Island becoming smaller and smaller as we moved forward, leaving history behind us. What had we just left behind?

Figure 3.32   Omelchenko with Brigit Bardo.

Figure 3.33   Children watching the ships on the ocean.

Figure 3.34   Church tablet on display.

What was waiting for us in the nearest future? We never know what tomorrow has in store for us. I saw a smiling face among passengers and thought to myself that Africa was smiling and believing in its good future.

With these positive thoughts we stepped onto the land, believing that everything would be alright with Luis Mbae, who took us to the airport the next day, and with all the people whom we met during this short visit in Senegal, who helped us learn a little bit more about this wonderful country.

INTERNATIONAL MISSION RATS

Daniel Chassignet, France

My honorable friend Robert Rail asked me a few months ago to become involved in his book *Surviving the International War Zone, Lessons Learned*, and now as a good friend I will bring my small contribution to this unusual collection of stories. I belong to the "Mission Rat family," and that means that, like Bob, I have been involved in different international missions around the world, trying to make peace, to keep peace, to teach, to train, or to advise. Before telling you two little stories about colleagues and myself and also to be polite, let me introduce myself. I am Daniel, a "Frenchy," and I belong to the French Gendarmerie that is a military institution with a civilian and military police purpose. Due to this particularity I am often away from my country and with my 34 years of service with the gendarmerie I have been selected, designated, or volunteered to join an international mission in a foreign country such as Lebanon, Bosnia and Herzegovina, Kosovo, Haiti, Liberia, Albania, Togo, and more, but the list is too long and I am not here to give you a geography course. All these missions have been different by their goal, context, danger, and funny stories like the one I am ready to tell you now. This happened during my mission in Kosovo when Bob and I were working together in the same unit. That day I proposed Bob to go shopping in a large U.S. camp located about one-hour drive from our location. We used to go there often to buy food and other stuff for our survival. Of course, before entering in a camp you need to go though several checkpoints and you must show your mission member badges that are visible on our uniform. Following the rules, Bob and I had our badges apparent and were wearing our respective uniform: U.S. uniform with U.S. flag sewed on the left sleeve for Bob and so for me with the French uniform. After the car was checked at the first checkpoint, we stopped at the second checkpoint for the ID check. I showed my ID first because I was driving the car and got the clearance from the guard to enter in the camp. Bob did the same but was requested by the guard to show his passport in order to prove that he was a real American citizen. I saw Bob was very surprised and looked deeply offended. To avoid any trouble with the security he stayed calm and did not argue. After we got the final clearance to enter in the camp Bob became very upset and I was laughing, telling Bob that the guards had more trust in a French police officer than a U.S. police officer. For a few moments I was very proud to be a French guest in a big U.S. camp and had to comfort Bob for the next hour.

Through the second story I am going to demonstrate that friendship in any mission between mission members from more than 60 different countries is very important and sometimes you share the rent of your flat or accommodation with colleagues from another country with different culture and language. When I was on mission in Kosovo, I shared one house with one colleague from the States and another colleague from Finland. Each of us was working in a different unit but after our duty time we used to sit together in our living room for dinner while we were watching a movie broadcasted by the local TV. Most of the movies in Kosovo are translated in German even if they are from the United States, France, Italy, or any other country. One evening Michael, my U.S. colleague, and I were sitting in the living room watching one movie with Sylvester Stallone and of course Sly spoke German in the movie. Besides speaking French and English, I also speak German. During the movie Michael started to laugh for the following reason: He said to me, "Daniel! The situation is very funny! We are here watching an American movie, translated in German and translated back to me from German to English by a Frenchman!" We found this situation very funny and found out that we were complementing each other.

I will keep these little stories in my mind. Also, these stories will not blot out the atrocities I have seen during my different missions but it allows me to keep my head screwed on the right way and to remember that sometimes we can still have fun in a world that is more and more crazy.

Figure 3.35 "Frenchy," on patrol in his favorite surroundings.

A SPOUSE'S VIEW

Janet Rail, United States

When Bob accepted his first foreign mission we were already "empty nesters." Both our children were grown and on their own which meant we had a lot of flexibility as far as my travel and vacation time with Bob. I grew up in the suburbs of Chicago and went to school with a very diverse cultural mix. I could say "hello" and "thank you" in a half dozen different languages. I had eaten in restaurants specializing in Greek, Italian, Scandinavian, German, and even African cuisine. I hadn't done a lot of foreign travel but I could handle it. I was ready to see the world and was confident I could go almost anywhere and blend in with no trouble—at least that's what I thought. Boy, was I in for a big surprise!

Adjusting

After 20-plus years of rotating shifts and rotating days off, I figured it wouldn't be all that different getting used to Bob being gone for a year. There was a huge difference! When you know someone is an hour away and can come home if there is an emergency your brain relaxes and you don't worry. Even when he is away at school or training in another state, he can still get to you in a reasonable amount of time. But when your No. 1 support is halfway around the world it's different. One of the other wives told me she sprinkled her husband's aftershave on the pillowcase so that when she was trying to fall asleep she felt like her husband was still close by. Some of the wives left a pair of socks or one shirt unwashed so every time they went to do laundry there was still something of their husband's in the house. Most of us rearranged photos or added a favorite picture to the bedside table. My favorite nightshirt for the first month was any of Bob's T-shirts. That way he was there with me when I went to bed.

Being able to communicate with someone when they are away is more than important. It's the one thing that saves your sanity. Bob's first mission was just before cell phones and Internet communication became popular. His house had one phone that worked most of the time if he stood still in the hallway and it wasn't raining or snowing. Phone calls from the States were expensive but would have been worth three times what we paid. It was being able to hear each other's voices that gave us the peace of mind we needed. During the rest of Bob's missions we had e-mail and cell phones available and that made a huge difference. Technology has really helped make foreign missions easier for families.

Bosnia

My first big adventure was Sarajevo, Bosnia. Bob had been in the country for three months so he had already sent me some photos of the area. I tried to learn a little about the country and the people. It was the site of the 1984 Winter Olympics which meant mountains and snow. Bob and another officer were renting a small house from a couple that had been given an apartment by the Bosnian government as compensation for their son's death in the war. They rented their home to peacekeepers but they would come to the house every day to tend their little garden and grape vines. They understood and spoke a little English and German and Bob had learned a few key phrases in Serbian, so between gestures and broken sentences we could communicate fairly well. The teenage girl who lived next door was taught English in school so if there were anything impor- tant that needed to be translated she would come over to help us.

My flight into Sarajevo was due to land in the middle of the afternoon. This was the best time to land because there was no working radar at the airport and most mornings were very foggy. As the plane started its descent between the mountains I could see all the little stone houses and cottages nestled in the hillside. Each little town or village had its own group of homes trailing up the mountainside from what looked to be the main part of a town. It reminded me of movie scenes of little villages in the Alps with laughing children and happy families. All that was missing was the cowbells. As we got lower to the ground I started getting a strange feeling that something wasn't quite right with this idyllic setting. A few hundred feet closer to the ground and I realized that most of the houses had no people near them. Roofs had huge holes or were totally missing. Bullet holes peppered the walls and the windows were shuttered or boarded over. You could tell where there used to be beautiful flower gardens with fences and walking paths. Now there was destruction everywhere. The war had destroyed the mountain villages and caused the people to move into the city. I learned later that there were so many land mines in all the fields most farmers had given up trying to plant crops—that was why the little garden at Bob's house was so important to his landlord. It was a safe place to plant his vegetables.

Bob met me at the airport and I was more than very glad to see him. Landing at an airport in a war zone is somewhat unnerving at the best of times. There is no taxiing up to the terminal and walking through an enclosed, heated ramp. The planes comes to an abrupt stop in the middle of the slightly too-short runway and one-by-one the passengers get off the plane and walk across the tarmac while armed officials watch your every move. In Sarajevo there is a sign in the airport that says "Unattended luggage will be blown up." They don't just take the unattended luggage and dispose of it like they do here in the States. They actually take it to the middle of a field and blow it up!

The car ride from the airport to the UN police training building could best be described as sensory overload. The photos I had been sent barely prepared me for the devastation I saw. Houses and office buildings that once stood proudly as monuments to Sarajevo's power in the Balkans were now piles of rubble along the highway. Businesses had been abandoned when the owner was killed or left the country. The damaged merchandise was scattered everywhere. Some of the apartments were slowly being repaired but it didn't appear to be any organized, state-run renovation. Each individual or family went back to their apartment, no matter which floor it was on in this huge high-rise complex and started trying to rebuild their own little, personal space. A few of the buildings had more than one apartment rebuilt on the same floor but many of the complexes had less than a dozen families that had "moved home." Other buildings were purposely being left in ruin as a constant reminder to the people of what could happen if the fighting were to start back up. Bales of straw were piled up to be used as a shield from drive-by shootings or hand grenades for the little house hiding behind them.

The smell of diesel fumes hung like a thick cloud over everything. The main street of Sarajevo was a boulevard, eight lanes wide with a train running in the median. It seemed to be clogged with traffic all the time. Drivers would stop their vehicles in the middle of their travel lane to talk to someone in another lane so cars would jump the curb and drive on the sidewalk to get around the traffic jam. Instead of rolling down the windows to let in air people would drive down the street with the doors open. The driver would have one hand on the steering wheel, the other hand holding a cigarette, his left foot holding the door open and his right foot working all three pedals. It didn't matter if it was stop-and-go traffic or traveling 40 mph, every door that could be propped open was open.

Pedestrians had to be careful no matter where they were. You had to stay on the sidewalk or at least some sort of paved surface at all times. There were so many land mines "planted" throughout the country even the parkways in the big cities were unsafe. Little bombs that were nicknamed "hockey pucks" were everywhere because it was so easy to place them just off the paved surface. An officer from the mine-removal team

Figure 3.36 It's hard to tell, but people were living in this house.

told us that it would take 100 officers working 24 hours a day over 100 years to clear the land mines out of Bosnia. Most of the land mines in the Sarajevo area weren't designed to kill you. They were made just strong enough to maim you so you spent the rest of your life crippled and in pain. This way you were a burden and a constant reminder of the war to your family. Both sides of the conflict put land mines everywhere they could. This was the first time I saw people truly hating someone else without having a reason for their feelings. From the time they were old enough to understand language they were taught to hate "the other side" just because they were on the other side.

Accommodations

Whenever it is possible, the UN tries to have its officers live "in the field," with the local people. This has some definite advantages and definite disadvantages. The officers learn a lot about the local customs, culture, and food which can make their job much easier, but when you have two ethnic groups sharing the same space it can lead to some tense moments. Which group is this landlord associated with? And shopping: Who owns which store? Which day is their holy day? (Friday or Sunday) What holidays do they observe? Who are your neighbors and how do they feel about having a foreigner living next door to them? If you are trying to blend into the community and have a peaceful place to sleep at night all these questions are very important. Both the Bosnia and Herzegovina and the Kosovo mission required the officers to live "off base."

The house Bob was renting was a few kilometers out of the city. Some of the fields had been cleared of their land mines and there were sheep and goats grazing. Most of the houses had been repaired or were being repaired so the area was considered "relatively safe." One of the things that I noticed was the lack of finished wood. There were plenty of sapling trees but 2x4s were very scarce so instead of bracing walls with 2x4s or 2x6s, they would simply strip the branches off a tree and cut the tree to the length they needed to brace the cement blocks until the mortar was set. Fences and walls were cinder block, stacked stones, or cement columns—no split wood or picket fences. The streets were very narrow and most yards were walled so there was no shoulder and no way to get around a herd of goats if it was walking to a new field to graze. More than once if a military tank had to go down one of the streets on patrol it would knock down half of the walls it passed by.

The closest food market to Bob's accommodation was a short walk down the street to a small building that was covered in bright blue tiles. There were two ladies that worked in the store that did not speak a single word of English (or German) but were always very cheerful and tried their best to help me find whatever it was they thought I was looking for. Paying for a purchase in any of the smaller stores was a bit tricky. Bosnia used Deutsch marks as their main currency but they were just starting to mint some of their own bills and coins. Copper was very scarce because of the war so there were very few "pennies." When you bought items from a smaller store and handed them Deutsch marks to pay for your purchase, they would try to give you Bosnian money as change and if they didn't have the right coins they would give you a little chocolate candy bar instead of pennies.

Bob's main assignment in both UN missions was instructing and testing the peacekeepers assigned to the mission from all the contributing countries (56 nations in Bosnia and 60 in Kosovo). Both missions were English-speaking missions which meant there could be 50 different accents in any conversation taking place in a classroom. This also meant there were some strange translations of materials that Bob had to correct. One of the strangest ones I saw was the American Red Cross First Aid manual that had been translated from English to Arabic, to Bulgarian, to Turkish, to Russian, and then the unfortunate Ukrainian officer who was looking at it, trying to translate it back to English and knew the words were not right. I never realized how important all the basic grammar I learned back in grade school was. It's a really strange feeling to be helping a high-ranking official from a foreign country when he is trying to write a speech for a visiting dignitary. He told me his head knew the words but his fingers could not write them in English.

Kosovo

When Bob was getting ready for his first mission in Kosovo we were told the situation was exactly the same and totally different than Bosnia, and that is the truth. Once again you had a country that has unbelievable natural beauty with mountains and forests that have been ravaged by an unnecessary war. There were the usual problems with electricity and gas supplies but this time it seemed to me that the spirit of the people was still broken. In Bosnia, the people were trying to return to their prewar lives, they were ready to move forward, but Kosovo was still struggling to survive from one day to the next. The war was still too fresh in their minds and they were still looking for revenge instead of peace.

Living conditions were worse in Kosovo than they were in Bosnia but that actually worked out better for us. I know that sounds backward but what happened was quite a few of the NATO and EU countries that had peacekeepers stationed in Kosovo sent products to the big cities to be sold in the little local stores. Canned goods, cookies, pasta, and personal toiletries had European labels. There are moments when you are very grateful for a name brand tissue that does not feel like sandpaper! Beef was scarce and high priced but chicken was everywhere. Because of the Muslim influx into certain areas of the country, trying to buy pork in Kosovo was not advisable. If the locals found out you bought it you could be the target for retribution and if the market was in the wrong area of town and foolish enough to advertise that they sold it they could be blown up. More than once a person would just casually walk down the street and a hand grenade would get thrown into the store that was selling the wrong things to the wrong people. Because the refrigerators are small and the electricity to them was limited, we shopped for perishable items almost every day. There were lots of little markets throughout the city so finding what you needed was more of a communication problem than a logistics problem.

Bob's first few months in Kosovo were spent in the rural town of Glogovac. He rented a house that was very similar to the one he had in Sarajevo. By the time I went to visit, Bob had been transferred to the International Police Training Center in Pristina, the capital city. His apartment was within walking distance of his office so there was no need for a vehicle. This was good because driving was even worse in Kosovo than it was in Bosnia. Most of the roads in the cities were still being "repaired" and the rural roads were muddy ruts. Not only did you have the usual congestion, there were donkey carts with a vehicle body placed over the bed of the wagon and a huge number of "modified" motor vehicles. They would take any kind of gas engine they could find and attach it to any kind of frame (metal or wood) so it turned two or more wheels (usually three or four). Then they put some sort of flat area on top of it that could be used as a seat, and you have a "Kosovo Harley."

Electricity for the entire country of Kosovo was provided by three antiquated, coal-burning generators that belched out a sooty smoke that covered everything. If you opened a window in the morning you needed to clean the table before you ate lunch. Windows and the outsides of all the buildings always had a grimy film on them and the air had an unusual oily smell. In the winter when it snowed, it looked like it was snowing gray snow. When I walked anywhere I would have to clean my glasses as soon as I got indoors because there would be an oily film on the lenses.

Figure 3.37   A common sight on the roads in Kosovo.

The generators were so old and in such bad repair there was always at least one of them "off line," being fixed, so electricity was rationed. Most of the time, the city would have power for four hours and then be without power for two hours. This cycle continued both day and night. (In the winter, it got a little chilly waiting for the heat to come back on in the middle of the night.) All the shops and offices had little gas generators to switch over to when the power went off, but there were a lot of homes that had nothing and they simply had to wait for the electricity to come back on. I never quite understood why they kept rationing power because every year, as a gift to the people, the government would leave the electricity on all day and night from Christmas Eve until New Year's Day.

Water was also rationed in Pristina. It was not considered safe to drink because there were so many cracks in the pipes and all sorts of contaminants could leach into it. All water for cooking or drinking had to be bottled water or boiled. Every night the water was shut off at some time between 8 P.M. and 10 P.M. and turned back on the next morning between 5 A.M. and 7 A.M. Taking a shower by candlelight is one thing but when the water is turned off when you are halfway through washing your hair you learn to bathe earlier in the day!

Christmas in Kosovo

Christmas in Kosovo was unique. Even though there were a majority of Muslims in Pristina, there were signs of Christmas everywhere. There was merchandise coming in from European nations and all the brand name products had Santa or holiday decorations on the packaging. So, to help the children "understand," Santa became Father Time and he rode a sleigh through the town on New Year's Eve, throwing candy to the children (the "elves" were shooting guns into the air in celebration). Christmas trees became "holiday trees." They were decorated with lights and little balloons. At the stroke of midnight on January 1st, the children would pop the balloons. Whether it was Santa or Father Time, if it's chocolate wrapped in brightly colored foil children of all ages think it tastes great.

Proper Perspective

In the insanity of a war zone, the only way to keep your sanity is to be a little insane. There are so many things around you that are beyond your control it becomes very important to find some sort of stress release. More than once I saw an officer skipping down the hall singing a children's song. Everybody laughed and the tension was broken. Any excuse was a good excuse for a party. There was always lots of food and drink and most important, laughter. (Some of the singing was really bad but that just helped with the laughter.) It helped the officers feel like they were part of a family when their own family was so far away. In Kosovo, one of the officers would announce his arrival by braying like a donkey every time he came to work. Before long, the other officers were responding with animal noises of their own. The chief of staff just shook her head and smiled because she knew all the animals were safely in her barnyard, ready for their shift.

Compensatory Time Off (CTO)

All of the UN missions Bob served in had CTO, better known to civilians as vacation time. He would save these days off until I came to visit so we could travel somewhere together and he could have a short time away from the war zone. We both knew that time away was very important. When you are living and working in a war zone it's like being at work all the time, day and night. You can never totally relax. (I think this is one of the reasons Iraq was harder on Bob. He was deployed to a forward observation base for a full year, far away from even the most basic comforts afforded the people in "the Green Zone," with no time away from the war.) Most of the time, we went on little trips to neighboring countries. In Bosnia we drove to the Croatian coast. We didn't need a map. We simply took "the road to the coast." When we were in Kosovo we flew in and out of the country because it was the easiest way to leave the country. It wasn't that these were exotic locations. The sightseeing was great but the most important part of every trip was that it was a time to relax and get away from the war.

There was one trip when we went to Greece from Kosovo by car. There are massive restrictions on people and packages coming across the border from Albania and Macedonia into Kosovo so it can take up to 12 hours to go through all the checkpoints. Because of this a fellow officer drove us to the Kosovo/Macedonia border where we walked across, carrying our luggage, to a hired taxi waiting for us on the other side of the border. He drove us through Macedonia to a resort on the sea in Greece. Leaving Kosovo was not the problem. Coming back would have been a nightmare. When we came back, the same driver brought us from the resort to the border. Trucks were in line for miles, waiting to show their papers so they could go through the checkpoint. It was late afternoon and our driver told us that most of the trucks would end up having to spend the night there, waiting in line until the morning when the border guards returned. Cars and taxis were also backed up but those lines were inching slowly forward. When our taxi was a few hundred yards from the border we thanked our driver, took our luggage, and started walking to the checkpoint. Every car we passed, every truck driver scowling down at us made me more uneasy. I wanted to drop my bag and run as fast as I could but I had to walk along with Bob, as if we were walking along a garden path. And then the final irony was feeling relieved to be going *into* a war zone!

Blending In

One of the most important things I learned while visiting Bob was the importance of "blending in." Muted colors and sensible shoes are always the best choice for a war zone. Don't expect things to be like they are at home. Life in the bigger cities is often referred to as "urban camping" and out in the country it's even worse. Forget the hair dryers and curling irons. There are times when you're lucky if you have hot water for bathing. And learn how to say "hello!" You would be surprised at how helpful it is just to learn how to say "hello" and "thank you." Don't try to learn a formal greeting phrase. It's that simple, friendly "hi" that tells the people you are trying to be a friend. If they do speak English realize that it's probably not their first language and it helps them understand you if you slow down your speech pattern just a little bit and try to stay away from slang phrases.

End of Mission

End of Mission—the second greatest three-word phrase in the English language! Just like anything else you look forward to, time moves so painfully slow when you're waiting for someone to come home from a war zone. Bob was coming home and everything was going to be exactly like it was before he left—right? Not quite! No matter how hard I tried to make everything look the same as it was when he left it was not the same and it was going to take time for both of us to re-adjust. All the little things he did before he left for the mission, like taking out the garbage—those little things that reminded you he was gone and made you miss him when you first had to do them. Well, now you've been doing them for a year and you don't even think about how and when you'll take care of them. You just do it and that means he has *nothing* to do. It's like he's a guest in his own home. After seeing so much death and destruction for a year it's very

105

easy to get overprotective of those you love. It's not that they are trying to control or smother us. It's an actual fear of something bad happening to us. Their bodies may have come home but there is plenty of the war zone that has come back with them in their mind. So I try hard to understand and start to let go of the strangle hold I have on every aspect of daily life. Now there is another person to think about when planning meals— When are *we* eating? What are *we* eating? I guess it's no more breakfast food for dinner. My life has been organized chaos while his every waking moment has been structured. Now he tries hard to understand and relax and slowly our lives fit back together. The Swedish contingent was told that it takes four to six months for returning officers to adjust to life back at home. From our experience I would have to agree. Second missions are easier on returning partners but there are still those few weeks of trying to return to "normal."

Friends and Characters

When I think back on all the people I met while visiting the Balkans I remember such a vast array of characters it would be impossible to come up with one most memorable person. There were officers who were over two meters tall, and when you're only 5 feet 4 inches somebody that's 6 feet 6 inches is tall! There were officers who spoke perfect English as a second language but could not understand even the most common, derogatory slang phrases and female officers who were determined to have something feminine on their uniform so they tied the little ribbon on the back of the beret into a bow or wore a belt buckle shaped like a flower on their gun belt. I became friends with an officer from Germany who patrolled the streets of the city where my father was born. I met UN workers with the whitest skin, blackest hair, and darkest eyes I ever saw. (They were born in Transylvania.) And I think both Penga and I were totally amazed that we had a common teacher in our education—my Bible school teacher in the United States became a missionary and taught Penga English in Cameroon. There were local women trying so hard to grow a few flowers in their tiny gardens—every inch of land is so precious when you are growing food for your family but they would plant one row of flowers so they had something to brighten up their lives. The local men working on their newly grafted plants—they would cut and wrap the new sprouts with the precision and care of a surgeon. There was the chef at the one restaurant that used a clever to whack off the quarter kilo of lamb (goat) when you ordered it. You didn't order lamb shoulder or lamb chops. It was just a hunk of lamb, whatever piece was next to get cut. I saw little children trying to play soccer in a school yard. If you kicked the ball out of bounds, passed the yellow "mine tape," you had two choices. You could send someone into the mine field to retrieve the ball and risk getting blown up or the game was over.

When you look past the first impressions and sit to talk with these people you quickly discover how very similar we all are. It wasn't an officer or local from another country with some unimaginable problem. It was girlfriends and boyfriends worrying about how being away would affect their relationships and how things would be on their next leave. It was husbands and wives worrying about how the stress of the situation was going to affect their spouse. It was mothers and fathers worrying about their families back home. What were their children doing? Was everyone still healthy? How were they doing in school? Was the roof still leaking? And vehicles! There was always someone's spouse or friend dealing with some sort of mechanical problem with some sort of vehicle. The country may have changed, but the problems were all the same.

I am old enough to remember being taught the ideologies of the cold war in school. We were told not to trust certain people because they were from "that area" of the world. These lessons of fear and hate were taught from misunderstood events in history. We were taught to blame an entire nation or race of people for the actions of a few. More than one conflict has continued long after necessary because we were not willing to believe that "anything good could come out of that area of the world." And yet, the best advice I ever received on accepting a person for who they are and not judging them for what someone else has done was from someone I was taught to hate. He said his grandmother always told him the fastest way to stop a war was to have both sides take off their uniforms so everyone could see how much we are all alike. Truer words have not been spoken.

4

French Island Hot Sauce

If you really want to know how very much the same we all are, just sit down with people from all over the world and eat with them. However, be prepared to be flexible and cast aside what and how ... and when ... and all the other quaint rules you have learned about dining. If you are willing to do that you will be subjected to an unbelievable rainbow of astonishing experiences.

After finishing our morning training, my United Nations International Police Task Force colleagues and I would break for lunch wherever there was food to be had. When you have a group of individuals from all over the world, from every different cultural and gastronomical background, every day that passes presents a new learning experience for us to consider and remember for the rest of our lives. Food was always a serious matter and not to be taken lightly, but there were those special moments that brought tears of laughter to the eyes of even the most serious of us. I remember when one of the French Special Forces officers that came from the islands sat down at our table. He was a slender built young man with an engaging smile. He carefully removed a small glass vial from his shirt pocket and proudly placed it at the side of his plate. It contained what I would guess to be about two ounces of a clear, golden liquid. He said it was sent to him by his grandmother who has a highly respected reputation on the island where he was born for her special hot seasoning liquid. I very foolishly remarked that I had tasted all kinds of hot seasonings in my life and that this was probably no different than one of them. He said to everyone at the table that it would be his pleasure if Robert would care to taste his grandma's special hot liquid. Everyone at the table stopped eating and looked directly at me! I had taken the liberty of opening my big mouth and now I would have to open that mouth for a second time to taste his grandma's sauce. I stood up from the table, looked at one and all, and said, "Put the cold water on my left side and the ice on my right side and don't stand between me and the bathroom." I learned a long time ago that it's better to have people laugh with you than at you. I drew my knife from my belt and just touched the tip of the blade into the clear golden liquid shimmering in the vial, and then I carefully touched the tip of my knife to the tip of my tongue. Nothing happened. There was no taste or flavor. I looked over at my French Island colleague with an expression on my face of, "What now?" He just said to all of us, "Just wait a moment, please." Suddenly I realized that I was breathing a little deeper and beads of sweat were starting to form on my forehead. The next thing I knew my entire mouth started feeling a dry burn that is difficult to describe but way too easy to remember. Out of the mercy of his heart my colleague poured me a glass of cold water and said, "A toast to my grandma." That was one toast I made in my life with serious conviction.

A few moments later after the excitement of the situation had subsided we were joined by a few more of our colleagues who were not present during my trial by French Island fire. They were all getting to the dining table late and were in a hurry to eat before the training classes resumed for the afternoon session. One of the late arrivals was a big, powerful officer from North Africa that was highly respected by all of us. He was a great weapons trainer and the entire international cadre looked to him for advice and consultation when it came to anything about weapons. In the blink of an eye, before anyone could say anything to intercede, our colleague reached across the table, dipped a piece of chicken that was on his fork into the golden hot sauce, and then put the entire saturated piece in his mouth. He casually swallowed the chicken and continued eating while we all sat there, amazed, almost mesmerized, watching and waiting. As we watched him, he realized that he was the center of attention. One of our Romanian colleagues placed a water glass in front of our fellow officer's plate and asked how hot the special hot sauce was. It was about that time the evil curse of the French Island hot sauce struck our esteemed colleague. It was like watching a fuse on a bomb slowly burn down his neck into his stomach. His face went from tan, to pink, to red. His breathing went from normal to puffing up his cheeks and blowing out like he was blowing up a balloon. He then slammed both of his hands, palms down, on our table and yelled out a lot of Arabic words I can't remember ever hearing before. I realized that this man was tenfold tougher than I could ever be; however, this was one eagle that flew a little too high and close to

110

the hot sauce sun and got burned. Had it been me, I would have had to be buried head first in the snow that was outside our barracks to survive the evil curse of the French Island hot sauce. The next day in a joking moment over a small, bland breakfast of eggs, cheese, and bread, my colleague told us that the only thing worse than the pain of the hot sauce going into his body was when the time came for the hot sauce to come out of his body. It was, again, another moment that brought us all closer together.

5

Interrogation by Torture

Let's make this very simple and easy for all of us to understand. It all starts with someone asking an important question to another person. The desired response to this question is whatever gives the questioner the information he or she is looking for. If the information is given truthfully and immediately, very little follow-up action is required. However, many times the response that occurs is silence, false information, or refusal to say anything. This can set a chain of events into motion, and some of these possible proceedings have the unfortunate potential of ranging between unpleasant and horrifying.

The concept of torture is as wide open to comment and interpretation as comfort and politics. It is a totally individual perception or point of view and dependent on the individual's interpretation of what is being imposed on him. On one end of the spectrum is the person who considers being without the comforts of shelter, food, or water for even a brief period of time to be torture. This perspective could be due to the lifestyle this person has been able to enjoy or it could be due to the level of empathy that person has for others and their perspective of their own life's circumstances. What that breaks down to is that some people on this Earth are enjoying a life that others would consider unattainable or even better than they could ever imagine. These are the people who suffer total emotional collapse because they are being scolded or yelled at during questioning. On the other end of the spectrum there are the more worldly individuals who have experienced the cold realities of life. These would include the thousands of people of the special military forces who have experienced "water-related" forms of persuasion and manipulation as a routine part of their training. They have endured these techniques for their own awareness and mental development, physical toughness, and personal discipline. Some of these individuals would even engage in similar practices of water persuasion or dunking as part of a contest to determine who would buy the next round of drinks on a Friday night at the local off-base bar. Many of these techniques are considered old-world challenges of fidelity and devotion. This is not to make light of some of the most vicious and atrocious practices that take place all over the world that are seldom discussed or even known to the outside world. It's these sadistic and disconcerting methods that fall within the general area of torture. They are comprised of the methodologies that inflict enduring harm on the mind of the victim, and inflict enduring harm on the body of the victim with the perspective that mind and body are by nature forever intertwined. But know this warning well: Whatever methods are agreed on by those in authority to be used on a person today, for whatever logic or justification, can, and more often than not will, be used on others in the future for other situations with different logic and justification. Interrogation by torture is a door that once opened is literally torn from its hinges and becomes an open passageway to the atrocities of the future.

During one hot and humid, wasted afternoon in the Balkans, one of my international police trainer colleagues and I were formally advised that the officers we were scheduled to train were delayed in their deployment to our location because of extreme West African weather. That's all the excuse it took for us to scramble out of the training barracks for an early lunch break. At that point in time life was good and we had a place to go to for hot food, running water, and electricity most of the time. Everything was great and our spirits were high. It was so much better than living on that chemically engineered, nutritionally complete goop in the plastic bags that they brazenly refer to as food. The food in the plastic bags really loses its appeal when you have to cut it open and squeeze it out of tubes, and the dessert is the same color as the main course. It was during these quaint circumstances I had the very interesting opportunity to have lunch with a distinguished officer from South America. Shortly after I had sat down with my food tray I was very politely greeted. The officer requested permission to share my table and have lunch with me. My first impression was that we were from two very different worlds. I came from the world of tactical policing where the officers did the dirty work or the grunt muscle work of the arrests and conflict responses. My lunch colleague, however, was clearly a textbook police administrator. It was not just his demeanor. From the top of the perfectly combed hair on his head to his unique expensive multicolored brown leather boots, and the perfectly tailored uniform that was worn between, I had the perception that this was a very precise and even particular individual that was sitting across from me. I have always had a very thick skin for tolerating people but I was feeling strangely uncomfortable with this person. I had a fork and a plate of hot food so I started to eat, and then for some reason quite unknown to me at the time, I stopped eating and looked across the table at him. My lunch colleague stated that we must find "pleasure in all things through organization and control," as he very precisely laid out his paper napkin and eating utensils in an uncompromising and disciplined display around his plate. It entered my mind that his method of eating was of far greater concern to my lunch mate than the food he would eventually be consuming. This sent up a red flag in my mind and I went into my "polite and constantly smiling" mode that I use when I am confronted or uncomfortable with the situation. He then asked me if he could inquire about my opinion on the reliability of reading body signs, such as were stated in the book I had authored titled *The Unspoken Dialogue.* It was another red flag waving in front of my face. He knew me. He knew the book I had written and lunch was no random meeting or circumstance. I had the distinct feeling that someone was trying to control me as much as the eating utensils he had carefully placed around his plate. He then shared with me that he had a great professional interest in my book and in my opinions about different strategies concerning interrogations. He was in charge of interviewing difficult criminal persons back in his own country. I asked him if a person is difficult to interview and the dialogue develops into deeper questioning did he consider that an interrogation? He said that they do not use or even consider that word. I quickly noticed that when he made that remark he broke off eye contact by looking down at his food and eating. That was a sure sign that he had just made a statement he didn't want to debate or discuss any further. I thought in my mind that if he could become that rigid in a casual conversation, I wonder how unbending and uncompromising would this person be as the interrogator of others? I concluded that this person sitting across from me was not an interviewer—he was clearly an interrogator. We continued to eat for a few more minutes, watching a small television up in the corner of the room that was broadcasting a show in a language neither one of us understood. I told him that when you are trying to interpret body signs the most effective reading will occur when you gather the greatest amount of body signs. Body signs are no more than a source of nonverbal communication and understanding. He said that he had heard of a clinic

115

where they always achieved getting the information they wanted without a single failure in their method or process. He made his statement and resumed eating. I felt like I was clearly being baited or manipulated, but I was keenly interested in what he knew or had heard. I told him that I was always interested in learning about other methods or skills. I saw a discrete smile of personal satisfaction form on his face. He carefully folded and placed his napkin on top of his plate and then proceeded to place his eating utensils strategically on the napkin. He had eaten only what he chose to eat and left the rest of his lunch that was not up to his meticulous standards on his plate. I was offered an excellent Cuban cigar to have with our coffee. Because I can't get them legally back in my own country, I accepted. I could see a developing structure to the story I was about to be told. It was being laid out not only on the table between us but by virtue of the organizational control my colleague was exerting over me and the conditions around us. Hopefully, the information would be worth my condoning his eccentricities. It's a common interrogation technique to control anything and everything around you, and he was doing just that with me. I wanted to hear this story, so the price to be paid was to let my colleague have his way. He was playing me and I was playing him for what I might learn out of this not so casual meeting. We were both playing the same game—the only difference was that we both had our own set of rules. For me, the game didn't matter. I just wanted to hear the damn story. With coffee being overstirred and cigars lit, he finally commenced with his story.

He said that there is a clinic that is not referred to by any name that has been in operation for many years. It is just a short plane ride from his capital. It is housed within a beautiful white two-story, modern rectangular building with no windows or signs. There are no markings anywhere on either the inside or outside of the building. The grounds surrounding the building are perfectly manicured and maintained. There are no other buildings in the area of this building. There aren't even any sheds or garages. There are several ponds on the grounds that have ducks and other water fowl in them as pets to be fed and watched. There are benches to sit on around the ponds and walkways going from all of the ponds to the clinic building. Everyone in and around the building is attired in white medical-type uniforms. All of the staff personnel display the most compassionate and courteous demeanor to all of the subjects of interrogation, that are referred to as "patients," that have been brought to them for "treatment." The patients are brought to their own comfortable private rooms and then personally advised by their doctor and staff of the times

116

their meals will be brought to them and the time schedule of their three-times-a-day treatments. The treatment times are scheduled in the morning, afternoon, and evening for all of the days they will be residents at the clinic. With the companionship of a staff member the patients are free to enjoy the grounds and walk around without any restrictions. They can walk about the ponds or garden area any time they wish. When it is their scheduled treatment times the patients are greeted in their rooms by staff members who gently and compassionately place them on gurney-type wheeled stretchers and secure them down very firmly to their stretchers for their own safety. The patients are then taken to the treatment room for their treatment sessions. The treatment room is an ultramodern operating room-type of atmosphere. The patient is then very carefully and courteously attached to an electrical control devise via electrical wiring all over key areas of their body, while being assured and consoled by the staff members that the treatment will result in their feeling much better after the session has ended. Then very interestingly, classical instrumental music is played in the background for about one minute. After this one-minute interlude, the expected intense electrical surge is delivered into the body of the patient, causing total mental and physical collapse, and loss of psychological focus and bodily control. With the focus on compassion and consideration, the staff then cleans and consoles the patient while telling them how well they did with their treatment and how much better they are now going to be in the future with continued treatments. As the treatments go on, throughout the day, day after day, and week after week, nothing changes. The conduct of the staff stays consistent with their display of kindness and consideration. No questions of any kind are ever asked during the treatment sequences or at any other times during the days and weeks of the treatment program. And the music remains exactly and precisely the same during each treatment, day after day, and week after week, for as long as the patient is in the treatment program. After all of the treatments have been culminated, the patients are then advised that their treatment program was successful and they are cheerfully congratulated. There are a couple of days where the patient is allowed to relax, under supervision, and spend some time by the ponds or just being wheeled around the grounds in a chair. Shortly after their conditioning, they are very warmly and compassionately escorted to a small, nicely furnished private office. This is where they sit down and casually talk to a different staff member they have never met before who is attired in regular business dress. This is the time that "control" questions are asked of the patient. These are questions where the interrogator already knows the answer. The "control" questions are utilized to determine just how responsive and cooperative the patient is to the interrogator. After a brief, but warm and relaxed conversation about other general topics of mutual interest, the "treatment program" is finally utilized for the purpose it was intended. The music that was played in the background at the beginning of every treatment session is now played in the nicely furnished private office far away from the medical setting. Approximately one minute into playing this same music that the patient was conditioned with, the imperative interrogation questions are finally asked of the patient. The response from the patients is varied but tragically dramatic. The responses range from a quiet fetal position to a hysterical convulsive response, and a myriad of other responses in-between. But in the history of the treatment clinic, all the patients submissively respond, and submit the vital information that is asked of them. I will always have a multitude of questions and even some doubts about my lunch with this person.

When in a culture and country that is foreign to you the key concept to remember is to intermingle and blend in, to try to become as one with your surroundings. In the Balkans the key to blending in was to remember the word "subdued," as in subdued clothing, subdued actions, and subdued expressions. First on the agenda is to go shopping with a local to get some clothes that will allow you to walk around without standing out like you have a sign on your back or a bull's eye on your chest. Shopping is an all day ordeal to those of us who hate doing it but there is no alternative to this critical exercise if you want to blend into any foreign culture. Having a local person with you will greatly help in two different areas. First is that they will hopefully stop you from buying something really stupid to wear, and second they will save you a ton of cash with helping you barter down the prices and not getting short-changed by paying taxes on your purchase when that clothing shop doesn't pay taxes of any kind. Remember that when you go shopping you are on the local menu, and the shopkeepers will eat you alive if they can, and they will do it with a smile. Subdued actions will also be of a great assistance to you in blending into the society in which you find yourself. Watch the locals closely on how they hand gesture. Nonverbal gestures comprise over half the communication between people the world over. Watch how they conduct their eye contact with you and then copy their actions and gestures, and even walk at their pace and manner. If you find yourself walking past other people on the street or if they are walking past you, you need to adjust your pace to match theirs in order to blend in. Subdued verbal and facial expressions are a final and critical key to blending in and not standing out. I still remember my first court case as a young street cop when a senior officer gave me advice I will never forget. "If you don't talk they will never know how dumb you are kid!" He could have said it a little more tactfully, but the essence of the concept remains the same. Talk if you have to and keep it brief, polite, and to the point. You'll know you are successful at blending in when other foreigners come up to you asking for help or directions thinking that you are a local. I got really good at playing this game—on my days off. If I had any shopping to do and was walking along the streets the locals would come up to me and ask for the time. Many times they would start a conversation with me before my limited responses alerted them to my being an outsider to their world.

These were the subtle skills I tried to hone to a fine edge to enable me to cull the information I needed about the physical torture sustained by those in a local clinic I wanted to visit. The first step was to stop by the German PX to purchase some gifts for the clinic staff. Like it or not this is a reality in most of the world we live in, and going with the flow or local custom makes things easier for all concerned. In most of the world it is not considered bribery, graft, or corruption to give a gift to a person of authority. It is simply considered a way to show your respect for another person and to thank them for taking time to share with you. With a couple of flasks of American whisky and several Swiss chocolate bars in my pockets, my local interpreter friend and I were off to a little-known quiet, side street on the outskirts of Sarajevo. It was a building that looked like all the others in the neighborhood. They were all built of stone and mortar many decades ago in a time when anything different was not tolerated nor condoned by the political crowd that was in power. The steps of the building announced their age to everyone that entered with their display of polished and badly worn treads. The steps were worn down so much from the foot traffic of the decades that they had actual concave impressions in the center of each stone step. The steps led to a massive weathered dark wood door with a huge cast iron knocker that had not worked for years. There was no buzzer, chime, or knocker to announce our entry. My colleague just walked into the building with me tagging along behind him.

Upon entering the doorway we were greeted by the stark but professional sight of a staff member. She was an austere sight as she sat behind a large, wooden desk that appeared to be as old as the building. There was nothing on the desk except some old stains and the scars of time. It was totally void of any papers, magazines, or even a telephone or intercom for communication. The greeting nurse was a conscientious older lady who was dressed in a clean and pressed, white uniform with matching white head scarf. Both were worn and frayed. After a brief introduction with the aid of my colleague, a chocolate bar was respectfully given to the nurse and she happily advised us where to go to see the doctor on call. It was rather eerie for me to be walking the hallways and listening to the sound of our footsteps echoing in the empty corridors.

After wandering the hallways of this mostly unoccupied museum-like building, we finally ended up on a floor and wing where there was a stench of medical activities and patient warehousing. Because there was no air conditioning the windows had to be left open to lessen the heat's effect on the patients and staff in the building, but there were no screens on the windows and the flies were drawn to the smell of disease that was everywhere. This caused a dreadful problem for everyone who was there. In the Balkans, as in most of the world, screens are a luxury most people have never even heard of, let alone had on their homes. After another formal and courteous introduction and chocolate bar, we were led by a cheerful nurse to the room where the resident doctor was napping between his tours of duty. I was quite taken back by the conflict I saw in the doctor. There before me was a very young and weary man, with the eyes of an old man full of empathy and pain. He appeared to be a doctor who had seen far more than his years should have allowed, but that was his lot in life. I remember being told by a senior international officer that people who live under severe conditions or conditions where they don't have a lot of worldly goods are usually in good cheer as long as they don't know that their situation in life is worse than others. With the doctor sitting on the end of his bed and me sitting on his chair by his small wooden desk cluttered with papers, my colleague and I explained how we wanted to considerately and gently interview the victims of torture from the Balkan war conflict that were under his care and supervision. The young doctor immediately agreed and stated that it would be good for the patients to talk about their experiences as a catharsis of healing, but he would require that his chief nurse be in the room with us any time we were with one of his patients. My colleague and I thanked the doctor for his cooperation and also for the nurse who would be with us for introductions and any other help we knew we might need. I slipped one bottle of whisky into a drawer in his desk, and opened the other for a toast to the hospital and its staff. As I started the toast staff members appeared out of nowhere with their own glasses. It was a very good thing I had brought so many chocolate bars because they were now all gone, with no one left wanting. In a life like the one these staff people lead, any time or excuse they can get to escape through celebration, even if it is only for a moment, is precious.

After putting on a tight-fitting white doctor's uniform smock, we proceeded down the hall to a small dimly lit room where the door was blocked open with an old wooden chair for air circulation. That's as close to air conditioning as these people living under these circumstances can get. The room was strangely cheerful in a macabre sort of way. The drawn curtains on the one window in the room were multicolored to match the blanket on the bed beneath the window. There was a small cushion on the one chair in the room next to a small round wooden table. The lady patient in the room quickly stood up when she saw us standing in the doorway. After a brief introduction by a staff nurse the chief nurse motioned for us to enter the room to meet the lady. In the limited light I could see the slightest smile coming from the patient's eyes over the small white towel she held at her mouth. I wasn't quite sure if I should be uncomfortable or not. She was a slight built person wearing a one-piece gray dress that looked almost uniform-like. There was no reason to draw out this meeting any longer than necessary. We told the lady that we wanted to learn what events led to her being in this place. When quietly asked by my colleague about what happened to her wrists and face she proceeded to stand up and recite to us as if she were an emotionless recording machine, spewing forth data. The words were coming out of her mouth but there were no feelings behind them. It was almost as if she was reading words off a paper that had no meaning to her. It was apparent this person had told her horrendous story many times by the methodical nature of her automatic recital.

She had been stopped just outside her village by several uniformed men who were demanding to know where her brother and father were. If she didn't tell them they were going to shoot her in the face. She told them that her father and brother were dead a long time ago, and that she was alone in a nearby house with other village women and children that had also lost their male family members. She said that this was not the answer they wanted to hear and it was then the pain began. The men began slapping her until she fell down and then they continued assaulting her by kicking her all over her body. Then she said she remembers in a fog-like state of mind that the men were standing above her, circled around her, just smoking and quietly talking for several minutes. Suddenly she was pulled up from the ground by her hair and rammed into a tree repeatedly face first. One of the men then wrapped her arms around a small tree while another man bound her wrists together with a piece of the barbed wire from a nearby fence. She said that she could hear them yelling at her, but that she could no longer understand what they were saying or what they were doing until they threatened her with a pair of pliers in

121

front of her face. No matter how badly they beat her, she said that she was resigned not to open her mouth to let them pull out her teeth, like she had seen them do to other people in nearby villages. It was at this point in the story she paused and looked down at the floor of her small room— her sanctuary from the world. She lowered the small white towel from her mouth. Not being the strongest person at seeing this type of thing, I found myself literally unsteady by the spectacle of this atrocity. At the same time I was equally enraged at the travesty of the circumstances surrounding this horror. When the victim had semiconsciously refused to open her mouth, the right upper lip was cut away by pinching the flesh of her lip with the pliers and then simply hacking it off with a knife. This allowed them the access to her teeth they wanted so they could continued to engage in their vicious and inhuman efforts. She took a deep and measured breath and continued to explain how one of the men would clamp the pliers down tightly on one of the teeth in her mouth and then another man would yell some kind of question at her. She said that at that point in the hell she was going through she didn't even understand what was going on around her let alone what they were yelling at her or what they wanted her to do or tell them. She was fading in and out of consciousness and all she could remember is the slowly lessening pain of the teeth being torn out; there was the yelling going on in the background that seemed distant and so far away, and the terrible waves of nausea that ran through her body as she faded in and out of consciousness as the situation seemed to go on and on unmercifully. We didn't need to look any closer to see that most of the teeth in the front of this woman's face were gone. It was also very easy to see that we didn't need to venture any farther on this journey into the hell that this person had endured. She had recounted enough of this life-changing horror—a horror so many others had also endured and unfortunately others will endure in the future. She said she wanted us to know that she was well cared for and thankful to the entire staff, but she wished that she would have bled to death so she would be with God now. The chief staff nurse patted her gently on the shoulder and talked to her in a reassuring tone as we exited the room. I didn't understand the words but the sentiment was obvious. The other rooms and the patients who occupied them were all different but all the same. The rooms were filled with men and women spanning in age from the young to the very old. The one thing they all had in common was that they were subjected to the inhumanity of others. The type of torture and the methodology they were subjected to may have been different but the result of the victimization was the same for each and every one of these devastated individuals. The same was true for their families who rarely came to visit them because of the circumstances of their existence.

This was not the only room on this floor and wing of the building, and this was not the only building in the Balkans, and the Balkans is not the only war zone that does or will ever exist with this procession of the devastated and disfigured. For my own personal sanity I just keep reminding myself that no group of people is all good or all bad, and that the conditions of a war zone are quick to wear down the veneer of civilization and reveal that which exists in all of us whether we want to admit it or not. I had acquired yet another set of emotional responses and perspectives when I would hear about one of my colleagues coming into contact with someone possessing a small roll of barbed wire or pliers and teeth in their pockets. I have found that the methodology and severity of torture is limited only by the creativity of a demented mind.

Combining the concept of physical and mental tortures with the exploitation of total terror is the display of a fatal act. An example of this is the impatient terrorists who line up villagers to determine who is helping "the outsiders" after they find the remnants of food or medicine in the village they are ransacking. They simply line up the innocent people of the village and ask one question to the first person in the line. If they do not receive the desired answer they immediately shoot the person who failed to answer their question in front of all the others in line. They then proceed to the next person in the line and ask the same question. The murderous response that occurred when the first person failed to answer now looms over the head of the next potential victim. This methodology is based on a vicious expediency, and so this barbaric situation continues on and on until the village is literally wiped out of existence. It does not end there, however, because these sadistic criminals simply move on to the next village to ransack and line up more innocent villagers.

Kidnapping and warehousing are a common type of torture that can be devastating to both the victims and their families. Unfortunately it is "unheard of" or ignored by most of the outside world. The victim is placed in a mental and physical limbo where the mind and body are put in a state of suspended existence for an undetermined time of detention. One minute they are driving down a road or walking down a street or shopping in a store, and the next minute they are seized and whisked away. And for all practical purposes, so is their life. They are taken to a facility where they are "kept." They are just kept, no more or no less. It's like their very existence has been sealed in a box and the box has been put on a shelf. All that's left to happen is for the box to gather dust as their memory fades and time passes. They may be placed in a room with others or alone, and the days, weeks, months, years, even to the end of their life, they agonizingly watch eternity crawl by. There is also another side to this dreadful psychological coin, and that is the duress caused to the families and loved ones of the people who have been kidnapped and warehoused away. No one knows where they are. They could be held literally in the same neighborhood as they were grabbed or they could have been flown out of their area, even into another country. Wherever the family turns and whoever they ask or plead with for help the family members and loved ones are met with closing doors and silence. As time passes it becomes as if this person has never existed. The reasons and logic behind each of these victims being seized and warehoused are as varied as the groups that utilize this method of isolation torture. This has become common for third-world government agencies and drug cartels. This game is played for the purposes of ransom, political or financial manipulation, and to maintain control of the victim and the families of the warehoused person.

I have very carefully chosen to end this chapter on torture with a comment on being taken hostage. Please bear in mind that the experiences you have just read about can and will happen to you if you are taken hostage. There are no statistics I can give you that tell you what percentage of hostages are released, but I do know that the longer you are held captive the greater the chance that the outcome will be bad. The final choice of what action you will take is up to you, if and when you are ever the subject of a kidnapping attempt. I can only state with extreme certainty that I made up my mind many years ago. I will fight with all viciousness necessary for my freedom regardless of the threats of weapons or the reassurance of humane treatment from my would-be kidnappers.

Whether it's the terror of instantaneous execution, the unrelenting pressure of time and isolation, the bodily pain that controls the mind, or the inhuman anguish of the mutilated body with a mind that has to live imprisoned within, it touches the conscience of all who know of its existence or practice. What we hear about gives us pause to think, but what we see through the eyes of understanding touches our way of thinking, and allows us to grow into a different and more knowledgeable and hopefully compassionate person.

6

The Bullet Gift

For some reason that still remains quite unknown to me to this day, I have always had the uncanny ability to make real friends—the kind of friends who would endure sacrifice at my behest. Be it my bold or foolish lack of pretense, or just not being the run-of-the-mill casual acquaintance, I have enjoyed the war zone fellowship of stray, mean dogs and great persons of enduring character, many with whom I suffered greatly on a daily basis. It's the sharing of the bad times and the good times that is the glue that binds persons together like no other glue can in any of the war zones that are scattered across this world of ours. It's not just what two people have in common but what they have shared in common. If a parent builds a model airplane in one room while his child builds a model airplane in another room they have building model airplanes in common. However, if they both build a model airplane in the same room working together then they are sharing and binding together, in the moment. This isn't limited to just a parent and child but to all people under all circumstances and situations. Under the extreme challenge levels of sacrifice, dedication, and mental and physical trials that exist in a war zone, the glue that binds us together becomes a permanent bond for life between all of us.

In Baghdad, the rooms where we taught and trained the Iraqi police officers were hot and dust-filled even under the best of conditions. The air conditioners, if they were working, fell short of doing their job of keeping the rooms cool enough for the officers not to sweat on their notes, their desk, and everything else that they came in contact with. And that insidious and ever-constant dust was everywhere! The dust had the color of brown sugar and the consistency of powdered sugar. When it got wet it

125

turned into a sticky syrup-like coating on everything. You would clean off the dust at the end of the day and then the very next morning when you walked into the room it would be covered by the relentless desert dust all over again. It was like the dust literally had a mind of its own and felt challenged to trespass on anything and anywhere it chose to venture. Most of us would put up or paint any kind of pictures we could on the walls just to encourage interest by the student officers in what we were trying to teach in that classroom. One of my fellow instructors did an incredible job drawing fingerprints on the wall of our classroom where we were teaching evidence collection. What we did took a ton of effort but well worth the result. First, we fingerprinted several of the students so we could get an example of the different types of print classifications. Then we put the prints we selected on an overhead projector table and focused the print image on the wall of the classroom. The next step was the most laborious and time-consuming of all. Each print was outlined by hand using a permanent ink marker and then filled in-between the fingerprint ridges. The result was better than awesome, and the 4-foot-tall fingerprints made the classroom a showplace. But no good deed goes unpunished. Shortly after finishing the prints I was reassigned to teach in another location. I learned to take it all in stride because there really was no other choice. I just went from one classroom to another, teaching the same courses to different officers under ever-worsening conditions.

The ever-constant bombs and other devices would go off nearby and rattle doors or even sometimes the desks. My standard way of handling this novel interruption to my presentation was to make light of it. If you are confronted with something or someone that is beyond your control it is a good strategy to relegate the circumstance to a group joke to keep the class anxiety level down. Whenever the big steel classroom door was rattled by a local blast going off, I would just calmly turn toward the door and say, *"Marhaba Ya Ah—Shucku Maku Gameal Ayleeown."* Very loosely translated it means, "Hello my brother, how are you this beautiful day?" After the first few times of me saying this the humor kicked in and even some of the students in the classes started saying it like a chant with a smile on their faces even before I could start. We had started a game, and the end result was that we had a small verbal pressure valve to release some of our pent-up aggravation and apprehension. Most of the officers lived close enough to some of the blast areas to be concerned about the safety of their loved ones, so I would dismiss the class for short breaks so they could use their cell phones to check on their families.

It was interesting how very quickly you became close to another person under extreme or difficult conditions when you shared them on a daily basis. In a matter of days I would go from being greeted with the formal, first-day greeting of *"Sabah el Hare oo Ahlan wes Ahlan"* (Good morning and welcome), with only brief eye contact to be polite, to *"Shuck Ku Ma Ku Sadeekee"* (What's up, friend?) and their hand placed on my shoulder. I know for a fact, that deep in my heart, any group of people is neither all good nor all bad, and that deep inside all of us are the same hopes and needs for ourselves and our loved ones. I know that all children sound the same when they laugh and when they cry, regardless of the race, religion, or other meaningless scars that were placed on them at their random births.

It caught me by surprise when I realized that as interested as I was in my students, they were interested in every detail of my life as well. However, they were extremely polite about asking any questions concerning my family and especially about any female members of my family. I also adopted this perspective when talking with them. There's a great story they told me to explain their point of view. When a wanderer in the desert needs water, food, or shelter and he comes upon an Arab Bedouin tent they are always taken in for three days and three nights as that is the custom of hospitality. However, one of the other very important customs is never to be impolite and pry into the personal life of a guest in your tent. Naturally any host is going to have a certain level of curiosity about who they are sharing their tent with, so how do they politely ask questions about their guests? They have a wonderful method of finding out all their necessary information without offending anyone. The way they find out who you are, what you do for a living, and where you came from is simple. First, they would ask, "When I pray to Allah to bless your parents for having such a wonderful child as you, who may I say should have peace be placed upon them?" "What is it that you do that I may ask for a blessing upon it, and that you be successful in all of your efforts?" "Which wind is it that I may give thanks to it for blowing you into my tent this day, the wind from the east, the west, the north, or the south?" They may not have the technical resources most of the rest of the world has but never underestimate their wisdom. The more we share with another person, the greater and stronger the bond between us becomes. Like a diamond, in order to forge a true friendship, it takes great heat and pressure, and that's just what we were enduring together.

There are many keys to opening the door to a great and lasting friendship, but the biggest lock is opened by sharing one's self. It was the custom on the first day of class for the instructors to introduce themselves and speak about their backgrounds. I would explain how all Americans came from different countries and even in ancient history they came from different continents that had no name at that time. And then I would compliment their culture as being so deep and rich in the accomplishments of language, math, and science that they had made while most of the rest of the world was still struggling to survive in caves. They would then very politely ask if they could ask about my family background. It was a sign of respect for them to ask about my father and his father. I told them it was my honor to tell this story to them. As I began to explain about my past and the past history of the Scottish people in Britton and how they traveled to the United States they went from sitting back in their chairs to now sitting on the edge of their seats and leaning forward to listen intently to my every word. I told them that I was a proud American Scot and I was honored to share my life with such a great people as them. They asked me why I said I was an American Scot and not a Scottish American like the other Americans who would refer to themselves by putting their ethnic name before the name of their country. With a very serious look in my eye I told them in a strong and clear voice, in Arabic, that I was born in America and put America first, because I love my country the same way they love theirs. They understood and respected my comment. From then on we would share many deep and personal conversations and I would always thank them for what they had taught me that day. I would also jokingly comment that I would not be foolish enough to play a game of chess for "a money wager" against anyone from the very land that invented the game. There is an Arab saying, "He that teaches me but one thing, I am his slave." I would repeat that to them whenever they would teach me or inform me about anything. They were always very impressed that I knew anything about their culture or history that was of a complimentary nature. The response to my using their own sayings of wisdom as well as other Arab sayings was always a polite and thankful smile and nod of the head. Many cultures are deeply involved in sayings and proverbs and using these words of wisdom and proverbs displayed my respect for their culture. Every day that passed was another link that was forged in the chain of understanding and friendship. From the very first day of class when no one walked up to me to greet me or shake my hand, to running the gauntlet of handshakes and back slaps we had now progressed to, was a living testament to the exchange of customs being critical to bond with any other culture. This sharing bond of understanding grew stronger and stronger as days grew into weeks and weeks grew into months and the months went on … and on and on.

I remember with great pride the day an Iraqi *Shorta* (police officer) from a class I had been training stopped me in the doorway at the end of the day's classes. He placed his right hand on his chest and then slapped his hand on my chest. The American training officer that was with me was startled and incensed that I had been touched by a student in that manner, and had no idea what the hell was going on between the Iraqi and me. But I saw the *Shorta's* broad smile, and between his broken English and my limited Arabic we were now, in that split second, more than just teacher and student—we were two officers from very different sides of the Earth who had come together. We were brothers with a bond that was cemented together with the glue of all of the bad and all of the good we were enduring together, like no other could be in a war zone. Then, standing just a foot away from me, he became quiet and reached down toward his weapon. Needless to say, the officer with me almost had a heart attack, but I just gave him a reassuring, "stay out of it" look, because I knew what was about to happen right in front of us. The Iraqi officer removed one 9-mm bullet from the clip of his pistol, kissed the bullet, and gave it to me. My unhesitating response was that I removed a 9-mm bullet from my Beretta's pistol clip and gave it to him. We then loaded up the exchanged bullets into our pistol's clips and hugged each other. The unspoken thought and meaning behind this gesture was "May my bullet one day defend your life." Word of the bullet exchange spread through the classes of other Iraqi officers. It would not be the last time I shared this honor with a *Shorta*, and I was deeply honored every time.

Of course no good gesture goes misunderstood. The officer who witnessed the bullet exchange wrote up a very formal complaint letter against me for the "transference and acceptance of unauthorized ammunition without documentation"; section number "whatever," article number "who cares." To this day I don't know what happened to this complaint letter or the fellow trainer who was supposed to be my assistant trainer. Wherever you end up in this increasingly small world you will have personal contact with the good, the bad, and the ugly. It won't be apparent from their appearance but rather from their conduct. Some will take that internationally needed step forward and share the best of their nation's customs and conduct while others will exist, labor, and participate, behind their own personally imposed shield of seclusion and indifference.

A Closing Thought: It's not just what we see around us in a war zone, or even what we touch. It's what reaches out and touches us. We must remember that what touches us the most also touches others. Remember always, in a war zone, all feelings and words, good or insulting, are more intense because of where we are when they are being said. Watch others, but watch yourself more.

7

Insurrection and Conflict

CIVIL UNREST AND PEACEKEEPERS

Ludovic Asan, Romania

From the very beginning I would like to mention that in my story you will not find any clear, full names or nationality of the international people involved. First, the names are not important, just the facts. Second, in relation to the nationalities, during my seven years of international experience I have learned that the peacekeepers should aim for the same things no matter what their nationality, religion, culture, etc. and police officers all over the world should act in the same manner for the benefit of the people whom they are serving.

From December 2002, I joined the United Nations Mission in Kosovo (after an experience in Bosnia–Herzegovina), and from December 2003, I worked as an instructor in the United Nations Police Training Center in Pristina, along with 20 other police instructors from many countries throughout the world. A police instructor was supposed to conduct the induction training to the peacekeepers after arriving in the mission area, guiding their first steps in the mission area.

I was really happy to be selected for this job as it was very suitable with my background (former teacher) and I considered it to be a safe job in Kosovo, a place which could be sensitive and volatile. My family was also very happy with this move since I was less exposed to any bad things or danger.

But I had to find out that in postconflict areas the security situation could deteriorate very fast and in this kind of situation peacekeeping also

131

Figure 7.1   Ludovic Asan in Kosovo.

involves performing duties that you are not used to or you are not really prepared for.

The riots/civil unrest in Kosovo in March 2004 were the events that changed my vision and perception about peacekeeping. After these events I learned to be more cautious and more aware of what is going on around me.

It was 17th of March 2004, a short time before the lunch break, when I went out on the balcony of the Training Center to smoke a cigarette. The situation in Kosovo was not that good lately, but at that moment we had about 100 newcomers in the mission and we were quite busy preparing the timetables and conducting the induction training.

At a certain moment our colleague and deputy chief of the unit, R.L., came and asked me to follow him to his office. At that moment I did not have any information about what was going on outside on the streets and I later realized that very few international police officers working in the nonoperational units like ours had this kind of information.

In the office I met two other colleagues, R.R. and J.G. , who were also called by our supervisor. He briefly informed us that the situation in Pristina was very tense at the moment due to the latest incidents that had occurred Kosovowide and one team from our unit was requested to send four instructors to Pristina Hospital in order to ensure that there would be no clashes between the K/Albanians (Kosovo Albanians)* present there and the possible incoming K/Serbian (Kosovo Serbians) who might come to see the medical situation of the Serbs who were wounded in the North in the past 24 hours.

I have to mention that due to an incident that occurred on the 15th of March in Mitrovica (three K/Albanian kids apparently drowned in the Ibar River after being chased by some K/Serbian kids†), in different places of Kosovo there had been clashes between members of the main ethnic groups and some people were reported to have been killed or injured from both parts. Apparently these killed or wounded persons were about to be brought to Pristina Hospital.

It was rather surprising for all three of us that instructors of the Police Training Center had to go to face people on the street without having the necessary protection equipment or any obligations in this sector (crowd control), but we understood that the situation was really serious and our presence was required. It was, however, clear for me that in this case of emergency, being a peacekeeper you also have responsibilities in maintaining the public order even if in your job description there is nothing of this kind.

Our team (deputy and the three instructors) left the Training Center at approximately 1230 hours in a 4x4 police vehicle and we headed toward the hospital. In the city, the situation did not look like that on a normal day. There were groups of young people here and there and the other inhabitants looked to be stressed and in a hurry.

We reached the hospital after approximately 20 minutes and the international police officer who was in charge of the operation explained to us what our role was. We had to block the access of the private vehicles from

---

* Usually, in the UN reports, official documents, and even in the normal spoken language the ethnic groups were mentioned as K/Serbian (Kosovo Serbian), K/Albanian (Kosovo Albanian), and so forth, to have the clear distinction with the Serbians from Serbia or with the Albanians from Albania, and so on.

† After the events in March 2004, an investigation revealed that the three kids died accidentally with no involvement of any other people.

the main entrance of the hospital in the front of the main building where the intensive care section was.

The only thing I had for protection was my Glock 17 pistol and my 34 rounds of ammunition. My colleagues also had only their handguns and ammunition, but the situation was quite calm in the beginning. None of us had his antiriot equipment which, in the given situation, could have helped us a lot.

We performed this task for about four and a half hours and we did not face any big problems to accomplish it. All this time, I estimate that hundreds of people were coming and leaving in order to check if their relatives were brought to the hospital and many drivers tried to pass our improvised checkpoint to go by car to the stairs of the entry in the Intensive Care Unit (ICU), but we were very strict in denying their access. In fact, on that particular road that we were blocking, it was obvious that three or four vehicles were enough to block the access for the ambulances that were coming every 15 to 20 minutes. Pedestrians were also a potential danger, so they were kept at a safe distance as well in order not to create a mass of people around the entry of the hospital.

Local police officers were also present and according to my assessment, they did a relatively good job, taking into account that most of them had not had much police experience (the Kosovo police force was created in September 1999) and also that they were not experienced in crowd control.

The situation in the hospital area was very tense. K/Serbians and K/Albanians were waiting not far from each other for their wounded or dead friends or family members, but international and local police forces kept the situation under control. When I look back now after some years, I realize that everything could have ended badly for us but at that time everybody's attitude was very positive and performing our task "as professional as possible" looked normal and not too difficult.

Meanwhile, in the city the situation escalated but we couldn't find out what was really going on. Shortly before 1700 hours, our team was called back in the Training Center for another appointment and another team from the Investigation Pillar replaced us. By that time very few ambulances were still coming and the crowd was not as massive as in the beginning.

It is interesting to mention that a member of this team who replaced us was a fellow countryman and while he was performing his duties in the hospital area, his private vehicle was burned down in front of his residence (which was vandalized) in Pristina—"duty above ALL."

Figure 7.2 The hospital became one of the thousands of buildings that were burned.

We left the hospital area and headed toward the eastern entry of Pristina, where at the bottom of Veternic Hill (Skopje Highway) we met one international police officer who was seeking help since his Toyota 4Runner had all four tires slashed. Other UN cars stopped at the spot and using our spare tires we could help our colleague leave the spot that might have become dangerous since night was approaching. While returning to Pristina, soon after passing a bridge we entered a large group of protesters who were heading toward Pristina. The situation rapidly changed into a critical one. Our colleague J.G. was driving the car and he immediately positioned the car on the extreme right side of the road and continued to drive very slowly in order not to hit any of the protesters. Their reaction was somewhat aggressive; they hit and kicked our vehicle but we did not lose control, and without reacting we came out slowly from their group. I really think that any reaction from our side in those moments (that seemed to be an eternity at the time) or just stopping the vehicle would have escalated the violence. We finally reached our Training Center and all four of us agreed that we were lucky enough to be in one piece.

Figure 7.3   Many rioters were proud of the destruction they achieved.

These kinds of things might have happened to many police officers during their police career but when it comes to peacekeeping missions it is always different. It is not your country and the people might be totally different in their behavior or mentality, and this can create more dangerous situations. That's why it is important to be fully aware of the places you go and the people's mentality, and not to lose control in any circumstance.

HOW RIOTS GROW

Bob Locke, United Kingdom

Wednesday, March 17, 2004, was a quiet day for the staff of the Induction Centre of the United Nations Interim Administration Mission in Kosovo (UNMIK), where we introduced the newly arrived international police officers to Kosovo and the workings of the UN. We had just received a batch of police officers from Sweden and were expecting a larger number

Figure 7.4 Anything that could be burned was burned.

of German officers that day. The next day the center would then assess their suitability for working in an English-speaking mission as armed police officers.

The day started fine and had become unseasonably hot for the time of year. At the time I was the acting head of the department. It was midday, all was quiet in the building, and I was working away at my desk with the police radio working in the background. As I was working I realized that all was not as it should be in Pristina. The police radio was reporting large gatherings of people on the main southerly route out of Pristina toward a large Serbian-populated village. I knew this was not good and the police officers on the radio, both at the scene and at control, were becoming agitated, both groups requesting the support of nondeployed patrols at the scene known as "the bull ring."

It was a quiet day so I decided to act and a quick search of the center's offices threw out three other eager officers—Robert (United States), Justo (Spain), and Ludovic (Romania). With nothing else other than a police radio and lots of enthusiasm, off we drove to the bull ring, unaware of what to expect and unable to receive any information from the very busy police radio control. It could not be anything serious because Kosovo had been reasonably quiet since June 1999. It was just another Balkan state in need of financial investment with the population fairly law-abiding compared to day-to-day street crime.

On the journey there, about 3 miles through what seemed normal daytime traffic, from our accrued information we discussed what might be happening. It would appear that earlier that day three Albanian children had drowned while swimming in a river in North Kosovo. The river forms a barrier between an Albanian and Serbian village. It would seem that the local media had reported that these children had been forced into deep water by Serbians on the opposite bank of the river and this resulted in the drowning. At the time we had no idea if this report of the event was true or not. Later it was revealed that it was not; tragically the children got into difficulties and drowned in the ice-cold fast-flowing waters.

When we arrived at the bull ring we could see a number of Kosovo Police (KP) and UN vehicles, all showing varying signs of damage, smashed windscreens, dented bodywork, and flat tires. Among these were the KP and UN police, watching large groups of people making their way past them south along the highway toward the large Serbian-populated village, with Albanian flags flying and people chanting. Farther south on the highway where it climbed away from the city, we could see that the crowd had been stopped by a barrier of NATO and UN vehicles in front of which stood a line of UN police.

From where we were, we quickly understood that it was time to move the damaged vehicles. Most were drivable with a minimum amount of work, however, those with multiple flat tires required taking usable tires from other vehicles there. This left a small number of vehicles either immovable or less a spare tire. I think in the end only one vehicle was left behind for the wolves, who were becoming more vocal and physical up at the police barrier.

The radio was now reporting that a serious incident was happening at a hospital and it was alight. I immediately informed control that my trusty crew was available to tasking, so they tasked me to go to Pristina Main Hospital and report back. It took about five minutes to reach the main ER entrance, which was besieged by upward of 200 people who did not seem aggressive—just vocal sightseers.

This was obviously not the location of the serious unrest; however, in the short time we were there the crowd was growing significantly and their vehicles were blocking the passage of the ambulances to ER, so we became involved with crowd and traffic control to ensure that a clear way was maintained for the emergency vehicles that were starting to arrive in increasing numbers, as were the sightseers. This was not easy. We were met with a lot of opposition and would have been overwhelmed if it were not for my crew's disregard for their own safety and forcing the crowds back just by their physical presence.

This situation was reported back to control who I could tell were not able to maintain command and control of the developing situation; I informed them that I would stay where I was until such time as I thought it was secure, which in the end was until around 1700 hours. The situation by then throughout Pristina and elsewhere deteriorated into mass lawlessness with indiscriminate shootings, arson, and physical attacks throughout.

By this time a U.S. support vehicle arrived at our location and issued Robert with a gas mask, riot shield, and news from the front. It was not good. I reestablished the old "lease-lend treaty" of the 1940s and managed to obtain gas masks for the rest of us, which was a godsend later that day.

With the arrival of a number of KP officers I decided to make my way back to base, which was situated at the main Police Headquarters, and on my arrival there I went to find who was in control and see what my orders were. The rest of the crew went about finding enough food and water for the next 24 hours. All was not good at the UN control. In fact, control was not a word to use but I was able to ascertain that I should take control of all my staff and that of the Police Administration staff, and then take them to the UN logistics to be issued with riot-control and personal protection equipment. This was a 10-minute drive on a good day.

I started gathering all my staff and those from the administration. This gave a total of 25 police officers and 6 vehicles. During this operation I found a group of 20 to 30 Serbian female and male UN workers gathered in one of the induction center classrooms. These were employed as cleaners and building support engineers to the UN Police Headquarters buildings. Their transport home, supplied by the UN, had not arrived and they were very agitated, not knowing what was happening to their homes outside Pristina and whether they would be safe where they were and, most importantly, they were without food and drink. I assured them that they would be taken care of and taken home in due course. I also assured them they would be given food and drink from our own supplies.

I then had to leave as we were being deployed to Kosovo Polje, a town on the outskirts of Pristina where there was a serious disturbance between Ethnic Serbs and Kosovo Albanians, in which a number of people had been killed and injured plus the destruction by fire of a hospital and school.

KOSOVO RIOTS

Greg Gronewold, United States

Wednesday, March 17, 2004, started like most every other day working as an UNMIK CivPol (United Nations Mission in Kosovo Civilian Police) officer in Kosovo. In looking back, one can hardly believe the drama that was to unfold in the coming hours and, accordingly, set the multiethnic province back months, if not years, in its pursuit of peace throughout the region, as well as the Balkans.

The temperament of the area has been justifiably described as resembling a covered pot of water sitting on a stove, constantly maintaining 210°F—just waiting for one more influence to bump the control over the boiling point. While those "bumps" did occur, the dramatic effects were underestimated by many and envisioned by few.

The first nudge of the stove controls occurred on Monday, 15 March in Caglavica, a Serbian enclave close to Pristina, when an 18-year-old Serbian was killed in a drive-by shooting. While such an incident in Kosovo was not that uncommon, such an occurrence always managed to bump the temperament up a notch, putting it at 211 degrees.

Then, the following day, four young Albanians were playing in and around the Ibar River in the Mitrovica Region of the province. While what exactly took place is not clear, a tragic accident occurred resulting in the drowning deaths of three of the young people. But due to heavy indoctrination of youngsters in the Balkans, the survivor related a completely false story to authorities, stating that they were actually chased by Serbs with dogs. In order to escape, refuge had been sought in the river, resulting in the deaths of the three. As one can imagine, this "news" spread like wildfire, severely heightened already stressed ethnic tensions in the region, and ultimately pushed it over the boiling point the very next day.

As is the case with any criminal investigation, searching for the truth takes time. From the moment the initial report of the drowning incident was received by the authorities, many questioned the truthfulness of the surviving victim. Too many details did not gel but while still continuing the search for the truth, the details, as outlined in the fictitious story, took on a life of their own among the public.

While the morning of March 17th was like any other in the mission, by the middle of the afternoon, demonstrations escalating to violence had erupted across the whole of the province. Calls for additional international officers poured in from all areas of Kosovo, stretching manpower availability to its limits. Emergency meetings were called by the Operations branch of UNMIK CivPol and as many officers as possible were immediately, temporarily redeployed to the various regions, fulfilling as many requests as possible for extra officers. By the middle of the afternoon, exactly 20 CivPol officers assigned to Main Headquarters remained there for its protection. This number was then bolstered by two contingents who had new officers recently arriving in theater and still undergoing the mandatory training before receiving their final assignments. Numbering 12 plus 18, this increased the strength at Main HQ to exactly 50, but one of the newly arrived groups had yet to be armed by their home country. At this same time, a brand new group of German CivPol officers had touched down at Pristina International Airport but were unable to reach Pristina due to the demonstrations. They were instructed to break out and don their issued riot gear immediately and attempts to get them transported into Pristina would continue. For them, this was a fantastic "Welcome to Kosovo."

By late afternoon, the first "parade" of demonstrators made their initial pass by UNMIK CivPol Main Headquarters. Estimated to number 3500, the 50 CivPol officers held their ground as the protestors made their way up Police Boulevard. By their second pass during the early evening hours, the newly arrived Germans had finally made their way into Pristina after much difficulty, and were assigned to guard the rear of Police Main Headquarters, which had been drastically understaffed until this time. After the second pass by HQ, word was received that a third wave was being organized for later that night and that all should be prepared for confrontation. Based on the ratio of CivPol officers to protestors, everyone at Main HQ was happy to welcome the arrival of the Special Police Unit (SPU) from Argentina prior to the third pass, and although a great disparity in numbers still existed, the general belief was that the line would hold.

Keeping in constant communications with not only CivPol Operations staff, but UNMIK Administration Headquarters as well (located outside the city center), word was later relayed that the demonstrators were once again walking up Police Boulevard sometime after 2200 hours that evening and those on the line were as prepared as possible for physical altercation. The protestors were first observed approximately 150 meters south–southwest of Police Main HQ advancing northerly on Police Boulevard where they temporarily stopped to storm another UNMIK administration facility. Rioters could be seen scaling the fence surrounding that complex and wreaking unknown havoc on that facility. This information was immediately relayed to

UNMIK Administration Headquarters at their compound outside of Pristina. During that same conversation, the CivPol officers were advised that plans were under way to quell this group of rioters, and this specific group should break up momentarily. The conversation had barely ended when the sound of a helicopter could be heard approaching the area from a southwesterly direction. Once it arrived above the demonstrators, tear gas canisters immediately spiraled to the ground from the chopper's side door and as projected, the group beat a hasty retreat from that location and therefore away from CivPol Main HQ.

In all, the serious unrest lasted a total of three days. Depending on the specific location of their assigned deployments, most officers lived at their offices for that time, with strict limitations placed on travel for a number of days thereafter. Officers were not allowed to travel alone, with all UN vehicles being restricted to secured parking areas when not in use. By the end of the riots, reported injuries to CivPol officers stood at 27 during the three days of unrest (13 of those Americans). In addition to the CivPol injuries, 38 members of the various SPUs also reported injuries, bringing the total number of reported injuries among the international law enforcement component to 65. While this was the first riot for many of the international CivPol officers, valuable lessons were learned by all.

One point that became very evident early on during the disturbance was that even though the local businesses, from the corner kiosks to the large stores, relied heavily on the business conducted by the international presence, they either closed or refused to trade with the CivPol officers for the first 24 hours of the uprising. Officers deployed to locations away from their normal work assignments were even unable to buy water and with many roads blocked with burning vehicles, it was extremely difficult to get them the basic supplies that were required.

Another serious problem pertained to the adherence of basic UN rules regarding the Kosovo deployment being a "nonfamily" mission. While this information was known by all CivPol officers serving in Kosovo, many officers had elected to bring family members to the theater on their own during their tour. Due to this violation of the mandate, many CivPol officers who had family members present elected to stay at their residences to protect their spouses and/or children, instead of reporting for their assigned duties. Besides those who did not report to work, there were other sworn officers who just chose not to report for duty during the riots or actually ran and hid from any engagements. While this problem was not encountered by all police contingents serving with UNMIK, it was noted as occurring more frequently among CivPol officers from certain countries. This same problem was also noted among the ranks of the Kosovo Police Service since many of them did not want to confront their own people during this time of civil unrest.

Once such a skirmish is over, there comes a time for debriefings and more planning meetings to avoid future shortcomings as experienced during the actual event itself. Next comes the initiation of new or altered procedures and everyday practices based on the many "lessons learned" from such an occurrence. And while these consequences are seldom popular to all of those involved, they generally are applied for a reason.

Within a very short period of time after the riots, a much stronger stance was taken by CivPol Command Staff regarding family members being in theater during a member's deployment. It was ordered that all CivPol family members be removed from theater, or the offending officer would be repatriated for ignoring this rule. This position, while generating quite an amount of discontent among certain contingents, remained strong during the tenure of CivPol Command Staff present at that time, and was fully supported by the appropriate personnel within UN Headquarters in New York. Even when this issue was later raised by a Contingent Commander during a theater visit by the head of the UN DPKO (Department of Peacekeeping Operations), the plea fell on deaf ears. As always, there are those who believe that such rules do not apply to them. However, with the rotating of CivPol Command staff over time to later include officers from countries identified as being frequent violators of this mandate, the enforcement of this rule started to suffer toward the end of UNMIK CivPol in Kosovo.

Another revelation came about months after the riots and did not set well with many CivPol officers, yet most have no knowledge of it to this day. Shortly after the end of this riot in Kosovo, a guarded rumor began circulating among a select few CivPol officers concerning UNMIK's required "support" of CivPols. (It is vitally important to note that rumors abound in such a mission, but while most lack any credence at all and are immediately dispelled, this one required some investigation.)

First off, one must realize that in many ways, CivPol officers in a UN mission closely resemble the concept of the "redheaded step-child." All CivPol officers deployed to a mission are only temporary "subcontracted" personnel. These officers are not employees of the UN, but are sworn officers from their home countries who meet certain criteria making them eligible to participate in such missions. With each member country being authorized to deploy a specific number of officers to a mission, the participating officer's base salary is paid by the contributing country, while the

UN pays the same daily per diem amount to every person, civilian and CivPol alike, who are deployed. (For those from certain countries, this per diem amount, called MSA by the UN [Mission Subsistence Allowance], can be 30 or even 35 times their normal salaries at home.)

To better understand the impact of this rumor, one must also have a little knowledge about certain aspects of participating in such a mission as well. Once an officer completes his/her initial in-country training, they are assigned to a specific job at a certain location. One of the first things that is supposed to happen when they arrive at their new duty location is that this officer must be included in that office's "Evacuation Plan." This plan encompasses a number of things including an initial evacuation muster point up to transportation to one of five UN evacuation locations through-out Kosovo. Such a plan exists in every office for everyone deployed under the UN "umbrella," including full-time UN employees, CivPol officers, and even local staff. (Local staff is citizens of Kosovo who are hired by the UN to perform certain job functions such as administrative support, translators, and building maintenance to name just a few.) At each of the five UN evacuation sites throughout Kosovo, adequate supplies and ame-nities, including food and water, were available which would allow UN personnel to live at these locations for a certain amount of time if such a move were necessary.

Now, hopefully with a better understanding as to why CivPol officers viewed themselves as being treated like "second-class citizens" by the UN administration, and a brief explanation as to the evacuation element of serving in a mission, a real eye-opener was revealed in the months follow-ing the riot. So now, back to the rumor.

Of major concern among the CivPol Command Staff following this riot was the fact that many officers were unable to obtain the basic neces-sities when operating in the field under such circumstances, especially drinking water and food. (Remember that the local businesses were closed or refused to sell anything to the CivPol officers during the first 24 hours of the riot.) Yet, the UN administration in Kosovo seemed to constantly change the subject when the CivPol hierarchy broached it. The rumor that reared its ugly head at this point was that CivPol numbers were not included in the "support" portion of the evacuation plan for the five major muster points throughout Kosovo, and were therefore not "entitled" to this form of assistance by the UN. To be perfectly honest, at this point no one wanted to believe this to be the case, but it had to be looked into.

One brick wall after another was encountered by the select couple of officers who were trying to verify or dispel this rumor as none of the

144

appropriate people from the administration side of the UN would even answer the relevant questions. After several months of casual inquiry, the exact person was identified as being responsible for establishing the amount of supplies to be maintained at each evacuation location and designating exactly who were entitled to them. Direct questions were asked and eventually, after a couple rounds of going back and forth, answered. At that point, the vicious rumor had become fact and the CivPol Command Staff learned that its officers were not entitled to emergency rations maintained by the UN, even if evacuation to one of the five approved sites throughout Kosovo were warranted and ordered. In regards to drinking water, it was learned that each evacuation site held a minimum of 50,000 liters of potable water in bulk storage. If the need arose, CivPol officers would be allowed to fill their own containers with water from the bulk supply tanks. So while UN employee numbers and even local staff employed by the UN were included in the maintained supplies, CivPol officers were intentionally left out.

Needless to say, the CivPol Command Staff was not willing to allow this practice to continue, at least without some input from their side, so an official memorandum was launched to the Head of Pillar I within UNMIK, asking that this issue be investigated with the appropriate civilian component. Basically, everyone who became aware of this practice within Pillar I was shocked and disturbed that this was the practice of record. A return memorandum eventually received a few weeks later from the UN Administration asked that the appropriate CivPol entity determine exactly how many rations should be obtained and stored for UNMIK Police, so after a fight, this battle had been won.

Countless CivPol officers experienced something new during the three days of rioting throughout the province, and hopefully, positive changes were implemented in the weeks and months that followed that will curtail a repeat of such an episode in Kosovo for both the citizens as well as those serving far away from home.

8

Eternal Hate

THE DEATH DAY CAKE

Spring in the Balkans is one of the greatest times of the year. After a very long and snowy winter, it was always so good to see anything that was even close to being green again. Everyone was looking forward to the warmth of spring and all of the promises that come with it. It was a time of putting away the good and the terrible of the past and all that was attached to it. However, the past for some is harder to put away and forget than it is for others.

It was a prized and long awaited day off—the perfect way to start this relaxing day was to spend a little extra time in bed on a cool spring morning. My partner and I were renting an entire home from an older, local couple who lived in the outskirts of the Sarajevo area. It was a typical, single-family home for the area. It was a two-story house that had red tile roofing shingles and dirty white stucco walls with an excellently maintained garden. The plumbing was lead-soldered joints, and the electrical setup was so fragile it would burn in the walls if you used any more than one appliance per socket or a small string of decorative lights. But we weren't in a position to complain about anything in this building because of the generous terms of our rent. We were paying about $US180 per month, and that included all utilities (for what they were worth). Our laundry was also included in the rent, being done in one day. The dirty pile of clothes was taken out of our rooms and by the next afternoon the clean clothes were carefully folded and set back on the bed. The place was spotlessly cleaned twice a week. After we were settled in for about a month I did my usual "honesty check" by leaving a bunch of paper German script and loose coins on the side of my dresser for a couple of days. After the third day my landlady became so upset with my frivolous money handling she put the money inside the dresser drawer with a note saying, *Yoo be care the mony.* As I had hoped, not a penny was missing. She and her husband who maintained the garden were great people with very high ethical standards and were also very careful to watch for any problems with the building when my roommate and I were away.

The morning was starting out great when I heard the sound of knocking at the door of the house. Balkan homes usually have only one door to enter and that door is always strong and mounted into a stone or steel doorframe. As I opened the door I became instantly aware that this was a special occasion because both of my landlords were very well dressed. The real giveaway that this was a special occasion was that my landlord was wearing his black leather vest that had a special pocket for his pipe. I cheerfully greeted them and motioned for them to please enter. As we walked through the kitchen door, over to the breakfast table, I noticed they were a lot quieter and subdued than they normally were. The old man didn't sit down in his favorite kitchen chair like he usually did. He simply stood beside the table as his wife placed a beautifully decorated cake in the center of the table. He gestured to me to try to explain that the flour of the cake had been sifted and that it was "super ok." The rest of the world sifts their flour before mixing and baking to determine the amount to be used in the recipe, but in a war zone the flour is sifted to get all the bugs out. Soon we were joined by a young neighbor girl who always showed up when they wanted to talk to me about a serious subject, or a problem they were having in the area. Before the first word was spoken I had the unsettling feeling that I was at a celebration that was more of a wake than a birthday party, and my gut feeling unfortunately turned out to be correct. All three of my impromptu guests were very quiet and just standing by the table, looking down at the cake. As my landlady started cutting the cake she had so carefully placed in the center of the old wooden table she began talking. As she started talking the mood of the room became clouded with overwhelming sadness. The young girl who was translating the landlady's words placed her hands on the landlady's shoulders, trying to console her grief. The girl then explained to me that this was the day that the landlords' son lost his life defending his country, neighbors, and family from the criminal invaders of their area of the Balkans. This is only one death story out of literally millions that are told to anyone who will listen about the Balkan conflict. This hatred has been an enduring cancer for hundreds of years. With tears in their eyes the cake was cut into slices. Then the yearly oath was made that while one family member remained alive, the cake tradition would go on and so would the pursuit of retribution and justice in the name of God and the deceased. This was not the time or the place for me to interject any of my own comments or views on the situation. Emotions were excruciatingly obvious and it was time for me to just eat my slice of cake and toast the soul of the deceased with a very small glass of local whisky. After only a few minutes, all three of my visitors left the kitchen, and after standing in the garden crying for a moment or two, they left the area. As I stood there in the kitchen looking at the death day cake, I tried to justify everything in my mind: the sight of the beautiful Balkan countryside, the tranquility of the fresh spring morning that lay ahead for me, and the reminder of vengeance that had lasted for centuries. When my roommate came back to the house he walked into the kitchen and yelled, "My gosh, this is so great, I've had such a taste for cake." I just stood there and watched him carve off a big piece of cake, flip it into his open hand, and chomp it down in less bites than it takes to eat a cookie. Not wanting to spoil the moment I thought it best to let him eat his cake without the burden of the story that went with this very sad occasion. Later when I told him about the landlords' visit, we both sat back with a cup of coffee and came to the conclusion that this historical and epic hatred will never heal. Even when the wounds stop bleeding, there will always be those who pick at the scars that are left behind.

THE LITTLE BOY AND HIS STICK

It was a wonderful day, even if I was thousands of miles away from home and in the troubled Balkans. Being of American Scottish decent I was always kidding my colleagues that the best weather for me was cool, overcast, and with the constant chance of rain. I would always tell them that there are no rainbows without rain.

I was in a great mood. I was off duty, at the end of my day of teaching induction training to a room full of international police officers for the United Nations and all had gone well. My ride had just dropped me off by the main road and I didn't have far to walk to my accommodation. The two types of roads we had to travel on in the Balkans were either broken asphalt with potholes, or narrow dirt roads with holes that were filled in with anything that could be gathered and dumped into them. The standing joke about the dirt roads was that they were made of either dry

Figure 8.1 Good Scottish weather in the Balkans.

mud, wet mud, or frozen mud. It always seemed so strange to see the local women sweeping the dirt road in front of their homes as I walked by, but this is what they did every day of the week. I could never understand how you can sweep dirt away from dirt. Are they sweeping and cleaning the street down to a layer of cleaner dirt? I never knew if it was just an effort of futility, or an outlet for frustration on their part, trying to keep a bit of sane routine in their shattered world.

As I walked by a house about a half a kilometer from my accommodation my attention was drawn to a small boy who looked like he was taken right off a picture on a tourist postcard. He couldn't have been more than five or six years old. Beneath a wild tangle of dark brown hair, two big, wide open, happy brown eyes looked directly into my eyes. A little voice came out of this postcard child and he said, *"Dobra Don"* (good day). And I responded by saying, "Dobra Don" back to him. After our exchange of the customary greetings the little boy returned to his task at hand. He was carving on a stick that was about as long as he was tall. His little face was very serious as he went about his task. He was very busy carving a point on the end of the stick. From the amount of wood shavings I could see all over the boy and the ground, he had been working on this for quite some time. A nearby woman walked over to where I was standing to watch the little boy carve. She greeted me by saying, "Hello American Police," in a polite but cold tone of voice. Her attitude was more clearly understood than what she said. It was very obvious what she really wanted to say was, "What do you want American? I don't want you here!" Her eyes didn't look at me—they looked through me. She was tired. Not just tired from the day of labor she had done but from the life she was resigned to living in such a forsaken place. I very respectfully asked the lady to ask the boy what kind fish he was going to spear when he used his stick at the nearby stream. The lady just looked at me with a very slight sinister smile. I asked again, and added, "Please ask the child." She reached out and gently touched the head of the child and asked him my question. He stopped sharpening the stick and looked up at me with a look that was tragically determined far beyond his years. He answered with an answer that was too long for a child of his age to make. After a pause, he returned to sharpening his stick with a new strength and focus in his little body. I looked at the woman, waiting for the answer to my question. I could see her body signs change in front of me. She stood up straight and proud and actually smiled. There was great resolve and pride in what she was about to say to me. She said the little boy told her he was making a very sharp killing stick so he could avenge the death of his uncles and father, over and over again for the rest of his life, and kill as many as he could for his God and family.

Like a farmer casts out seeds on the fertile soil of his land, so too here in the Balkans the seeds of hate have been cast out on the fertile and impressionable minds of the children. It has been this way in the past and it will be this way in the future. I have heard it said far too many times by the locals that the flames of the Balkans can only be extinguished by the shedding of blood. But it's that very same blood that waters the seeds of hate as they are planted in the hearts and minds of the children who walk these intolerable dirt roads.

9

Eternal Hope

THE SCARF

Being a patrol officer in a war zone is not like anything you could ever imagine. The only thing you could count on is when you were supposed to start your patrol and where you thought you were going to be patrolling. Past those ideas the options were wide open to every heartrending, ludicrous, dreadful, and forbidding thing that could possibly happen. The shift I preferred working was six at night to six in the morning. I liked working in the darkness. It was kind of relaxing for me to hide in the night and no one else wanted to patrol in the shadows. My partners would say they hated not being able to see the enemy but I thought the enemy couldn't see me either. I never used my lights and liked to park up on high ground with my engine off, not making a sound, just waiting for whoever or whatever to make their first mistake in the darkness.

After each night's "tour of duty" my shift would meet with the next shift and go on the road to brief them on what had happened that night and any problems we thought they may encounter on their tour of duty and how to handle those possible incidents. It was important to suggest these ideas with the local police because we were not just working with them, we were training them. These officers didn't have an easy lot in life. They walked to their assigned patrol station in this small village regardless of the distance. They ate their meal before their tour of duty and usually didn't eat again until they walked back to their homes. They rarely enjoyed the luxury of a ride to work or bringing something with them to eat on patrol. Most of the international officers attributed the local officers'

Figure 9.1 This police station was one of the best in the area.

slim physique to fitness and not to being in a state of borderline starvation most of the time, a circumstance they endured without complaint.

One of the Kosovo police officers I would see every morning was a tall, slender, young man who was always wearing a clean and pressed uniform with polished shoes and a matching uniform scarf around his neck. He was there every day without fail. I don't think I ever saw him take a day off. My attention was first drawn to his eyes. They seemed to possess an unusual, wisdom-like quality. I'm at a loss to completely explain or describe the look in his eyes. His eyes were clearly relaxed but yet alert and intent on every detail around him. His eyes appeared to reveal an understanding of the world around him to a level far exceeding his youthful years. Every morning when I finally drove in he would greet me with a slight smile and say "excellent day to you." I would always ask him if he was assigned to car number 404 and he would get red in the face and say, "Please, Robert, do not use that very bad word." The word "car" to my Kosovo colleague was a slang term that refers to the reproductive part of the male anatomy. There was the time when my wife mailed a bunch of magazines to me and I noticed one of them was an issue of *Car and Driver Magazine*. This caused quite a commotion when I just

154

happened to leave it lying out on the briefing table in the squad room. (I have to admit I just couldn't resist the opportunity.) Through his jokes on me and mine on him we developed a very strong big brother/little brother relationship. On one particularly hot day, I asked my young friend if he was going to be wearing his scarf with the collar buttoned up on such a hot day, or be like me and patrol with an open collar. He stood close to me and put his hand on my shoulder and said very quietly that he could never be like anyone else and asked me if he could talk to me away from the others. We stepped outside and I watched in a state of controlled shock as he unbuttoned his collar and carefully removed the scarf from around his neck. From just under his left ear to just past the midway point across his throat, going under his chin was an indescribable scar. I could see that it was an old scar from a wound that must have literally opened up the entire side of his neck. I could also see without even looking closely the jagged crisscross of crudely gouged-in stitch marks that closed this wound and brought the two sides of this horrendous slash together. My young colleague began to tell me that several years earlier he had been with other youths of his village when they saw some soldiers they hated passing down the main street of their village. As they chased the soldiers, throwing rocks at their vehicles, he made the mistake of running too close to one of the vehicles. To the horror of the villagers who were standing along the roadside, one of the soldiers reached out from his vehicle, grabbed the boy by his hair, pulled him up onto the side of the vehicle, stabbed a bayonet into his neck, and then ripped it across his throat. The soldier thought the boy was finished so he just let the body fall to the ground. The boy fell onto the road and then rolled into the ditch. Some of the local women grabbed him out of the drainage ditch. Without hesitation and literally out of nowhere, more women came and pinned him down while others crudely stitched his neck closed. The locally distilled alcohol drink was poured on the raw wound and then it was covered with mud and wrapped as tight as they could wrap it. He told me that according to the old women of the village, the real battle began when the fever came. He was told that every hour and every day that passed brought him closer to his loved ones and farther from the hands of God. Each old woman of the village took credit for his survival because they all had their own secret healing broth that they took turns feeding to him. As he slowly started to cover his neck with his scarf he told me something that truly amazed me. He said that every day when he gets up and looks in his mirror and sees the scar that could have resulted in his death he pledges to his God that he will not

155

be like the man who tried to take his life. He will always remember that all people are to be treated fairly whether they are part of the enemies of the past or not. He said that the scar will remind him as a police officer to be just and fair to everyone for the rest of the life God has given to him as a gift.

A LIFE FOR HIS FAMILY

Siegfried Robatsch, Austria

My second mission with the United Nations Mission in Bosnia and Herzegovina (UNMIBH) was from July 2000 to July 2001. As an Austrian police officer I was part of the IPTF (International Police Task Force) in Sarajevo for my first mission. I was assigned to ITSS (Internal Training and Support Section) to train other officers. On this mission I wanted to be on land, working with the local police and people.

This UN mission was a monitoring mission and I was finally going to be working at a police station. I was assigned to Gradiska in northern Bosnia and Herzegovina. The city is on the border of Croatia, situated in the Republika Srpska. In 1995, the Dayton Peace Accord divided Bosnia and Herzegovina into two areas with two separate governments—The Federation of Bosnia and Herzegovina (primarily Bosnian citizens) and the Republika Srpska (primarily Serbian citizens). These two states are separated by an imaginary line called the Inter-Entity Boundary Line (IEBL).

The trip from Sarajevo to Gradiska took us through Banja Luka. We traveled through a beautiful, natural landscape filled with forests, rivers, and little lakes. Unfortunately, the scars of the civil war that raged from 1992 to 1995 were still apparent everywhere we looked. Destroyed houses, villages, and mine fields filled the landscape. The land mines caused many children and adults (both women and men) to lose their arms or legs—and even their lives. The horror of the war seemed to touch everyone.

The UN mission in Bosnia had officers from over 50 different countries serving in different capacities. The Gradiska mission had officers stationed there from many of the various nations serving in Bosnia. This station was responsible for monitoring the boundary line and the border crossing into Croatia. It was also responsible for monitoring the local

Figure 9.2 Siegfried Robatsch.

police activities from the two police stations in the area (approximately 50 kilometers in circumference). All officers from the UN police station in Gradiska reported to UN Police Headquarters in Banja Luka (Bosnia). I secured private accommodations and was given my assignment—I was to be a police monitor and advisor to the local police; I was ready to start the daily routine of mission life.

I was able to have a lot of direct contact with the local people of Gradiska. I spoke with them at the police stations in town and in the police stations in the surrounding villages. During my spare time I played football, ate at local restaurants, and attended various events. Much of the language spoken in the area was English and German so I was able to learn quite a bit about this border town.

Gradiska is a small town right on the border of Croatia with only one bridge across the Sava River to take you in and out of the country. The Sava River forms the natural borderline for approximately 200 kilometers in the north between Bosnia and Croatia. The standard of living is largely farming and agricultural. Recently, many bunkers and underground silos have been found that are filled with items from the time of Stalin. Ammunition, armored vehicles, and even rockets have found their way to "the market." In town there is also a large free market that has everything from original artwork to copies of art, electronics, CDs, clothing, and anything else you could want. All the trafficking and trading, and the large amount of customs fees have helped enormously to revitalize this city.

The Bosnian Civil War has had a huge impact on this area. There is still fighting to this day and it will probably continue for many more generations. Approximately 30,000 Bosnian people lived in Gradiska and the surrounding area. They were expelled from their land and told they had to leave the country. All their houses and possessions were confiscated. The mosques were burnt. People were captured, tortured, and murdered. Serbs that were living in houses and apartments in the Muslim regions were forced from their homes. The result was refugees of both Bosnian and Serbian background being forced into other European countries. There was no state government that both groups could agree to. Many people became refugees within their own land, looking for a new home in the correct part of their own country. All these incidents caused a great strain and ethnic division. To this day, this is the biggest problem for the people of Bosnia. Although it appears to be calm, there is always constant tension and problems between the two ethnic groups. Just recently, when preparing for the official dedication of a new mosque, 30 armored personnel carriers and a contingent of 300 UN officers were called in to the town to assist the local police in keeping order. There was even an evacuation bridge built over the Sava River in case there was trouble and large numbers of people had to be removed quickly.

In between this hatred, the ruling parties from both sides and various NGOs (nongovernmental organizations) decided to try to reconcile the situation and return the refugees to their homes. The United

Nations Agreement for Displaced Persons and Refugees in Bosnia and Herzegovina was created. Serbian refugees had to give back the houses they were living in to the Bosnian owners. Likewise, Bosnian refugees in Serbian areas had to return the houses they were occupying to the Serbs. Enforcing this agreement did not always go smoothly and trying to coordinate things so they ran trouble-free and according to the paper (contract) was not easy. There were structural defects, destruction, abandonment, and mistrust. Many times you had the Bosnian owner and the Serbian refugee living together in the home until legal matters were resolved. Another problem was the fact that Bosnians did not want to return to the Serbian part of the region and Serbs did not want to return to the Bosnian part of the region even if their home and all their possessions were there. This is always a problem in a civil war and it is still a problem today in the Balkans.

In this area of the world that was filled with joy and sorrow, disappointment and hatred, I made it my task to walk from my apartment to work at the police station every day. My path led me into the community, through a park, and past businesses and shops. In the morning I saw people waiting in long lines at the local government office for assistance payments (welfare) and work assignments. In the parks I saw many homeless people who spent the nights on the park benches, working for companies and stores as day laborers, trying to earn some money to help them survive. In the evenings I saw people who were downtrodden by life trying to find something to eat—anything edible.

Each morning as I walked to work I saw a man that had spent the night sleeping on a park bench. He stood out from the others who routinely slept in the park because he did not act as worn down by life as the other homeless people around him. At first I did not believe he was truly homeless but there he was again and again on the same park bench. I tried to speak to this man to ask him what events had occurred in his life that led him to spending the nights outside on a park bench. (I do need to comment that even though he was old and the clothes he was wearing were old and well worn he did not appear unkempt.) Unfortunately the man did not understand me. I felt sorry for this gentleman and decided that I had to do something to try to help him, so I asked an interpreter from the station to come with me to talk to him.

The next day I met with the interpreter and we went together into the park to talk with this man. Because I came back to the park with an interpreter the man became very nervous. He told the interpreter that he had a small room and that he was no longer sleeping in the park. I tried

159

to make it very clear that I only wanted to help and that I wanted to find a solution to help this man. He was very quiet and was still not totally comfortable with the situation but after some time he agreed to go with us back to the UN police station. When he showed us his ID, he also presented a certificate of discharge from a hospital where he had been a patient.

Once we had gained this man's trust he told us his tale. A story that shows how men can become almost superhuman with all the things they are willing to endure for the love and affection they have for someone else. With great pleasure and satisfaction he quietly told us how he came to be in his present situation.

He came from a mixed family (Bosnian and Serb). His wife, a Serb, was already deceased at the beginning of the civil war. Two adult children belonged to his family and they had lived with him and his wife in their little house. They had to do this because they were a mixed family. This made for a very difficult situation with a lot of need. During a physical examination he was diagnosed with lung cancer. He was told that he had a life expectancy of one year. He was to be admitted to the hospital where his cancer treatments could be carried out.

Prior to his hospitalization the civil war had so radicalized this area of the country that there was a great risk for all Bosnians of mixed marriage. They were regularly persecuted and robbed of their possessions. The only chance for his children to have a reasonably secure future was to get them out of the country. He sold his house and everything else he could and sent them with the money to the Netherlands to escape the war and build a future for themselves.

You have to imagine being in this situation—your spouse has died, your children are now living in the Netherlands, there is no future ahead for this man. He is in a part of the country where he is not welcome. He doesn't even have a home, only the hope that his daughter and his son will be better off once they are settled in their new home.

Many people would consider this a tragedy but he told us that this was a relief, satisfaction, even a means of joy for him. He could help his family before it was too late.

In the hospital he was treated but with only the barest necessities. He was feeling worse and worse. There were times when he thought death would be his only relief. Because of the Dayton Agreement (the General Framework Agreement for Peace in Bosnia and Herzegovina) foreign aid came to Bosnia and medical assistance also came to the hospital. There was treatment for his pain, chemotherapy, and much more. The cancer slowly started to get better but it took three years of treatment. One day a doctor came into his room and told him he was cured. The cancer was gone. He didn't know if he should be happy or disappointed.

When he was being discharged from the hospital he was too proud to tell the officials that he was homeless and destitute. Through minor jobs, support from acquaintances, and sleeping in the park or barns he was struggling his way through life.

He did not want his children to know the situation he was in. Things were still too dangerous for them in Gradiska and he did not want them to return. They were to know only what their father told them about the situation. The interpreter and I became very aware that this man was luckier than a lot of people in similar situations.

Through various NGOs we were able to get this man admitted into a nursing home immediately. His children were notified and told that everything was being done to take care of their father and that they would be told of any new details in the future.

This event caused my UN colleagues and our associates, both Bosnian and Serb, to think about the situation in this country. How do you compare material values, power, and control over another culture, ethics, and religion to things that are truly important? The facts show what someone can achieve even when they outwardly appear to be old and frail; war, power, personal threat, murder, and torment will be defeated when there is love, a sense of family, and a willingness to give, even from someone who is supposedly weak.

To this day in Bosnia and Herzegovina ethnic cleansing is still the biggest problem for the realization of a single government that will be able to identify with all its citizens.

A FAMILY LOST

Ali Dikici, Turkey

The Srebrenica genocide occurred in July 1995, during the last year of the war in Bosnia (1992–1995). It was the single worst atrocity during the war and in Europe since World War II. In July 1995, the world's first United Nations' "safe area" became the site of Europe's worst massacre. It happened in the Bosnian village of Srebrenica—and was a turning point in the vicious war between Bosnian Serbs and Bosnian Muslims in the former Yugoslavia.

161

When I start working for the United Nations IPTF in Bosnia and Herzegovina in 1999, Hasan Nuhanović was assigned as a language assistant to me. We were together for almost two years from June 1999 to May 2001. When I first met Hasan, I thought he was the angriest and saddest man in the mission. As a Bosnian Muslim, he was one of the few survivors of Srebrenica genocide whose entire family was expelled from the UN compound into the hands of the Bosnian Serbs and have been missing ever since. His personal story was tragic and almost incomprehensible. His parents and his little brother were killed, while he survived. During my stay in the mission he told me how he had been trapped in the little town of Srebrenica for three years, besieged by the Bosnian Serb army with his parents and younger brother, along with 40,000 desperate refugees and betrayed by UN forces. Starving and fearing constant bombardment, Hasan worked as an interpreter for the Dutch Battalion of Peacekeepers, deployed to watch over the first UN "safe area." As a UN interpreter he was present at many of the crucial negotiations and decisions that took place. So, he places the blame squarely on the shoulders of the UN, who disarmed the Bosnian Muslims and then reneged on their promise to protect them. He has, in fact, spent the research of his life trying to track down where they died, who killed them, and exactly what took place. One of his undying hopes is that, in fact, one day his parents' bodies will be exhumed.

The story that Hasan told me about the genocide horrified me. He narrated some unbelievable scenes from the massacre and he accused the international community for what really happened in Srebrenica. Hasan's sad narrative was particularly touching, as many Bosniaks who had worked for any UN and NGO in Bosnia during the Serbia and Montenegro (SCG) aggression may find similar to their own personal experience. Thus, I drafted this article on the grounds of what Hasan told me but I also quoted from other sources that support his claims. You are going find a horrible story in the following sections about what happened the day the Serbs arrived to destroy the town, massacre its menfolk, and drive their widows into exile—with Hasan's words. It clearly reflects the innocence and naivety of Bosniaks of 1991–1995 in dealing with arrogant UN and other foreign military personnel.

While Hasan and I were patrolling in our area of responsibility, he explained step by step what really happened in Srebrenica in 1995. When he spoke about the genocide in Srebrenica, it was possible to see on his face the tragic fate of his parents and his younger brother, cold-bloodedly evicted from a UN office, turned over to the Serb forces, and then murdered, and how it has completely devastated his life.

Hasan and His Family in Srebrenica

In 1992, Hasan Nuhanović and his family left their hometown of Vlasenica when their village was taken over by the Bosnian Serb Army but got only as far as Srebrenica as refugees. "In the beginning of the war, I escaped from my hometown because we knew that we were going to be killed if the Serbs catch us." When they arrived in Srebrenica, they were able find an abandoned house; they suffered through severe famine, shortage of water, and other life-threatening circumstances. In 1993, Hasan and his family witnessed the arrival of the peacekeeping troops from the UN. They were elated to find what would appear to be salvation, and Hasan volunteered as an interpreter, and after six months became an official member of the local UN staff. From April 1993 until July 1995, Hasan worked as an interpreter and translator for the UN Military Observers (UNMO) and the Dutchbat team guarding the demilitarized enclave of Srebrenica. From inside the UN's safe area, he became a firsthand witness to much of the distress and the actions taken by both the Serbs and the UN forces.

Hasan and his family displayed their hospitality toward the UN soldiers. "I had established a custom to invite all newcoming officers I have dealt with daily, home for a dinner. My parents, my brother and I lived in a house not our own, being refugees from Vlasenica, together with another 20 persons. Despite all our poverty and misery, due to the fact I had been a paid interpreter, I was able to buy some food supplies." His mother made up some Bosnian specialty for these foreign guests. His family thanked them for coming to Srebrenica. These aliens in the uniforms, choking in good Bosnian food, would manage to spill it between bites: "Hasan, tell your mother she is great cook."—one Gary, another Paul, Derksen, William, Tony, Mark Foster, Dutch Captain Andre de Haan, dozens of them.* However, other members of Dutchbat Team were not so close and friendly toward the Bosniaks. Hasan told Robert Fisk in 1996 how, at the last Ramadan feast before the fall, Karremans had been invited to drink *rakija* with the Muslims. "I told one of the UN officers to tell Karremans

---

* Hasan Nuhanović, "Srebrenica as an S-Word in The Netherlands," Srebrenica Genocide Blog, available at: http://srebrenica-genocide.blogspot.com/2006/12/dutch-medal-of-betrayal.html (accessed August 12, 2009).

I was happy because it was the first time I had seen him smile," Hasan told me. "I saw Karremans giving the officer a return message for me. His reply was: 'You are an arsehole.' "*

The Fall of Srebrenica and Shelter in the UN Base at Potočari

On July 9, 1995, the Serbs took 30 Dutch peacekeepers hostage. With Serb troops tightening the noose around Srebrenica, panic took hold. Finally, the Bosnian Serbs under General Mladić overtook Srebrenica on July 11, 1995. After the fall of the town, the terrified population of the enclave split into two. Some 15,000 made off over the mountains toward Bosnian-held territory. Another 25,000 streamed to the Dutch UN base at Potočari on the outskirts of Srebrenica, seeking protection from troops charged by the UN Security Council with providing protection. Some 5000 got inside the base, which the Dutch then closed, leaving 20,000 outside. Hasan and his family sought shelter at the UN base and he hoped that the UN troops would protect both him and his family. The situation was terrible there: "There were 6000 people. They were told to sit down by the Dutch soldiers. They were not allowed to go to the toilet—so they did everything here. The temperature was 35°C. The place stank so much it was almost impossible to breathe."† However, at least, it was a safe place. "Being inside meant you live, being outside meant you die. It was very simple." On July 12th, the Serbs began sporadic killing of people outside.

---

* Robert Fisk, "Our Shame over Srebrenica," *Independent* (July 12, 2001). Likewise, Hasan tells how other internationals were ungrateful: "When, late night on July 12th, sometime around midnight and day after the fall of Srebrenica, I learned that at least nine bodies of men killed in the presence of Dutch soldiers were seen before the base, we were inside Dutchbat base in the improvized office where Andre de Haan was in charge. I said to my mother and brother, who stood next to me and de Haan, what I just learned and my mother fainted. She understood then and there, that all of us will be killed, both her sons and her husband. I caught her in fall and placed her carefully on a bench nearby. She went yellow in face. In that moment, few feet from me there was de Haan, and next to him German nurse, Christina Schmit, as well as Aussie MD O'Brien. They've just turned their back on us, pretending that nothing was going on in the room. My mother was losing consciousness, yet they were standing and just talking. Just as if nothing was going on around them. Just as if my mother was a plain piece of furniture in that room. That same de Haan, just few week ago ate Bosnian cabbage rolls at my mother's (while the rest of the people in the house were starving) and made several compliments how good her cooking was." See Hasan Nuhanović, "Srebrenica as an S-Word in The Netherlands" (op. cit). Much later, after the genocide, Hasan contacted those aliens who had eaten his mother's dishes. They all behaved as if nothing happened in Srebrenica.

† Duncan Staff, "Srebrenica: The Search for a Terrible Truth Goes On," *The Guardian*, Tuesday, October 13, 2009.

General Ratko Mladić delivered an ultimatum—5000 people, mostly men and boys, had to be expelled from the base. He also asked for a skilled interpreter to translate his orders to the Dutch UN commander, Colonel Tom Karremans. Hasan was assigned for this task. Following the "negotiations" with Mladić, the Dutch UN peacekeepers decided to hand the civilians over to the Serbs. On July 13, the Dutch ordered the refugees sheltering inside the base to leave. Hasan was instructed by Dutch colleagues to announce that decision. "UN Dutch battalion authorities gave me a megaphone and told me to tell the crowd to start leaving the base in groups of five. There were executions of several groups of men and teenage boys in front of the base, and the Dutch saw it all. The question is how the Dutch could continue to expel people knowing what was happening in front of the base. And this question has never been answered."

Hasan Nuhanović spent the night of July 12–13, 1995 with his parents and brother in an improvised office in the base, taking orders from the Dutch officer, Captain Andre de Haan. The next morning, between 5 and 6 A.M., De Haan gave an instruction to Hasan, "'Hasan, tell your mother, your brother and your father that they must leave the base, now.' He was looking at me and them, while behind us stood three well armed Dutch soldiers. Everybody was looking at us—as if saying—what are you waiting for? Outside, right in front of Dutch base, Serb soldiers were killing Bosnian people."

In fact, Hasan's father Ibro could stay in the compound because he was one of three representatives of the 30,000 refugees inside and outside the base who took part with Dutch senior officers in supposed "negotiations" with General Mladić. The Dutch Major Robert Franken told Hasan to explain to his father that he could remain on the base. Hasan's father begged a Dutch major for his family to be allowed to stay. "Sir, what about my wife and son?" hoping that he would say "let them stay, too." He said, "Listen, tell your father if he doesn't want to stay he can leave too. And there'll be no further discussion." His father had three seconds to decide whether he wanted to stay on the base, to go on living with his elder son, or go and die with his younger son and his wife. He chose to leave. And Hasan was yelling, "'I'm coming with you, I'm coming with you, so I'm coming outside the base.' When my parents realized that I was really going to come outside the base they turned around and they told me, 'Listen, Hasan, if you can stay, you stay, you don't come with us.'" The soldier told Hasan that he could remain with them as he was a UN interpreter. The Dutch didn't send Hasan out, as a piece of plastic was hanging on his chest, upon which, beside his name, was written "UN." Hasan desperately sought permission for his family to remain as well. But because of the agreement with the attacking Serbs, the remaining civilians would have to go. Hasan continues: "At the moment, when my family was told by the soldiers to leave the base—they were told to get out, you know, just get out—I couldn't see the difference between the Serb troops and the UN Dutch peacekeepers."

The brother of Hasan Nuhanović, Muhammed, was also an employee in the base, and was also one of the people who had to leave the compound. Only those who were officially employed by the UN were allowed to stay. Hasan's brother may have been helping the Dutchbat contingent, but had no contract with the UN. Hasan kept begging them to leave his brother at least. Despite Hasan's pleas, Dutch Major Rob Franken decided that his brother must quit the compound. Muhammed got up, looked at Hasan, and said: "Hasan, don't you beg them any more. I'm going out, f... them. You stay here, if you can." "And he left me—forever. Him, my mother, my father, and all other Bosniaks from the base." He did leave, together with his father and mother, in one of the busses waiting outside the camp, never to be seen again. Hasan says "My name was on a list of people who could stay in the base. My parents asked me to do everything I could to save my brother, and for two days I was trying to get his name on the list. They put his name on—maybe just to get rid of me—then erased it at the last moment. I was walking alongside him as he walked out of the base, trying to apologize and saying: 'I am coming with you!' He suddenly turned around and screamed at me: 'You are not coming with me! You will stay here!'"*

"I saw the Dutch battalion deputy commander sending my family out, and that's the last memory I have about my family." Hasan Nuhanović watched—mutely and helplessly—as his closest relatives were led away to their deaths. In spite of his pleas on their behalf his family was forced to leave and was sent to their deaths as victims of the Srebrenica Genocide. His stunning account of the fall of the town had reached its terrible climax with the moment when he had to watch his family being thrown out of the haven of the Dutch base and into the hands of the Serb army, knowing they were going to their deaths. "I brought my brother [to Srebrenica] to serve him to the Serbs on a plate," says Nuhanović. "I thought I did the best thing at that moment, to bring him to the safest place in the region,

---

* Duncan Staff, "Srebrenica: The Search for a Terrible Truth Goes On," *The Guardian*, Tuesday, October 13, 2009.

which was the Dutch battalion base, not knowing they were going to hand him over to the Serbs. If he had gone to the forests with his friends … many of his friends survived. At least he would have had a chance to run and fight for his life."*

The commander of the Dutch base, Colonel Tom Karremans, left his deputy, Colonel Franken, to oversee the expulsion, or "evacuation" as it is known. Under the eyes of Dutch soldiers, the Serbs then separated women, children, and the elderly from men and boys—the latter taken away for summary execution. "The Dutch just stood there. Some of them turned around and walked back toward the factory [where the refugees were gathered inside the base] and forcibly expelled them. They did nothing to save people, even though there was an opportunity to do so," he says. Hasan recalls the scene: "They just planned everything to efficiently empty out the camp. Just tell the people to walk like cattle toward the gate. What happened in July 1995 was the final episode of genocide, of mass killing, of mass murder. The only thing I did not expect—because I expected bad things to happen—was that the UN peacekeepers, the Dutch battalion in this case, was going to assist the Serbs, to hand over these people to the Serbs, like my family."† In that same moment, on the tallest building of the base, there were two flags flapping in the wind—the flag of the Dutch kingdom and the flag of the United Nations.

Hasan blames Dutch soldiers: "They all knew. There were court preliminary hearings in The Hague against the state of Netherlands, where several Dutch officers actually admitted in the court. It's in the court records that they did know that some people were already being killed outside of the base, but they still decided to hand over the people who were inside the base to the Serbs, who then killed them. In five days, Serbian forces slaughtered over 8000 Bosnian Muslims, mostly men and boys. Initial reports from the head of the UN mission in Bosnia made no mention of the atrocities." According to Hasan, victims perished "with the active connivance of UN troops." The Dutch peacekeepers should share a larger portion of the blame. One Dutch soldier, by refusing to allow some Muslims to remain in the peacekeepers' compound, was effectively condemning civilians to death.

---

* John Chipman, "The Bones of Srebrenica," CBC Radio's *The Current*, July 11, 2005.
† Joe Rubin "Srebrenica: A Survivor's Story. Interview with Hasan Nuhanović," *Frontline World*, Bosnia: The Men Who Got Away, March 28, 2006, August 12, 2009.

Hasan's Struggle and Search for His Family

After the war ended, Hasan had spent his years trying to prosecute those who were responsible for the death of his father, mother, and brother. He has contributed his story to documentaries, newspaper articles, and television programs in an effort to ensure that the mass murder of 8000 Muslims from Srebrenica is not forgotten. He was unstoppable in his determination to get at the truth.

Hasan searched for his family, driving through the Bosnian countryside, talking to anyone who might know what happened, praying that the stories and the rumors weren't true, that they had somehow escaped the mass executions and the mass graves, that they were alive somewhere in the hills or maybe being held in secret prison camps. When I left the mission in 2001, he had already been searching for his family for six years. Then, slowly, he learned the truth. He has since learned some details about where and how his family was killed. "My brother and father were probably taken to the soccer field in Bratunac, along with 4000 other men and boys," he said. "On the same day, my mother was taken to a prison in my town in Vlasenica. She was actually killed there." Nuhanović gave up looking for his family, and started looking for their bodies. In the evenings and on weekends, he hunted for the remains of his murdered family. "There is no closure—closure only comes when we die," he says. "But I need to bury them." Finally, partial remains of his father, Ibro, and mother, Nasiha, have been recovered from concealed mass graves but there is still no news of the fate of his brother Muhammed. Ibro Nuhanovic's funeral took place in the cemetery opposite the Dutch base at Potocari on 11 July 2007. Hasan says that once he has found and buried all his family members, he will dedicate the rest of his life to pursuing justice for them. "I don't want to talk about the details because some of these bastards are still living in that town. Apparently there were six of them. First, they tried to rape my mother. At that time I think she was 48. So how would you feel if you drove through a town in which five or six thugs who tried to rape your mother and then kill her still live like free men? This whole eastern part of Bosnia is soaked in blood."

Since the end of the Bosnian War Hasan Nuhanović has campaigned to establish and publicize the truth about the genocide. He has given evidence at the International Criminal Tribunal for the Former Yugoslavia at The Hague. He played an important part in establishing the Srebrenica Genocide Memorial at Potočari where the remains of many of the identified victims have been interred. Hasan has a message to the Serbs: "The

Serbs must accept that this genocide happened. This grandiose memorial should be a reminder. If they can't accept that, I don't see how we can live with them again."

Nuhanović works closely with other survivors and relatives' organizations, including the Mothers of Srebrenica in Sarajevo and the Women of Srebrenica in Tuzla. He has written a book of chronology of the events at Srebrenica, *Under the UN Flag: The International Community and the Srebrenica Genocide*,* in which he examines the responsibility and guilt of members of the international community who were either direct participants on the ground or indirectly influenced or were capable of influencing those events but failed to fulfill their commitment to protect the Muslim population of the besieged "safe area" under UN Security Council Resolution 819.

It's true that the blame for Srebrenica belongs mainly with General Ratko Mladić, Radovan Karadzic, and their followers; they are the ones who compelled Srebrenicans to make the bitter choices they did. But it's also true that the Dutch peacekeepers in Srebrenica and their superior officers in Sarajevo and at the United Nations in New York had a duty to the world and their own honor to do better than they did. Hasan says, "The massacre committed in Srebrenica against my people was done by the Bosnian–Serb army and police. But the role of the international community—the UN peacekeepers, the United Nations in New York, the European Union and NATO—were very, very shameful because many things could have been done to prevent the massacre." Hasan adds that ignorance of those parties continues after the war. "International community and involving states are trying to forget the Srebrenica massacre. They are doing nothing to help us, the families of the missing, to find out the truth about what happened to our loved ones." And Hasan puts a serious claim. "There are various sources of information suggesting that a deal was made a month before the attack on Srebrenica when General Mladic was apparently promised by the top UN officials that they would not bomb his troops on the ground anymore; they would send no more air strikes against his forces."†

Hasan openly claimed the Dutch government that initially denied its responsibility and blamed others for the fall of Srebrenica and the

---

* During my stay in Bosnia, Hasan was collecting all evidence and data to finish his book as a person present at numerous important meetings and in contact with many people. He managed to publish the book in 2006. For this book, Nuhanović undertook the effort to interview an additional 100 people where other sources remained indecisive or information was not yet available at all.
† Joe Rubin (op. cit.).

genocide that followed. However, the Srebrenica massacre led to long-running discussions in Holland and it quickly turned into a national scandal and trauma. Hasan's role is great for this trauma. "While some were claiming that ex-members of Dutchbat 3, the unit of Dutch military which found itself in Srebrenica on July 1995, suffer from PTS (posttraumatic stress), while part of Dutch public opinion truly accepted the excuses that Dutchbat 3 was also a victim of Srebrenica events, while Dutch officials were publishing one report after another in 1995, 1998, 2002, and 2003, I was going from one place to another both in the Netherlands and in Bosnia repeating the misfortunes that had befallen my mother, father and brother whom those same Dutch soldiers, before my very eyes, handed over to Serb soldiers at the gates of their military base in Potočari, Republic Bosnia-Herzegovina."* So, Hasan blamed the Dutchbat not because it did not do enough, or because it did nothing, but because it did do a number of things that were wrong. Hasan attempted to pursue the Dutch authorities in court and to seek compensation. In order to seek redress for the death of their relatives, Hasan Nuhanović and the family of Rizo Mustafič, a UN electrician ordered by his employers to leave the Potočari base, have taken legal action in the Dutch civil courts. The bases of the action include allegations, inter alia, that the Dutch State was involved in genocide and violated fundamental human rights by handing Nuhanović and Mustafič's family members over to the (Bosnian–Serb) enemy.

After the capture of Karadzic in 2008, "there is some kind of relief," conceded Hasan Nuhanović. "But there is absolutely no place for euphoria. This should have happened years ago." "Karadzic," he said, had "lived much better over the last 13 years than most of the survivors."

Conclusion

When I first met with Hasan in 1999, he seemed to be full of anger and rage due to the loss of his family. We chatted many times about the incidents in Srebrenica. We visited different places, NGOs, institutions, and so forth, related to genocide. Once we went to his hometown Vlasenica for official paperwork to get back their house, occupied by a Serb family. I could easily observe the hate in his eyes due to the "international betrayal" of his people in 1995. He always seemed to be stunned by the memory. He was still under the influence of the incidents and it heavily wraps his entire life, even his dreams. "After the Srebrenica massacre, I had terrible dreams,

---

* Hasan Nuhanović, "Srebrenica as an S-Word in The Netherlands" (op. cit.).

like I'm flying over scorched land, and everything is destroyed and black. And there are many graves, and one grave opens up suddenly under me, and my mother comes out of the grave and says to me: 'I don't like you!' For a long time I couldn't even bear to look at signs or newspapers in the Serb Cyrillic alphabet," he said. And he talked about his endless struggle with guilt. "I'm trying not to think about what happened to me here," he told me. "It was as though my mind was telling me that my mother didn't like me anymore because I hadn't managed to protect my brother's life. It was just a nightmare and it still is a nightmare," says Hasan. "It's not finished yet because I still don't know what happened."

It has taken him years to begin to deal with his traumatizing experiences in Srebrenica. "But in the end," he said, "I realized I was weary of living with my rage, and of replaying the past. I wanted a future with my wife and daughter more than I wanted revenge. I wanted a normal life." When I contacted him after years he seemed well, and he said, "That's because I've decided to live for my daughter rather than die for my mother." However, it will be very hard for him to forget everything and establish a new life from the beginning. "I don't think I will ever be able to forgive or to forget, but I can live—I mean, I have to live with it. And I think I have to see some justice done in court. And that's the only way in which justice can be done, I think. And the International Criminal Tribunal for the Former Yugoslavia (ICTY), the tribunal in The Hague, the International Tribunal, covers the part of the story where the Serbs who killed those people, but I am not trying to have a court case against those UN peacekeepers or parts of this whole system that has contributed. I mean, that has basically assisted and helped the Serbs get hold of these people."*

If there is to be any hope of reconciliation in the wake of the Srebrenica massacres, people like Hasan Nuhanović must learn the truth of what happened to their loved ones. Hasan's view, after all that, as to if reconciliation is possible between Serbs and Muslims, is as follows: "Really, I don't think you should ask this kind of question of people like me. My whole family was killed. Maybe you should ask other people who have not suffered as much as I have. And there's a great part of the population that has not been directly affected by this war. So, you know, this part of the population that have lost entire families, and our lives have been ruined completely, I don't think we are the ones who should be dragged into this kind of issue, you know, on reconciliation and things like that.

---

* "Srebrenica Remembered," Transcript, *CNN Live Event*/ Special, aired July 11, 2005.

I have already too many problems to deal with in my life. So, this is, you know, I have this mourning that is going on for 10 years now. There's no closure for me. My relatives have not been found. I couldn't bury them. Those who have done this have not been punished. So, I mean, how can I have closure?"*

Leslie Woodhead from BBC says, "It was a somber occasion, but afterwards Hasan told me about a little Serb girl he had spotted on his drive to Srebrenica that morning."I looked at this girl and I asked myself: 'She's a Serb—do you hate this girl?' And the answer is, 'No.' This little girl and my daughter should have a future."†

A FUNNY INTERNATIONAL SITUATION

Yitvah Penga, Cameroon, Africa

This I would like to share with you. While in Kosovo for my very first peacekeeping mission I was posted at the police station at *Skenderaj*, as it is called by the Albanians, and *Serica* as the Serbians call it. This town is in the Mitrovica region. I went out on patrol with one language assistant to a village around upper Kopiliq and to my great surprise while driving through the village I could hear the young people shouting, "Zizag, zizag, zizag!" This shouting was accompanied by people, both old and young, coming out of their various houses. I asked my language assistant what was going on but he would not tell me and only continued laughing. At one point I decided to stop the patrol van. I asked my language assistant again what really was the problem. At this juncture I could see the people running toward the vehicle. Some had the courage to come close to us while others stood far off and were just looking at me. My language assistant told me that *Zizag* means *Black man* and many of these people had never seen a black man before. Some of them were happy to see one while others were afraid to see a black man in their land. I then gathered courage and went out of the patrol van. I noticed one very old lady closing her eyes as a sign of disbelief of what she was seeing. So I moved toward a young boy and greeted him with a handshake. I watched the young boy, after greeting me and touching my hand, move behind and try to wipe his palms, hoping to wipe out the black color that he thought I

---

* Ibid.
† Leslie Woodhead, "Srebrenica: A Survivor Moves On," BBC News, Monday, July 11, 2005.

must have left on his white palms. I started laughing and the old lady ran back to her house. The others were asking questions through my language assistant. "Where does he come from?" and "Is he living in a jungle?" My language assistant decided to give me the answers in Albanian without the town's people knowing so when I gave the first response in Albanian they all shouted, "He speaks Albanian!" More of them came running out again and a young man asked me, "Why are you speaking Albanian?" I told him I was also an Albanian and he said, "NO. We don't have black Albanians." So after spending some time there with them I decided to leave the village to continue my patrol in the other areas but I promised them I would be back. Some few days later I came back to that same village. This time around I brought some loaves of bread with me and as soon as I drove into the village, the children started shouting, "Zizag has come! Zizag has come!" All those who were away and had only been told about my arrival in the village now had the opportunity of seeing me this time around. I gave the bread to the children. Some of them refused to take it while others took it and started eating it right in front of me. I told my language assistant, "Now the ones eating the bread care less about the color of the hands that gave them the bread and have some human feelings that some people in the world are black."

Editor's note: Perhaps there is much to be learned from bread, children, and a clever international officer bearing the gift of understanding.

CHICKEN HOSPITAL

François Vigneron, France

In 1999, I was deployed to the International Training and Support Section, International Police Task Force, Sarajevo, Bosnia, and Herzegovina. I was appointed as a contingent rotation officer in this UN mission. I was working in the same office with one Russian officer (Evgueni O.) and I was really happy when we received a new monitor from the United Kingdom (Zbignew S.) because I was hoping to improve as much as possible my "so poor English" with my fantastic French accent. Unfortunately, when Zbignew arrived, he immediately started to speak Russian with Evgueni. I was so disappointed. In fact I even tried to learn the Russian language! The Russian language is really easy after you drink a few glasses of vodka. But after a couple of minutes I did remember that I was French and I really prefer red wine. That's why I decided to create a "French Red Wine Club."

Figure 9.3   Bon appétit.

Two police officers eagerly joined me. They decided that I must be the president because of my great knowledge of wine and they would be my two vice presidents. With Evgueni and Robert from the United States we decided to have this weekly red wine meeting and discussion. We always had a really great time talking about everything and nothing, and how we could start to rebuild a new world. I remember this one very special evening when Bob explained to us his new idea for making a lot of money when he would be back home—the "Chicken Hospital." First of all he would find a building that had a street on two of its sides and entrances on both of these sides of the building. The hospital side would be for the poor, sick, or injured chicken, brought to the hospital by the unfortunate and desperate owner. It would be well organized with a waiting room with a television, and a sympathetic nurse, with special accommodations for all of the animals to rest in while waiting for their own special doctor. But life is really bad and even with the best of the best doctors they cannot find it possible to "cure" the poor animal. Of course the owner has to pay a lot of money for this desperate medical intervention, and of course a special and very expensive psychological team has to announce the unfortunate bad news to the owner and offer him as much comfort

174

as possible ... and also a free drink at the small restaurant located on the other side of the building, just behind the hospital. On the other side of the building the deceased chicken would now be respectfully and deliciously embalmed in a mixture of salt, pepper, eggs, and flour (in case there are vehicle tire marks on its poor little body that need to be covered). Then it is cooked in oil for its final departure from this world. The small, but nice, brand new restaurant would serve a complete menu of chicken breast, chicken nuggets, fried chicken, and many other very respectfully presented "recipes!"

After several bottles of red wine we thought this was such a great idea! Even now, when I want to eat some chicken, I walk around the building just to be sure that there is no chicken hospital nearby.

Viva the French Red Wine Club! Thank you for all this marvelous time we had together. It does not matter if the mission is quiet or difficult; do not forget to have fun when you can and to smile all the time.

10

War Zone Insanity

THE TOILET BBQ

There are two sides to every coin, no matter where on this world of ours it was minted, what it's worth, or what it looks like. Every river on the face of this Earth has an upstream and a downstream. Unfortunately there are even some people who have two faces. Whenever you travel far from the place you call home, remember, whatever you find that appears to be strange or unusual in that foreign culture, it will find something equally strange or unusual in your culture. It's the precarious and hilarious balance of cultures we all share in this great world of ours.

The United Nations International Police Task Force missions were and still are an incredible eclectic assortment of officers from every far-reaching point on the globe. There are even spots from places you will never see on vacation travel maps. Bringing this inconceivable collection of officers together for predeployment war zone briefings and induction training was beyond challenging. The only things we had in common were our dedication to the mission we were deployed to and our pride for our own country. Most of the rest was quite unique to say the least. I could never understand why the administrative officials would deploy equatorial African officers to the Balkans in the middle of winter. As if the culture shock were not enough for these officers to adjust to, they had to cope with snow and ice as well. For most of these officers it was the first time in their lives they had seen or touched the "painful cold white." The Scandinavian officers' sense of humor didn't help matters very much either. They would post pictures of polar bears around the dining hall and the training rooms, warning one and all about the dangers of being torn apart and eaten by these gigantic snow monsters. Then, they would stick an old boot in a snow drift by the training barracks and stain the snow red with a little cheap wine. There were actually several times when we had to go on the transport bus to reassure the officers and coax them out of the bus and into the training barracks because of a "decorated" snow drift. I remember one day having an officer from Ghana tell me that he looked forward to having a "Sveedman" officer come to his country so he could have some fun with him in the brush country of his West African nation. Having been there myself I can only imagine what "fun games" he would consider playing. Even when the African officers were deployed to the Balkans in the summer months they were still chilled to the bone and extremely upset with the country they called the cold white hell. They would sit in the training classes wearing heavy overcoats with stocking hats and gloves while we would be teaching in just a polo shirt. Many of the officers we were close to would ask us what they should eat or drink to make their blood thicker so the cold would feel less severe. We just said that time was the best medicine and that they would do very well in the near future.

One night we received an urgent radio message that we had fires and injured student officers at one of the residential barracks. When our training team, the medical transport, and fire units arrived on location we were rather taken back at the sight in front of us and at a total loss for words. Some of our Middle Eastern colleagues had mistaken the western European style toilet for some type of a cooking unit. After all, it was nice and clean. It was in its own small cooking room. It had its own sink for preparing and cleaning food, and water flowed through the cooking station for cleanup later. It even had a roll of paper to clean up with right on the wall next to the cooking station. The cooking station even had a two-piece hinged cover. One of the hinged pieces was for the grill to be placed on while the other provided a cover for the cooking station while it was not in use. Yes, they thought, this is a well-organized kitchen. With the chicken and vegetables well washed in the food preparation sink, the water in the cooking station was carefully drained and the paper on the wall was used to properly dry the cooking basin. First, paper was placed into the bottom of the cooking basin and then small twigs that they had gathered from outside were placed over the paper in the porcelain basin. Larger twigs and sticks were placed into the basin and the fire was lit. As the fire burned, the meal of the chicken and vegetables was cooked and served in the small kitchen room to several of the officers. Life was good and so was dinner until someone decided to clean the cooking station by flushing the big white porcelain unit. When the cold water of the toilet reservoir was flushed into the hot porcelain basin, the result was a devastating "commode bomb." The explosion propelled razor-sharp shards of porcelain material into the walls and doors of the kitchen/bathroom and unfortunately, but not seriously, the shards also went into the face of that contingent's chief. I can't begin to express the effort it took all of us to contain our remarks and comments during the first aid and transport of the chief to a German MASH (medical field) unit. We knew it was unbecoming of an officer to find any kind of humor in the injury of a fellow officer regardless of the circumstances, but after all, we were only human, and containing ourselves was beyond our abilities. The attending doctor was a very serious German major with a very serious demeanor. As the doctor curiously looked at the injuries to our colleague's face while he lay on the stretcher under a massive surgical light, we all remained emotionally restrained—for the moment. Then the doctor said, *"Was ist das?"* (What is this?) We advised the doctor it was cuts caused by toilet porcelain. The doctor stopped looking at our colleagues face, took off his glasses, and turned to face us. Not believing he understood us correctly he stood straight and said, *"Was sagst du?"* (What did you say?) We told the doctor the injuries were incurred by our colleague while cooking in a toilet. The silence was deafening until our colleague on the stretcher said in a very loud and clear voice, "Can somebody get this shit out of my face." That was the end to any professional demeanor or restraint we could have possibly had left in us. We all just exploded into laughter including our friend on the stretcher. Even the ultrastrict, totally disciplined doctor lost control, covered his face with a white towel, and staggered out of the operating tent laughing. We could hear the doctor explaining in German to someone outside the tent about what was going on. Before we knew it the operating tent was flooded with other doctors, nurses, and medical aids, to the point where there was literally nowhere left to stand. Our dear colleague had become a "kitchen" celebrity.

THE SHATTERED COMMODE

Greg Gronewold, United States

Was it due to an extreme gastric incident? How about a manufacturer's defect? Maybe it was caused by unintentional impact with a heavy metal object? No, the cause of this destruction was none of the above.

Unless you have traveled outside of the United States to locations in Eastern Europe, or points farther east, you have probably never encountered a "Turkish toilet" when nature called. (Although we commonly referred to them as a "Muslim toilet" or a "Turkish toilet," you will find them in many countries besides Turkey, including the Middle East.) But you quickly get used to looking for the symbols on the door to the restroom, whether it be the letters "WC" (water closet) painted on the door, or maybe a plaque affixed to the door portraying either a pair of high-heeled shoes versus loafers to indicate the male or female lavatories. Any of these notices provide the adequate information to assist you in locating the appropriate facility.

Now imagine that you have absolutely no idea that there is another style of commode used in the world. So you open the door and come face to face with that in Figure 10.1. Yes, my friends, that is a Turkish toilet, which is also called an *alaturka*, or the *elephant's feet* model toilet. (This photo was actually taken in a public restroom in Bulgaria.) Needless to say, there is no sitting allowed so while keeping your personal property securely in your pockets, you "assume the position" and go about your business.

Things have changed over the past few decades and while you find a good number of these models still in use in various parts of our world, you generally will not have to hunt for too long before finding one of the "sit-down" models close by that we Americans are more familiar with.

But this type of educational information is not the purpose of this piece. It is merely required so you can understand the problem this can cause.

It was a morning in July 2002 when the Deputy Director of Logistics entered my office and it took all of about two seconds to see that something was wrong—very wrong. With no warning, the ranting and raving commenced, asking how something "like this" could happen and who in the world could have done this. Interjecting a word every now and then, I managed to settle the source down enough to find out what he was talking about. It was then I learned that a commode on the third floor had broken. (Oh yes, it was "in use" at the time—just in case you were wondering, and it is assumed that it had provided the occupant with a "wild ride.") The complainant then went right on in to see my boss, who he reported to directly pursuant to the chain of command.

Now realizing that you are not able to "zoom in" on the photo of the destroyed commode, I can tell you that the reason for my visitor's outrage could be found on the right side of the large broken piece of porcelain seen toward the lower left of the picture. Yes, there was a distinctive boot print

Figure 10.1 *Alaturka*—also known as—a Turkish toilet.

on the rim. (Also, be thankful that you cannot zoom in on the photo or else you would see more than just broken porcelain.)

Basically, someone had been standing on the rim of the commode doing his business when it "gave way," shattering into many pieces. Unfortunately, this is not the end of the incident.

Upon completion of the brief meeting held in the adjacent office, I was instructed to prepare an e-mail to be disseminated "en masse," to every single CivPol officer in Mission (somewhere around 3300 officers), instructing them that standing on the sit-down style of commode was not allowed (for obvious reasons). The message was to include a photo of the destroyed toilet. By that afternoon, the message was written, approved, and launched.

Less than five minutes after punching the "Send" button, visitors were standing two and three deep in my office, the phone was ringing nonstop, and my e-mail account was even livelier than usual, thanks mostly to my fellow Americans. Yes, folks had seen the message! Amid the endless

Figure 10.2   Results from standing on the rim.

laughter, I soon learned that the message I had sent was already making its way around the world via the electronic society we live in today, along with the help of the notorious "Forward" button on all e-mail accounts. I'm not sure that even one American saw the serious side of this situation. (Take this opportunity to look at the photo of the destroyed toilet once again, noting the protruding piece of porcelain toward the rear of the remaining bowl. Now that could have caused a very serious injury!)

Before it was over, one fellow American had even written my boss that it might be appropriate to include a block of instruction in future indoctrination training for new arrivals in mission on how to properly use the sit-down style of commode. That idea was quickly quashed when my supervisor replied to the author that this was indeed a good idea, and therefore, he would be recommended to provide all the demonstrations.

While this was not the first commode I recall being destroyed in mission by "improper" use, I do not remember hearing of another prior to my departure almost three years later.

DEMENTED "WAR ZONE" DRIVING

If you die in a war zone, the overwhelming odds are that it will be some type of circumstance or situation that will be related in some insane, twisted way to a vehicle. Your last moments will probably be spent either looking at the underbody of some vehicle that has driven over you, or flying without wings over some vehicle's roof after getting "lift off" from a friendly bumper, or just getting too close of a look at a vehicle's hood ornament, or making a fatal leap from the front bumper to back seat via the windshield, or getting embossed via a tire indentation that is rolling over your body, or a burning, exploding, or shot-up vehicle, that you had the bad luck to be inside of, outside of, or just too damn close to. This also doesn't rule out the possibility of several of the above-listed causes of your unexpected demise being combined in some truly novel way. This of course is in addition to the constant threat of being rear-ended by another vehicle that's going over twice as fast as you are and the very last thought on their mind is using their brakes, or your unexpected involvement in a head-on collision with some person with a death wish that doesn't comprehend the concept of driving on their own side of the road.

Having a vehicle in a war zone is more of a situation of opportunity than it is of ownership. It's similar to getting a driver's license. Most of the locals don't want to be troubled with all the paperwork so they don't apply for a license. If you are part of a unit that has its own vehicles then you are very fortunate indeed, and I hold you in "quiet" contempt (especially if you are bigger than me). But if you are relegated to being part of the rest of the war zone rabble that has to scrounge up their own vehicle as need dictates, it's best to carefully consider the situation of vehicle commandeering. Quite a large percentage of vehicles in a war zone have been stolen from other countries and then driven back into the war zone. They have been reissued new, fraudulent serial numbers and then through the "purchased efforts" of corrupt local police, new papers and license plates are issued for the stolen vehicles so they can be "legally" operated in that war zone country. I remember hearing about an antagonizing ad that was displayed in a major German newspaper that read, "Come to Kosovo for your holiday, your vehicle is already here!" Most of the license plates are exchanged with other vehicles on a regular basis, and that's if the vehicles are displaying any licenses at all. Ignition keys are always optional.

The rules of the road in a war zone are simple: There are no rules and too often there are no roads either. You drive to where you have to be regardless of what's beneath your wheels or under your butt.

I remember one day when several of us got into a vehicle to run off to a nearby base camp to get some hot food. The "new guy" who was with us on this never-to-be-repeated journey remarked in awe and wonder, "Where's my seat belt?" He had no idea how lucky he was to have a ride to the base camp never mind a seat to sit on. Starting the vehicle is *always* the second thing you do when you're getting ready to operate your vehicle in a war zone. The first thing you do if you want to continue to survive in one piece is the onsite inspection of the vehicle. You might have keys for the ignition; not having keys is only a slight inconvenience. Hopefully there is enough gasoline (Is the gas gauge working?). You can always spot an experienced war zone officer by how skillfully he rocks his selected vehicle from side to side while listening for the sound of the splashing gasoline inside of the vehicles tank telling him just how far he will get in this vehicle. Inspect the outside of your intended vehicle like your life depends on it because it does! It's best to keep your vehicle in a dirty condition at all times. This is so it doesn't stand out as a target, and so you can tell if someone has been tampering with your vehicle. There will be the telltale sign of a clean spot where someone has been trying to alter something or even brushed up against the vehicle. It would be wise for you to spend more time looking *under* your vehicle than you do looking *in* your vehicle. Again, please let me caution you, with no humor intended—even though some of this chapter is intended to be rather dry wit—beware of anything clean on a dirty vehicle and *do not* pull on any loose wires to see what the hell they're connected to … Or they could be connected to your partially filled coffin! If you see anything that you don't understand or if it looks the least bit suspicious, back off and get a bomb team out to handle the situation, whether it's your vehicle or anything else you see.

Don't make the foolish effort of getting a closer look, or it will quite likely be the last look you make of anything. Even if your vehicle has been parked in a secure or protected area, you still must go through the same careful "lookover" you would normally. Just like you have a morning routine when you first get up, you also need to establish a survival routine of inspecting your vehicle and all of the cautions that go with it.

That round thing you're holding in front of you when you are driving is used to aim the vehicle. Grip the steering wheel with both hands and line up the center of the hood in your line of sight like it's a weapon or a rifle. This is how you aim your vehicle down the roadway if you

Figure 10.3 It's not just the mud. It's also the land mines that could be in the mud.

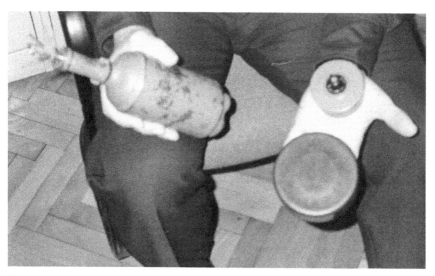

Figure 10.4 The small land mines are not designed to kill. The insidious strategy is that when they cripple an officer it takes not only that officer out of the battle but several others who will now have to transport and care for the wounded officer.

Figure 10.5 Mines this big are designed to destroy and kill everything that detonates them.

Figure 10.6 There may or may not be a road around the corner.

Figure 10.7   If you can't go forward always make sure that you can still back up.

have a roadway to aim it on. Any road signs you might happen to see along the local war zone streets are merely suggestions for your driving style. They should in no way be considered a limiting comment on your driving behavior. As far as any other vehicles that are on the war zone roadway, the relationship between you and them is relegated to the perspective of "lead, follow, or get the hell out of my way." Always base your right-of-way perspective on the size of the vehicle you're driving. The bigger the vehicle you're operating the greater the right-of-way you have on the war zone streets. Armored personnel carriers and tanks have the right-of-way because they have the ability to go over you or through you if you don't swerve or run out of their path. I remember one bitterly cold Balkan afternoon where the thick, powder-like snow crunched under my feet as if it were saying, "Go home, go home," with every step I took. One of the locals had kindheartedly parked his vehicle in the middle of the street, on the bomb-cratered center line so traffic could have enough room to pass around his vehicle if they drove up on the sidewalk a little bit. Unfortunately for this person and his unique parking style, he didn't take

187

Figure 10.8   Be ready for oncoming vehicles or animals at any time or place.

Figure 10.9   If you can make it through, then you call it a road.

Figure 10.10   Do you see the roadway?

into account the room needed for a tank to pass his vehicle in that small space on the Balkan roadway. After returning to the scene of his gross mistake in judgment with a bag of groceries in each arm he found himself standing in the middle of the street staring at what was left of his vehicle. It was now relegated to being about one foot tall and autographed with a tank tread. Our friend just accepted the fate of his compressed vehicle and wandered home.

Most of the vehicles you will encounter in a war zone will have manual transmission, which is commonly referred to as a "find 'em and grind 'em." You select the gear you need at the moment and force the gear shift to that position hoping it doesn't destroy too much of the transmission. Some more advanced drivers do prefer using the petal that's referred to as a clutch. It does help make the transition from one gear to the next a little smoother. Most of the vehicles will come with an interesting array of pedals proudly displayed at your feet by the manufacturer. Notwithstanding this entertaining selection of motoring options, the best choice in a war zone is the stomping down of the acceleration petal. When driving in a war zone it's always best to consider the fact that you will be safer and more difficult to be hit by enemy gunfire or a roadside bomb if you're a moving target. When another vehicle is driving too close to you or trying

Figure 10.11 Nothing is for certain or safe. Inspect everything repeatedly!

to parallel you, step on the accelerator! When pulling out of a camouflaged parking area, step on the accelerator! When pulling into a cramped parking space, step on (this technique can help make a little bit more parking room) the accelerator! When passing by any suspicious parked vehicles or objects, step on the accelerator! When passing by any suspicious persons (no matter how attractive they appear to be), step on the accelerator! When you are in doubt about anything while aiming your vehicle down the imaginary street you think you are on, step on the accelerator!

One of the major pieces of vehicle equipment that's used constantly, far beyond excess, is the horn. Whether you're in a war zone or you're on holiday or leave in some other foreign country you'll be subjected to "the language of the horn." I say the language of the horn because in each country you travel to, you will notice that there are slight but significant differences in the use of this international vehicle toy. In some countries, or regions like the Balkans, the horn is used constantly and mindlessly every second any driver is in his vehicle. In other countries, such as Egypt or Jordan, it's used as a social "hello," or a "get out of my way *yella* (Arabic for *now*) please." Throughout most of the European countries it's used to fend off other drivers but in a less than courteous manner, its intended meaning somewhat similar in many ways to the use of some distinctive hand gestures.

FIGURE 10.12 The road you see in the valley is farther away than you would ever believe.

Figure 10.13 As the wheel turns, it pulls on the barely detectible wire.

Figure 10.14   Then the wire pulls the pin out of the grenade.

Figure 10.15   And this is where you could have been.

Another piece of vehicle equipment that is sometimes used is the headlights. In some areas of the world such as the North African area around Egypt, the locals feel little need for using their headlights or driving lamps. I never really got a valid answer from any of the locals as to why they considered the driving lamps unnecessary even at night. When I would ask the question, I was always given a look of total confusion. I think they must have considered using the headlights as unnecessary as using the vehicle's heater in the desert or trying to use their "always" broken air conditioning. When I told some of my close friends I could get a ticket in the United States for driving without having my headlights on or not restraining myself by using the seatbelts, or using my horn without an emergency reason, they just about fell over on the floor laughing. (It was just like the time I told my Russian colleagues I needed a license to go fishing and they asked if Americans also had to have a license to eat the fish.) When it comes to operating a vehicle anywhere in the world the main thing to remember is that you must be open minded and very flexible and ready for anything you might drive into—literally!

I remember seeing the common sight of the Bosnian drivers speeding through traffic on a hot summer's day with the driver's side door propped open. The easiest way to do this was to use the driver's left foot. It made perfect sense to them because you can get more air flowing through the vehicle with the door propped open than you can with the window rolled down. Now how can you argue with that?

What we refer to as potholes in our own countries becomes a major life-threatening circumstance on a war zone street. These potholes generally break down into two categories. Some of the potholes are big enough to swallow your entire wheel while others are big enough to swallow the entire vehicle you are aiming down the road. The common local driving behavior on these muddy bomb-devastated pathways is to drive very fast and swerve around any and all craters they can see. It is also imperative to swerve around any crater that has standing water in it because there is no way to determine how deep the pothole could be. This means that there is no right or left side of the road when you are driving. You are trying to go in one direction and the locals are trying to go in the other direction. The locals will drive on the right side and then the left side and then the sidewalk on either side of the roadway. I have even seen them take an abrupt turn and drive between the local houses whenever they feel like it even if there is no road. When they're stopped (or physically pulled out of their vehicles) and asked why they're driving like a homicide looking for a place to happen, the locals just look at you with a blank and confused look on their faces, as if to say, "What did I do?" They truly have no idea what is normal because in their world this *is* normal.

If you happen to be driving along and see a section of roadway where the potholes have been nicely filled in, *do not* drive over the filled-in potholes! These filled-in potholes may have been properly filled in by local street workers but these potholes could just as easily contain a land mine. Never take the chance of driving or even walking on disturbed ground or roadways. If you find yourself having the terrifying experience of driving into a mined area, stop! Exit your vehicle with your weapons and radio on your person and do not touch the ground. Exit your vehicle through the vehicle's window or door and climb up to the roof or top of your vehicle, then slide down the back of your vehicle and get the hell out of the area by walking in the tire tracks your vehicle has just made. Never walk in another person's footprints when you have tire tracks available to walk in. Just because the other person luckily got out of the area without being blown up doesn't mean you will be as fortunate. Make sure you are far away from the threat of any explosive device before using your radio. That's the only time it's safe for you to use your radio to call for help. Never take the chance of your radio signal triggering an explosive device. When it comes to land mines don't play the odds or take any chances, because sooner or later the land mine will detonate, and you will become another tragic lesson for others to learn from.

I do remember that there were consistent reports of deaths among people who didn't roll down their windows while driving. It wasn't that the windows themselves were so deadly. It was when they were throwing hand grenades out of their vehicles, the hand grenades would bounce back off the glass and very nicely detonate inside the vehicle. (Now that's what I consider the perfect example of instant social justice.) Unfortunately another common example of hand grenade use gone wrong was the novel method the locals had for fishing in a war zone. Because hand grenades were easier to get than bait, and a whole lot faster whether the fish were biting or not, there were many times when a hand grenade was thrown a little bit too far and it landed in the boat of nearby fishermen. Fishing with that unique method and/or driving on the war zone streets both were problematic.

There are several general perspectives to keep in mind when you are in or around a vehicle, whether you're driving, being a passenger, or being a pedestrian. Most tanks are not equipped with a horn, so don't expect them to signal you to tell you to get out of the way because there is a better chance they will just reduce the height of your vehicle to the height of the surrounding road kill. Tanks and their steel cousin, the armored personnel carriers, announce their presence by two rather spectacular and "one of a kind" means. The first way they catch your attention is by virtue of their immense size when you find one of these steel dinosaurs bearing down on you. The second way these behemoths get noticed is that unsettling feeling you get when you actually feel the ground shake under your feet or your vehicle from the movement and weight of one of these modern-day battleships of the land.

Just like you have vultures circling in the sky above road kill, you also have the vehicle-stripping pirates circling around on the ground searching for anything they can steal at the expense and misfortune of others. Using constant awareness hopefully you won't be the subject of anything circling above your head or around your feet. Any vehicle left unattended or unprotected, anywhere, is fair game for someone to strip any and all of the parts it contains. In most war zones it's not unusual for the car behind you to give you a little nudge if you don't react quickly enough to their constantly beeping horn. Most of the locals will drive around with enough friends in their vehicle to help push it when and if they become stuck or for some other situation. You might think of it as a type of insurance when you see a vehicle that's loaded down so heavy the shocks and springs of the vehicle are just about down to the frame. The strategy is in case they need to do an emergency repair there is more than enough manpower to literally pick up the vehicle to change a tire. There are also more than enough passengers available to help settle any disputes with another vehicle that may occur because of the driver's novel display of driving skills. The passengers have the advantage of a cheap form of transportation while the driver has the back seat funds available to keep his fuel tank filled to the brim.

There are several things you must keep at the forefront of your thoughts when driving in a war zone. Most local drivers will simply stop abruptly in the middle of the street to talk to a friend who is passing by. For most of the locals, parking their vehicle is never a problem. They simply park anywhere the vehicle fits! Wherever the vehicle stops running, whether it's because it runs out of gas or it breaks down, that's where it will be parked for at least the next 24 hours. If it runs and can carry the weight of a person, it's considered to be a vehicle no matter how it looks or how it's constructed. Remember, when you want to use the services of a taxi the usual requirements for a person to be considered a taxi driver are simply to obtain and display the little yellow sign you see on top of their vehicle.

They come in many forms and with many names, and all of the war zones have them on almost every street corner and bend of the road. They are the unofficial checkpoints, tollway booths, inspection sites, excise pay stations, visa stamp stops, license examination posts, and on and on. They are there for one basic reason: to make money for the thugs that man these posts. Sometimes they'll be uniformed or partly uniformed and sometimes they won't even bother to try to look official. When you have the occasion to pass through these spots in a marked vehicle you will only see their deceiving smile and a friendly wave of the hand telling you to go through. But if you have the occasion to pass by one of these impromptu checkpoints while operating a local civilian vehicle you will very quickly become aware of the money-fleecing scam they are perpetrating on all the locals passing through. I was always amused when I was stopped by one of these scams while I was operating a civilian vehicle. They would almost strut as they approached the vehicle but when they would look in the window and see my uniform or international police identification card, they would literally fall over in shock.

In most war zone situations these operations are used as part of a unique revenue-generating system. The "checkpoint" would surrender some, if not all, of the ill-gotten gains to the crook with the highest authority. The money flowed upward from the checkpoint "officer" to a local police officer, to the local sergeant, to the local lieutenant, to the local captain, to the local police chief, and then to the local mayor, each one taking his "share" of the money. The trail would continue all the way to the top whether it was the local officials or the black market that controlled the area.

There is one checkpoint I will never forget, and it still makes me laugh to this very day when something reminds me of it. A good friend and I were driving in a local civilian vehicle that had a full tank of gas and a valid license plate (that by itself was unique) from Sarajevo to Makarska, on the coast of the Adriatic Sea, for some hot food and a small escape from the war zone, when we were flagged over to the side of the road by an incredible sight. We were heading to the coast on the only land mine free road we knew when we came upon the law enforcement joke of the century. On the left side of the road we saw a potbellied man that was just slightly older than us wearing some type of a uniform shirt. It had a silver badge carefully stuck on it and the bottom part of the shirt was unbuttoned because of his massive protruding stomach. He was wearing a dirty gray hat and a pair of blue pants with bright white gym shoes. He was standing next to his "police vehicle," holding a portable hand-held radar gun in his left hand. The plug at the end of the power cable that should have been inserted in the cigarette lighter or 12-volt outlet adapter was swinging in the breeze for one and all to see. As we approached this poster boy of international enforcement we saw him motioning for us to pull over and stop our vehicle by waving the paddle sign he had in his right hand. Paddle signs are used widely throughout the world, with stop printed in red on one side and go printed in green on the other side. Waving that sign for all it was worth, there was no doubt he wanted us to stop. We exited our unmarked vehicle and were immediately scolded by our red-faced officer for getting out of our vehicle without his permission. He then arrogantly showed us the digital readout area of the radar gun. The registered speed of our vehicle would have been flashing on the display indicator if the radar unit had been working. Instead of flashing numbers, we saw "55" printed in red ink. He had very carefully printed out the numbers on a piece of white paper and taped it across the broken display indicator. He started shouting, "You look! You look! You look!" We showed him our international police credentials and laughed while saying, "*Dobra don, kock ko stai*?" (Good day, how are you?). He shook his head from side to side while looking down at the ground. All he would say to us was "I sorry, I sorry" in his local language. After gathering up all of this officer's toys, so as to stop this errant business, our thoughts returned to the hot food that awaited us down the road at the coast. We both knew there would be other questionable "checkpoints" but none with the flair of this entrepreneur.

LASTING IMPRESSIONS

Our perception of the people around us is of great importance, but even more significant is how we are perceived by those who are around us day in and day out. People who know me know full well that I'm going to say what's on my mind while the thought is still swimming through the gray matter of the frontal lobe of my little brain, but there have been countless times in my war zone life that I have had to handcuff my mouth and just learn from the negative example I was dealing with at that moment.

I remember when I was serving in the Bosnia mission with the International Police Task Force. My wife had come to see me in the war zone, and prior to her coming I had advised her how to dress and conduct herself so she would blend in with the threatening surroundings and so she would not stand out in a crowd (or anywhere else for that matter). Being that she is a born and raised Chicago girl of German and

Swedish heritage that was all I needed to say. When you grow up in the Chicago area of the United States you have the advantage of meeting and living with people from all over the world who have come to the Chicago area to make it their new home. In a way it kind of makes the rest of the world seem like a big Chicago when you do get the opportunity to travel overseas. We have neighborhoods in Chicago that are literally populated with representatives from the majority of the countries of the world. It has always been my wife's nature to be tough, strong, and wary. When I went to the airport in Sarajevo to pick her up I proudly noticed how well she blended in with the locals with her dress and mannerisms. Even the people she was with didn't know who she was until she either spoke quietly in English or displayed the requested passport at the airport customs counter in Sarajevo. The other side of the coin was the wife of a partner of mine who could be considered the poster child for what not to do when entering a war zone. As I was standing on the tarmac of the landing strip I was amazed, amused, and more than stunned to see the sight of this lady as she exited her plane. She stopped at the top of the mobile stairs that had been hand-pushed up to the plane's door, and as she came off the plane, she waved her white scarf high in the air while shouting "Hello, hello, I'm here." It should be noted that in the Sarajevo war zone area the basic color was gray. The clothing people wore was gray, the vehicles people drove were gray, the grass was gray, the sky was gray, the sun itself was gray, and, most of all, the faces of the people were gray and the words that were spoken were gray. Any bright color or loud sound was out of place and quickly caught the attention of everyone as being "different." Different is a very bad thing to be in a war zone where people are shot just because they make a good target in some sniper's sights. She waved and talked loudly to her fellow passengers as she hurried down the exit ramp. The other people getting off the plane were doing their best to ignore her but literally everyone on the ground that could see her was staring at her in disbelief. She was dressed in a yellow coat that matched her bright blond hair, and she lavishly displayed gold jewelry around her neck and wrists that shined like a light in the bright sun as she waved to everyone. I could only think about the image of a bright yellow deer with a big red bull's eye on its flank, sporting a rack of horns adorned with gold chains on the first day of hunting season. The first major rule when traveling in and out of a war zone is to go unnoticed in dress and conduct and to blend in with the surroundings. The second major rule is to obey the first major rule on pain of being shot or kidnapped. What you do and what you wear and how you act with and around others should never make you stand out.

Sarcasm by any other name is still sarcasm. When you scorn or mock another person it's simply put into the perspective that you are being rude and offensive. The common retort from a person who has chosen to be the classic jerk is that they didn't really mean it that way, or that they were just kidding or teasing. An insult is never a joke to the person who is receiving the personal assault. I remember the old saying that the wounds of a weapon will heal but the wounds caused by words will bleed forever. I remember having an English-speaking colleague from North America with us in our training unit in the Kosovo mission. In less than one month this person had alienated just about everyone within range of his dry witless remarks through his constant stream of cheap comments. I say just about everyone because there were a few people who always walked past the door to his office and never stopped in because they had heard about the negative reputation he had already acquired. When working with colleagues from non-English-speaking countries I found myself to have a position of great respect and admiration for their efforts to speak my native language as well as they did. I always told them that I wished that I could speak their language as well as they spoke mine. It not only put them at ease when I would say such a thing but it was also the truth for me to compliment their efforts. For a non-English speaker to be able to comprehend a subtle innuendo in a sarcastic greeting or comment is very difficult to say the very least. I know how I felt about being insulted when I was in a foreign country. The sarcasm from this obnoxious colleague would start in the morning and continue throughout the day until he left his office. I remember the saying one of the Italians told me when the subject of our crude friend came into the conversation, and it's the same saying that's common in many countries: "Everyone brings joy into this world. Some when they come and some when they leave." This master of sarcasm would start with a morning greeting that included remarks like, "You don't look as ugly as you did yesterday, eh," or "Did your parents have any good-looking children, eh?" and as the day progressed we heard "Time for me to have lunch but you look like you already ate, eh," "Take off the ugly mask and sit down, eh," "I've got a minute to listen to you, tell me all you know, eh." It even got to the point that when there was a greeting or get well card to be signed by all of the members of our unit, he would be passed by because he couldn't even resist writing some nasty phrase on the card. It was customary that when the time came for one of our unit members to end their mission and go home, we would all gather at some safe local restaurant and celebrate with food and drink. An end of mission of one of our colleagues was an excellent excuse to have a great time with one another. When it came to the wonderful day that this person was at the end of their mission and being replaced by an intelligent and "likeable" colleague from Democratic Republic of Congo, we all felt like a great weight had been lifted off our shoulders. The difference between the outgoing officer and the new, incoming officer was quite the match with the famous horror story of Dr. Jekyll and Mr. Hyde. When it was time for the end of mission party for our sarcastic colleague I was totally amazed when I dutifully but unenthusiastically trudged into the restaurant. In every sense of the word this evening did not feel like it was a celebration; it was more like the feeling when you attend a wake for someone who has died. As I walked into the restaurant I noticed only 5 other people sitting at the long table that had been set for about 24 attendees, and they were all busy eating and not even talking to the "guest of honor." As I walked up to my soon-to-be former colleague I extended my hand and wished him "Best of luck back home." Unfortunately, in his usual manner he said, "You don't have anything better to do tonight, eh?" I withdrew my hand, smiled, turned around, and walked out of the restaurant. It felt great to watch his jaw drop, and enough was enough! A short distance from the restaurant where the end of mission party was being held there was a small, quiet cafe. I needed to eat before I got back to my accommodation because there was probably no electricity for me to cook with anyway. The electricity in most of the war zones you will be deployed to will quite likely be on a schedule of a couple of hours on and then several hours off. As I walked into the small dining room I was happily surprised by the sound of my name being yelled out by several of my colleagues who had also decided to forgo attending the end of mission party for our sarcastic colleague. We all agreed that eating a small dinner in peace with friends was better than consuming a big free feast in the presence of a truly sarcastic human being. He was just another living example of what we never wanted to become when we were representing our respective countries.

MAN'S BETRAYED FRIEND

One night we were told by some of the older men of the village that another child had been killed by the wild dog packs. This was upsetting news for all of the officers and a terrifying situation for all the people of the village who had children, big or small. During the Balkans War when food was scarce and starvation plagued the villages that were at the foot of the mountains, the people couldn't feed themselves let alone their pets and the dogs they used for protection for their homes and sheep herds. So they made the heartbreaking choice of setting their dogs free to fend for themselves, to survive or starve in the mountains. But now this ugly part of the Balkans War was coming back in the darkness of night, preying on those who had cast them out. Regardless of all of our personal feelings about our own pets, we had no choice but to help defend the village. We would set out on moon-bright nights (and unfortunately on many other nights) to do what must be done. In the dark of the night we perched ourselves over a ravine to shoot at the dog packs as they would sneak into the village from their mountain lairs. They would roam the town all night and at first light of dawn, we would shoot at the dog packs again as they crossed back over the ravines to get into the mountains. Between the curtains of sunset and sunrise we would go out quietly, on foot, without the noise of our vehicle scaring the dogs away. We would walk the narrow streets of the village shooting any pack of dogs or rabid singles. We would see the local people watching us from their windows, and knew that these people were developing a close bond with us because of our efforts to protect their children. In a way I find it very strange to say how safe I felt around these people and how damn proud I felt when an old man stepped out of his warm and safe home to give me a sip of hot tea.

This was an extremely important gesture of support and respect from the eldest male of the home. It was both a kind and critical gesture that would be repeated many times throughout the night. My return gesture would always be to place my right palm on my chest and nod my head and smile. I found this gesture to be valid and welcomed throughout most of the world I would see in the years to come. It simply expressed by gesture, "From my heart I say thanks to you." Some of my international colleagues would just say "No thanks" to the offer of the tea. I could see the local men's quiet reaction to the rejection of this important gesture. I told the officers if they didn't trust the tea or didn't want to drink it to just touch it to their lips, but never to refuse this gesture because when they refused the tea they were also insulting the "honor of the household." I knew that family honor and self-respect were two of the very few things these people had left. It was important to at least leave them with that. I was told by a local man in my first mission deployment to the Balkans that the wounds of a battle will heal but the wounds of an insult will bleed forever. The standard approach to keeping yourself safe and well taken care of in most foreign environments is to ask to speak to the eldest male of the household first and compliment him on how strong his male children look and how respectful you are of his home. After you have

Figure 10.16 When staying alive is the priority, living conditions don't seem to matter.

done the proper greeting, just sit back and prepare to spend a very long time drinking more tea or something else that tastes like turpentine. Then you will meet everyone, and I do mean everyone. Know this well. This meeting is very important to them, as it should be to you. Everyone you are introduced to by the eldest male "will never forget you." They don't say what they don't mean, and they stand by what they say. Whatever you do, do not make an idle promise or dismissive or sarcastic remark. They consider your word as your bond whether or not you do.

HOLIDAY STEW

When you are dealing with multiple cultures, religions, and climates, "traditional" holiday customs are as varied as the people celebrating. Some of the holiday confusion resulted in a very happy mix of celebrations that put all the customs and beliefs into one impossible-to-understand pot of stew. It was impossible to understand how they decided to celebrate certain things in certain ways but to change it was a task beyond the ability of anyone. So we all just sat back and enjoyed all the religious days, and

Figure 10.17   Shelter is the priority, not how the world views your home.

Figure 10.18   The locals can and do live anywhere they can find shelter.

Figure 10.19 No matter how they live, they still have self-respect and survive day by day.

holidays, that were mixed together. One of my fondest sights was seeing Santa Claus going down the main street of town in a sleigh being pulled by a donkey, throwing candy to the children while shooting an AK-47 machine gun into the air, and yelling "Happy New Year." The novel twist on the Christmas tree was also quite amusing. The tree would be decorated with balloons and on the stroke of midnight the little children of the house would break the balloons on their "New Year's tree." In Bosnia especially, the people loved displaying Christmas lights for most of the Muslim holidays, and of course even with people getting killed from the falling bullets, no holiday was a holiday without the firing of every type and caliber of weapon into the air. Fathers would sit in front of their houses, drunk out of their minds, and laughing at their very young sons running around shooting an AK-47 machine gun up into the air that was half as tall as they were from gun butt to muzzle. Festivities and tragedies were always just around the corner from each other.

11

A Matter of Perspective

Janet Rail, United States

When Bob was stationed in Bosnia, there was a small canteen just inside the gates of the Italian contingent's base camp. It was run by an NGO (nongovernmental organization) in conjunction with the United Nations and provided a safe place to eat for all the peacekeepers—safe because the area was secure so you could relax a little, and safe because the food was clean and cooked properly. The first couple of times I went with Bob to eat there it was a little unnerving—we walked through a maze of barbed wire and sandbags to the gates with armed guards while other officers were in the guard towers looking down at us with machine guns at the ready, but like so many other things in a war zone, it soon became almost second nature to smile as I showed my ID card and motioned that I was part of the group. Once inside the little restaurant we could sit indoors if it was cooler weather or out on a large, covered deck if it was warm. Sitting outside safely was a special treat. Being able to relax and not having to worry about who was watching you was really appreciated by all the peacekeepers. The building protected the view from two sides and the Italian training grounds blocked the snipers' sites on the other two sides. More than once we watched the Italian peacekeepers conducting fighting or shooting drills while eating lunch. This was just one more event that became "war zone normal." They were never too close to us because there was an area of land that had not been demined between their training grounds and the canteen. Two rows of barbed wire separated us. I was told if I threw a coffee cup over the edge of the deck there were good odds

I could hit a land mine. You definitely didn't chase after any bread roll that started falling off the deck!

Because this canteen was right next to the ITSS (International Training and Support Section) building almost all the peacekeepers in Bosnia ended up eating there at some point in their mission. I was told that there were many conversations between people from very diverse backgrounds at those tables on almost a daily basis and I believe it. In the short time I was there I met and talked to some of the most memorable people in my life.

One afternoon while Bob and I were having coffee, a gentleman walked in. I refer to him as a gentleman because "officer" does not do him justice. He was immaculately dressed. His uniform was spotless and he had a white, silk scarf around his neck that was carefully tucked into his shirt. He was smoking a cigarette with a short, mother-of-pearl holder, carrying it European style in his hand. His handlebar moustache was perfectly waxed and curled evenly on both sides of his mouth. After getting his cup of tea he saw Bob and came over to our table. In perfect British (with the expected Far East accent), he asked if he could join us because he was very upset and wanted to talk to Bob. We assured him he was always welcome at our table and asked him what it was that "was troubling his heart."

The colonel told us how he had spent his entire life training and being in the military service of his country. It was early in his career that he and his instructors discovered that he had a wonderful gift from his God that allowed him to have an expert eye for shooting. He had an uncanny ability to hit even moving targets with great ease. He felt very blessed because not only did he have such a great gift but also he knew how to use this gift to help others and his country. It was his job when he was at home to be driven up and down the streets of his city so he could deal with the sick, beggars, or homeless people "in the most prudent fashion." In a very calm and proud manner—not boastful, just proud—this officer told us how he had dealt with over 200 unclean people. It was because of his special gift that all these people had been taken care of in the most merciful manner. None of them had ever suffered for one second. He had done what his government said needed to be done and he had used his talent to extend mercy to those who needed to be eliminated. It was good for everyone. But now he had been sent to Bosnia and he was upset.

The colonel had told his commanders and other officers with the UN peacekeeping force about his talent. He knew that his driver was not with him in Sarajevo but he was confident that another peacekeeper could drive him and he would still have his sure aim. If they would just allow him to patrol the streets, even if it was only after dark, he was positive he could make a huge difference in the amount of the nightly violence. He knew that Bob worked in the training center and he was wondering if there was anyone in that section who had the authority to grant his request "to use his talent" while he was serving in Bosnia, or did Bob have a vehicle so they could go out together at night. Bob told the colonel that he did not have a vehicle and that he didn't know who the proper authority was to present the paperwork to for a request of that nature. Bob suggested that perhaps there was another way the colonel's talent could be used while he was in Bosnia. Bob calmly tried to reassure the colonel that his time in Bosnia was not a waste and that we were sure there would be a way to put his gift to use that would be more acceptable to the mission in Bosnia. And then just as if we had been discussing the weather, we finished our conversation, said our good-byes, and went back to Bob's office. I think we were both a little quiet for a while, and when we were alone Bob asked me if I realized the significance what had been discussed. I assured him I did. There are a lot of things that become "normal" in a war zone, but some things will never be "normal" no matter where you are.

12

Children Lost

LITTLE GIRLS AT PLAY

The spectacle before us was more picturesque than any oil painting on canvas could ever reveal. The Balkan countryside was one of the most astonishing visions that could ever be seen anywhere on the globe. It was a never-ending carpet of hills and green valleys that were constantly interrupted and divided by the awesome splendor of snowcapped mountains and the white water rivers that raged around them. The azure sky flowed down into crystal blue lakes that were sheltered by this magnificent isolated scene.

It was this idyllic setting my fellow police colleague and I were patrolling. We found ourselves hard pressed to even imagine anything could go wrong in this seemingly paradise on Earth. It was a cool day with a bright sun and just enough clouds in the sky to contrast the sea of blue over our heads. It all seemed to gently wrap around the sun. At first glance we saw a totally peaceful scene. I will never forget how perfectly harmless everything appeared to us as we drove up the winding dirt road to a man sitting on his wagon next to a field filled with little girls playing, running, and laughing with each other. It would soon become apparent to both of us what a malevolent and horrendous situation we had come upon. As we drove up to the old wooden, two-wheeled horse-drawn wagon we became the recipients of a look of disgust and a smirking smile of total distain from the slender man with the hawkish facial features sitting in the driver's seat of the wagon. He just sat there motionless, looking straight ahead, rhythmically moving his arms up and down with a clock-like precision as he smoked the cigarette he cradled in both his dirty hands. The field full of five- and six-year-old little girls playing together paid little to no attention to us as we walked over to the side of the wagon to see if anyone needed our help. As soon as we got to the side of the wagon, the man took off his small gray stocking hat and waved it at us in a motion that was easy to interpret—total disdain. He was signaling for us to go away and leave him alone to his business. Our interest was piqued and being upset with being insulted and treated so rudely, we both decided to check out the situation a little further. We now felt the need to satisfy our police curiosity. As our friend, the man, grumbled to himself, we took it upon ourselves to inspect the back of his wagon and began to search for whatever might be in it. As we searched the wagon, the man just sat on the front bench seat and smoked and grumbled and talked to himself in a language we didn't understand. I noticed how his smoking became faster and his grumbling became louder as we searched closer to the area of the wagon that was covered with a small, carefully tucked down piece of canvas. When my professionally curious colleague who was in the wagon yanked up the tucked-down canvas, the man spun around like a top on the seat he was sitting on. He grabbed my colleague by the arm that was holding the canvas and said in perfectly clear English, "no you!" My colleague's response was instantaneous, explosive, and totally unexpected by me because I couldn't see what he had uncovered from where I was standing on the ground outside the wagon. He seized the man by the neck with his free hand and shook him like a pit bull shakes a rat, shouting directly in his face, "Brass, brass, brass, brass!" This sorry excuse for a man was using these innocent little girls to collect brass ammunition casings from the mine field. My partner then hurled the man from the seat of the wagon through the air like a stuffed toy onto the dirt road between the wagon and our patrol vehicle. We had both heard of this horrendous tragedy going on in this countryside but now it was more than just a story we were being told by tearful hospital workers. It was a real situation and it was our ethical responsibility to handle this insane practice here and now. We picked up and pinned this piece of human garbage masquerading as a man against the side of our patrol vehicle and established our point of view. We shouted in his face, "No girls for brass!" As we demonstrated to him our displeasure with his macabre business choice, he cried back to us, "Ok no brass girls ok, ok, ok ... " Suddenly we became aware that there were many eyes watching the indoctrination this repulsive monster was getting. The girls had stopped gathering brass from the field and now were frightened by what they were seeing. My partner and I had to calm down from our anger and quietly convince the little girls to walk directly to us trying to get them safely out of the minefield. We threw the newly rehabilitated man back up on the bench seat of the wagon and thankfully retrieved all the little girls out of the minefield without a single land mine detonating under any of their little feet. We put them in the wagon with all the candy and water we had in our vehicle to give them. We slapped the horse on the butt to start it on its automatic walk back home down the road to its village. We both breathed a sigh of relief that we had not lost any of the little girls. This was definitely not a reportable arrest situation or a community contact where a commendation would be forthcoming, but that didn't matter to us as long as a wagonload of little girls was slowly on its way back to their village. Most adults who walk on a land mine do survive, but they live the remainder of their lives in a horribly mutilated condition, as burdens to their already struggling families. When a child steps on a land mine they usually die because they are lower to the ground and sustain greater injuries to their vital organs and head. The exploitive and criminal practice that too often results in these injuries and death is just another sad aftermath of not only the Balkan war zone but all of the other war zones in the world. Starvation and need compel parents to "rent out" one child so their other children can eat. Vendors of death and suffering drive their wagons through the local villages asking parents for the use of their little girls to pick up the brass casings that were discharged when the weapons were fired and left on the ground of the surrounding minefields. The brass is sold on the open market for whatever blood money it might bring to the butchers who traffic in this human misfortune. They use little girls as a practice due to there being "less chance" of a land mine detonating under the lighter bodyweight of their small feet. Of course there was also the obscene perspective many of the local families had that if given a choice they would prefer to lose a girl instead of a boy. Boys could be more useful working in the fields when they got older, whereas girls would just become a burden or be married off to another family. In this part of the world there are no retirement accounts. There are no pensions, social security plans, or even bank accounts. The only retirement a family has is the land they own and the sons they have who will support them by working that land when they become too old or ill to do so themselves. I know full well that what we did that day was against the law, against any code of conduct, and against all of the rules we both had agreed to abide by when we came to this land so very far away from our own. But when it comes to preventing the loss of innocent life, there should never be a choice or hesitation in the matter.

The next morning as I sat with my colleague eating a great breakfast of eggs, grilled bread with cow butter, and some type of meat that remains unknown to me to this day, I remember how we ate our breakfast quietly, with deep reflection on what had happened the day before. We were very "quietly" satisfied with what we had done, and what we had stopped. We knew that our effort would not stop this barbaric practice, and that it probably would go on as long as there were minefields that had brass in them, but for that day and that time, we were content that there was a wagon full of little girls going home to some village somewhere with a man who would never forget us. There comes a time in the life of any war zone officer when the situation he or she is confronted with calls for more than just a decision or action that represents the badge that is pinned to his chest. It calls for swift justice for the innocent from the heart that lies beneath the badge that no one else can ever see.

BLOODSTAINED APPLES

It starts in the early spring, when everything begins to turn green and the rich black soil is soft and can be dug up easily with little or no effort. It's commonly said that Balkan soil is so fertile it can grow anything that grows anywhere else in the world, but nowhere else on this planet is the soil so tainted with such bitter hatred. This is the time of year when the ground is soft enough to be corrupted with the seeds of hate that some with no heart and an evil soul have planted in this ancient soil. There has been blood in the dirt of the Balkans for hundreds of years and the only thing that grows from this sad legacy is the generational fire of hatred that will never be extinguished.

When no one can see them, these evil people sneak into the orchards and gardens of their enemy. They cunningly calculate where they think the branches of the apple tree will grow. Deviously figuring how the branches will bend down to yield their fruit to the children who long for this crisp treat, they bury land mines where they think the children will stand to pick apples. For hundreds of years the conflict in the Balkans has relentlessly struggled with various groups claiming, losing, and reclaiming what they feel is "the land of their fathers." The existing mind-set is, "If I can't have something I will do my selfish best to deny its benefit to you regardless of what it will cost me." This is the premise on which this unspeakable practice is based. The men who plant these small black antipersonnel land mines studiously plan where to "plant" them around the apple trees. Due to the limited number of land mines they have available to them they select the site for their deranged purpose that will do the most damage. Smaller trees where the branches are lower to the ground are better than mature trees where the apples will be too high for the children to even try to pick them. They want to be sure that none of their devices will simply lie in the earth undetonated. They use their cunning perspective to insure the maximum loss of life for the least amount of effort and land mines that are placed. When they are selecting the apple trees they look for a tree that has signs of a worn path leading to it. This assures them that there is someone who is regularly looking after and pruning the tree. They carefully and precisely measure and calculate where the branches will bend over the deadly mines concealed in the ground. Months later the children of the local village come to pick the apples from their trees like they have done for so many years. They walk on the deadly ground, happily looking up at the delicious apples waiting for them, just within their reach, and their foot pressure sets off the land mine under their feet. The instantaneous and merciless blast shatters and propels the leather of their shoes and the shattered bone fragments of the foot, up into the lower body of the victim, causing more damage than just the tragic loss of a foot or a leg. Usually, the tragic outcome of this inhumane scenario is the loss of the foot and/or the leg to blast, massive soft tissue and bone damage and also a severe infection resulting from blast fragments penetrating the lower body of the victim. Bystanders who were too near the victim at the instant of the detonation can suffer the same consequences. Most of the ground debris and even the very bone fragments of the victim's foot and lower leg are propelled by this miniature bomb blast at a force equal to the speed of a bullet. This shrapnel radiates outward from the blast site, thus causing an extensive expansion of the blast area and further suffering to other victims in the area. There is a greater percentage of children who die from land mines than adults because the children are simply lower to the ground, thus placing their vital organs closer to the detonation or blast point.

There are no uniforms worn by the men who plant this evil in the ground, and there are no uniforms worn by the children or adults who are the victims of this horror. This tragic action cannot be considered justifiable in the mind of any sane person. The only harvest that will ever come from this apple tree will be the ongoing generational hatred caused by the senseless loss to each victimized family. There will never be enough bloodshed to quench the flames of hatred that are being harvested from these trees.

GYPSY CHILDREN

I will always remember the sad sight of packs of gypsy children who ran the streets looking for anything they could find to fill their stomachs or their pockets. I say "packs" because that's what they struck me as being. They were like a pack of wolves in almost every way, with the exception of having an instinctive loyalty to the pack. They might not have been swimming in water or had the fins and teeth, but they did remind me of a school of piranha fish, ready to devour anything that got in their way. Be they wolf or piranha, they certainly were something to contend with by virtue of their numbers, and every war zone country has packs of them. The heartrending circumstance of their desperate existence has relegated them to being exactly what they appeared to be. They lived in a world of constant hunger and the overwhelming fear of tomorrow's hunger that is always just around the corner. The few bites of food they consume are burned off their malnourished little bodies by their constant, aggressive life on the prowl.

When you see someone confronted by one of these foraging packs you will instantly become aware of the common body signs that are displayed by all of the pack members. The unsuspecting and emotionally touched "victim" will be approached by one or two of the children, reaching out with their hands, palm up, in a begging gesture. Their bodies will be bent over in a submissive posture and they will continue to get closer and closer to you until they are within range to actually touch you. If the victim makes the mistake of actually placing money in their hands, all hell breaks loose. With the smell of money in the air the rest of the pack rushes in, surrounding and overwhelming the well-meaning and sympathetic victim. The begging instantly transforms to "reaching and taking" as the flurry of little hands from the surrounding pack quickly probe and seize anything and everything from every pocket and place that could conceal something. It is also quite common that during this ambush the victim will be jabbed with a pin or needle or even stabbed with a knife. This is done as a distraction to literally strip them bare of everything they possess. Just like in the Charles Dickens novel, usually there is an evil "Fagan" (adult who oversees the group and teaches them how to rob others), waiting to take the money from the children just as they have taken the money from the victim. First, the children become the victims of this tragic war zone circumstance, then they become the victims of the theft of their own ill-gotten gain from the very same criminal Fagan who orchestrated their attacks on victim after victim while he waited out of sight to rush in at the last moment to take from them what they had taken from another. They are the victims of being children in a war zone and having little choice between the life they were living or death by hunger or a vehicle that could strike them down while begging and stealing in the streets. Most important, they have lost the one thing that all children have a right to hold on to for as long as they can within their hearts and minds—and that is innocence.

If you are one of those people who simply must give something to the packs of beggars on the streets please consider a safer alternative to giving them money. Carry some loose candy in your pocket and when confronted by a child or a pack, toss the candy in the opposite direction you are walking. The children will usually be able to eat the candy before the repulsive Fagan can take it away from them, even if this reprehensible criminal has the urge to chase them down and steal candy from a child.

13

Communicating

INTRODUCTION

I think I know what you said. I know you said it but I don't know if what I think you said is what you meant to say. And I may not have meant the same thing as you though I did at the time I said what you thought I meant … what were we talking about?

International communication is one of the biggest obstacles you will have to overcome on any war zone deployment. If you think you were having a difficult time understanding the accent of a fellow countryman from a different region of your own nation just wait until you are trying to communicate with a person from another area of the world. Even when a mission is designated as speaking a certain language, you quickly learn there is the spoken language you are used to and then there is a multitude of variations of that language. Add a couple different accents and improperly used slang phrases and you have War Zone English (or French). International efforts at understanding can result in some of the most hilarious and some of the most tragic moments that can ever occur in a war zone. People have literally lost their lives over a situation of miscommunication.

Fortunately there are a couple of very simple things that can limit the number of problems you might encounter when dealing with people from other cultures and language bases. First of all, stay calm about the communication problem between you and the other person whether they are standing in front of you or trying their best to make you understand through a static-filled phone connection. If you start to get upset about the difficulty of understanding that person it's only natural that they will also get upset. So just smile, slow down your talking speed, and even if you don't feel relaxed, try to make the effort at looking and sounding relaxed and calm. Whatever you do, never raise your voice to be better understood. Unfortunately it's very common (and can even be funny) to have someone start to raise their voice to be better understood until they get to the point where they are literally yelling the same word or phrase over and over that was never understood to begin with. Louder and louder is not the answer to any question. The louder you speak the greater the tension and frustration in the conversation. So just take a deep breath, talk slowly, at a normal volume level, with a smile on your face. Even when you are talking on the telephone, the other person can hear the difference in your voice if you are smiling. Carefully watch the body signs and gestures of the other person to help you understand what they are trying to say. Also and very important, watch your own body signs! Make sure they are displaying an image of being relaxed and in control.

BODY LANGUAGE

I remember the slice of hot pizza I was holding in both my hands because it was just too big to hold in one hand. The waiter who I had become friends with over several months, walked by on his way back to the kitchen with a smile on his face saying, "My pizza too big for you?" The pizza was too hot to eat, but I was too hungry not to eat, and too impatient to wait until this slice of heaven cooled down. It was warm inside this little pizza restaurant because it was heated by the oven, but it was still a great place to be because the alternative was the severe cold and icy conditions of the Balkan winter. All seven of the very old but very clean wooden tables were covered with faded red and white checked tablecloths. My entire world was a small table with two old wooden chairs and a soon to be consumed pizza. As I sat happily devouring my pizza with my back positioned against one of the walls so I could watch the door (which was my standard practice), the man sitting alone two tables away caught my attention. I couldn't understand what he was mumbling quietly to himself but his body gestures were screaming out that he was extremely upset with my uniformed presence in the restaurant. He sat at his table with a body posture that was hovering over the cup of tea he was guardedly consuming, sip by sip. He would take a sip, tightly holding the cup with both hands, quietly mumble something to himself, and then give me a scowling gaze from the side of his eye, without even the slightest head movement. I learned many years ago that when a person deceptively looks at you from the side of his eye it never means anything good will be coming your way. His legs weren't stretched out in front of him in a typically relaxed manner. They were pulled back, tucked and braced under his chair. As the moments passed I had the growing feeling in the pit of my stomach that this very disgruntled person was about to become the victim of his own, soon to be out of control emotions. He was starting to establish a routine of body signs to display the growing anger that was building inside of him. He was taking a deep breath, and then a sip from his cup, and then firmly placing the cup down on the table while mumbling something to himself and then staring at me from the side of his face. All too soon the breathing became like the snorting of a bull, and the cup was emptied in one gulp and slammed down on the table with his right hand. His first physical act of violent expression was done to the cup and I knew that I would be part of his next display of emotions. He stood up abruptly sending his chair sliding across the floor, and stepped forward toward me with his left foot. His body posture was now leaning in my direction and his quiet mumbling had changed into loud comments I did not understand. His eyes were narrow and fixed on my eyes. His teeth became tightly clenched with his jaw lowered. I then saw his shoulders rise up, getting ready to deliver his punch. As he closed the distance between us he threw a table aside. This was a textbook example of a personal attack about to happen. I knew this as a fact because I'm the one who wrote the textbook, *The Unspoken Dialogue*. That soon to be attack was now in progress and as quickly as it started, it was over. He was now resting quietly and contently on the floor. My friend the waiter came out from the kitchen and just smiled as he put the table and chairs back where they belonged, and dragged my fellow diner across the floor into the kitchen. The outstanding pizza was now gone, and so was I, but I remembered to leave a very nice tip on the table, to ensure a smile from the waiter upon my return to this great pizza restaurant in the future.

THE FISH PATCH

When I was in my upstairs office of the police training unit in Kosovo, I would have the pleasure and honor of officers from over 60 countries coming through the door to say "hello" to me. Many of the officers had confidence in me that they could come to me if they needed help or advice. I always considered it a very important act of trust to be asked for assistance and I always tried my best to help the other officers. When you help a person in need they remember, and it's always better to have a thousand friends than a thousand Euros. The big trick in making sure you are giving them the assistance they need is to understand them and have them understand you. I always remembered the important things first, and that was candy. Thanks to my wife I always had a supply of jelly beans in a jar on my desk. Whenever a person would come into my office I would greet them with a big smile, no matter what their attitude was when they came through the door. I am a great believer in greeting everyone with a smile. If they hate or dislike you it drives them crazy to see you happy and if they are a friend they are happy to see that you are happy. Either way it pays to be nice. When my colleagues would come to the office door I would motion with an open hand for them to come in and have some jelly beans. If they wanted to talk to me they could sit in the chair next to my desk. No matter what language they spoke or where in the world they came from they all understood my gesture invitation for some jelly beans and a place to sit.

There was one time, however, when I thought I was doing so damn great with all of my gestures and interpretations of the other officer's body signs that I ended up with quite a surprise. One of the highly prized items that were traded back and forth between officers was the insignia or shoulder patch that the officers wore on their uniforms. These shoulder patches came in all different colors, shapes, sizes, and flags. They were great to see and even greater to have as a keepsake of serving with these officers. Trading patches were some of the better moments of the war zone experience. There was an officer who was looking at my white board where I displayed all my extra patches from home when he saw a patch from one of the police departments in the States that he really fell in love with. He repeatedly exclaimed, "Wow! Wow! Bob! Ok, you give I give back better, too?" I said "yes" and then tried to say something in his language that caused a big smile on his face. I took the patch he so admired off the white board and gave it to him right there on the spot. As he happily walked out the door he repeatedly said, "Tomorrow, me you tomorrow." I have found by my experience and the experience of others that you barter with strangers and not with friends. With friends, you freely give them what will make them happy and in the end that gesture will come back to you with more than you could have imagined in the first place. I have seen many foolish officers choose to barter with a friend and by the time they finished all that was bartered was the friendship itself.

Figure 13.1 It's not what you receive; it's all about the giving.

When "tomorrow" came I had to teach in the morning and missed my friend coming to the office to bring me what I expected was going to be a really neat police patch. I was told it was on my desk in my office. What I actually got will bring a smile to my face until the day that I die.

Lying on my desk when I entered the room was a salted fish in a clear plastic bag. I wonder just what the words I spoke to him the day before really meant in his language.

14

Day of the Bull

A glorious festival atmosphere had taken over this little isolated village nestled deep in the Balkan Mountains. Surrounding this little village with its scattering of red tile roofed homes were the mountains that had protected it since time began and isolated it from the influences of the ever-changing outside world. The snowcapped walls of jagged stone that comprised the circle of mountains were a stark contrast to the lush green valley that sat sheltered in the center of the mountain ring.

No postcard picture could do this stunning sight justice, as long as the eye of the camera didn't focus too closely on the people themselves, but today they were happy. This was the long awaited day a Swiss agricultural group was bringing about two dozen cows and a couple of breeding bulls to the village as part of a special program from the United Nations and European Union to help Kosovo after the war. This donation was valued far beyond all possible words of thanks that could ever be spoken. The old people of the village had tears of joy in their eyes while the young children ran and played. As UN officers coming from countries where the cattle breeders have vast genetic resources available to them we all knew it was impossible for us to understand the importance of this breeding infusion into the local dairy stock. The village had been isolated in this valley with one road in and out and that was only passable for a couple months each year. The winter snows turned the road into no less than a suicidal effort in getting out of their beautiful valley to the world beyond, while the spring rains were responsible for washing out what little roadway there was and it was already in a dangerous condition. They existed for generation after generation in scenic separation from a world they knew little about. As we entered the valley and this little village the first matter at hand was our warm greeting by a thankful and always hospitable proud people. We had made it a point to eat well before we arrived in the village because of the hospitable reputation of these people. As is the custom, we were treated to food and drink in abundance. It is a matter of both pride and honor that the meal set before us be more than we could ever want. We ate modestly and drank lightly of the potent Balkan whisky, and then pretended we were very full, because we knew full well that what was set before us was quite likely several days' worth of food and if we ate it all they would have to go hungry because of their generosity.

I am not the most knowledgeable person in the world when it comes to knowing good dairy stock or cattle when I see them, but this was not much of a situation for comparison between what these people had for cattle stock and what was soon to be unloaded in front of them. The few cattle we could see were a sad sight indeed. They had been isolated and inbred for literally decades if not at least a couple hundred years with little chance of any cross-breeding in their bloodlines ever making it through the mountain pass. The cattle were not as big as they should have been when you compared them to the sheep that wandered among them. They were small and frail, and producing little milk for a village that depended so much on being self-sufficient by necessity for survival. There was nothing that came out of any of the cattle stock that wasn't utilized in some extremely resourceful way, from milk to fertilizer to the total use of the final remains. The expert from the Swiss agricultural group quietly told us that the new cattle would do very well with all the grazing and hay that was available even though they were three times the size and weight of the present cattle. The present small herd of stunted cattle wasn't even consuming a noticeable amount of the food that was available to them in the valley. He said that the milk production and related cheese production would be increased anywhere from three to four times from what was presently being turned out by the villagers through near-futile efforts.

The hour and the time had come for the "adoption" of the cattle to the families that had been chosen. Adoption was the word that was used by the very serious and joyous villagers. As the rear cargo doors of the first truck swung open the gasps of total awe and amazement could be heard from the crowd of villagers. As the cattle were slowly and very carefully walked down the truck's ramp they were each met with all the reverence and respect you would give a head of state or a major religious figure. It was beyond any and all words to describe the feeling in the air as the cows and bulls were being turned over to the families. The entire family would approach the animal, singing quietly. An adult member of the family would then give it some special weak tea water to drink as the children placed wreaths of flowers around the animal's neck and gently pet the animal constantly. They would then slowly and beyond joyously lead the animal away to its new home where it would be magnificently spoiled for the rest of its existence.

A symbiotic relationship between any two living things is always the best that could be hoped for in this world of ours, let alone in the conflicted and tragic world of a war zone. But here in the center of the Balkans, isolated by a ring of mountains, life will go on as it has for countless centuries, with a new and positive future and a new glimmer of hope for man and beast and all who come after them.

15

Less Becomes More

The very first time I saw this man I was stunned by his sheer size. He had come to the United Nations International Police Task Force, Training Division Headquarters in Kosovo to meet with a fellow colleague from his faraway North Sea country. I was walking down the hallway about 10 meters away with another partner of mine when my eyes caught sight of him and I actually stumbled as I was walking. The partner I was with was a former European heavyweight judo champion for two straight years and was tall enough that he had to actually bend down to get through a doorway. This modern-day Norseman strode across the hallway in two relaxed strides and when he stood behind my partner, the relationship in size between the two of them was astonishing. My partner now looked like a small child in the presence of this truly enormous man. It wasn't just the height of this man that set him apart from the rest of us. His shoulders were close to the top of the door frame and so wide he had to turn sideways in order to go through a doorway into a room. He displayed a quiet, polite demeanor and moved in a very athletic, almost cat-like manner as he walked down the hall. We were introduced to him by his fellow countryman, and then as was customary, the officer from the training division proceeded to introduce his friend to all the other trainers who had their offices on that hallway. If we were in the office our doors were left open and any visitor would simply knock on the door-frame and say hello. As this gentle giant made his way down the hall a small group of curious officers seemed to form behind him, not quite sure if they could believe what they had just seen looking through their office doorway. In about the middle of the hallway, a petite, dark-haired member of our training team was busy reviewing a classroom presentation in her office. The Norseman very slowly and politely bent down under the top of the doorway to her office, leaned in, and said, "Hello, you are pretty lady." The "pretty lady" let out an ear-piercing scream and almost fell out of her chair! The gentle giant unsteadily responded with, "Please, sorry to disturb. Please, sorry to disturb." He was very embarrassed, and she was very embarrassed, as they shared a moment of uncomfortable silence the crowd of onlookers that had formed chose to tactfully disperse and leave these two alone. As we left we could hear the quiet laughter and conversation in the background. In the weeks and months that followed I remember seeing the two of them walking together and being in their own little world, a world they had created in the middle of a war zone. Born and raised thousands of kilometers apart and coming from different cultures, these two had now found each other. While in the company of her Norseman escort, no man passing by would risk even a glance at the pretty lady. All who walked by were quietly respectful of this couple, and gave them a very wide berth.

On several occasions I saw my Norse colleague walking by the river. I noticed that from time to time there would be a certain spring in his step and an air of purpose in his demeanor as he would stride along the riverfront carrying a heavy bag that seemed light for him to carry. One day while I was one of my own after-work treks I saw a truly wonderful sight. Just over the hillcrest on the other side of the river was a little gray, red-roofed house that looked as though it was build for a postcard picture. There were laughing, little children running and playing around this little house, and there was a very peaceful happy Norseman sitting on a tiny little stool near the doorway of this loving happy home. As I watched from a discrete distance I saw an empty bag tucked into the back of the belt of my Norseman colleague and watched as he was respectfully given a large cup of tea that looked tiny in his huge hands from the man and woman of the house. I realized then that I was given the gift of seeing the other side of this man with a heart as big as the warrior body that carried it. In ancient times the ancestors of this man were the fierce unmatched warriors who boldly sailed the unknown world seeking to test and challenge their abilities at the very cost of their own lives. I had seen enough and been there too long as it was. It was time for me to go on my way.

The very next day would find me at the PX gathering up a bag full of food staples and some little toys, and a few other little items that cried out from the shelf for me to buy them. With a warm feeling in my heart I wrote out a little note that said, "For the house down by the river," and then proceeded to walk over to where my Norse colleague was deployed, sneak into the building, and leave the bag by his equipment locker. He had reminded me of an important lesson I needed to keep close to my heart. But no good deed goes unpunished; someone saw me sneak into the building and told my massive colleague of my secret gift to the river family. The next day I was paid a visit by my Norse colleague. He literally darkened my office doorway with his presence. Fortunately for me he was displaying a very big smile and said in a slightly loud voice, "Robert, nice bag of goodies for those with little, nice man." He then reached down, picked me up out of my chair like I was a small child, and gave me a "thank you" hug only a bear could have matched. I was almost recovered by the time I saw him walking in the direction of the little house by the river from my office window. When we choose to have less by giving to others, we somehow come away with more in our hearts. What becomes less of that which we can hold in our hands becomes more of what we can feel in our hearts. It feels good for all of us to think back on moments such as these where people with goodness in their hearts built small islands of compassion in the middle of a war zone.

16

Red Wine in Eastern Europe

It was my first foreign mission with the United Nations International Police Task Force, and there I sat in total splendor in my little office watching the electricity go on and off. The water was also turned on and off but we had to drink bottled water anyway so the only annoyance was the lack of water flow to the pipes of the toilets. Such was my glorious life in the war zone of the Balkans. I was extremely fortunate I thought that I was so very skilled and knowledgeable about literally everything and had little else to learn in my life. After all, I was coming from the most developed and intellectually superior country in the world to a backward country devastated by conflict, or so I thought. I was doing my very best to hide behind my inflated self-image for protection. I figured if I just smiled and kept my mouth shut there would be a limit to the amount of mistakes I would make and the embarrassment I would have to endure in front of all the other internationals I was working with.

While I was earnestly engaged in doing very little at my desk, the training section chief opened my door with his size 14 shoe and declared to one and all that I was the lucky bastard who was going to the sunny beaches of Eastern Europe for an SAT (Selection Assistance Team) mission. I was scheduled to be a testing officer for skill competence in a war zone. They would have to demonstrate the ability to shoot a weapon, drive a vehicle, and other skills before they would be allowed on this lucrative mission. Yes, I said lucrative—extraordinarily lucrative. In their home country they were earning $US200 to $US300 a month where as with the Police Task Force they would be earning over $US3000 a month in expenses alone. They would be making about 12 years' worth of pay in one year. For me, the $3000 was for my monthly expenses because I was also getting a payroll check from my country. Even without a penny from their home country getting to go on a war zone mission was like winning the lottery for these officers. This was a major life-changing event to them, and there were many others from countries that were far worse off. Many officers from Asia and Africa make approximately $25 to $35 U.S. a month with a couple of bags of rice thrown in. Sometimes if they have been promoted to officer grade there is also a place for their family to live, but in far too many cases this promotion to officer grade requires bribe money that they just don't have and their families can't afford. For these officers, they would be earning over 10 years of pay for every month they serve in the mission. This is such an incredible financial blessing it's easy to understand why they so desperately want to go on missions and what it means for them and for their families.

I thought it was great that I was getting out of my field training office until I found out, among other things, that there were no beaches where I was going. Our section chief was an incredibly unique individual and more than just a character. The officers who had worked with him said he would tell them, "Mess up mate, and I'll roll up my sleeve, reach down your throat, grab you by the ass, pull you inside out, and throw you to the dogs in the street." I am proud to say that I never gave him cause to even unbutton the cuff on his sleeve. As time went on I grew to have nothing but respect for this very tall and lean chief of training, who stood in front of his officers in conflict and behind them when we needed him. We never had to ask where he was—he was with us.

There was only one possible problem with the SAT training. My assigned partner was going to be a Russian Army Major. I was more than slightly concerned and interested about how we were going to work together after decades of cold war conflicts between our countries. During our first informal meeting about the SAT mission where we were given our orders and responsibilities, I noticed a small amount of blue and white horizontally striped undershirt exposed under his gray uniform shirt. The undershirt colors signified he was SpetsNaz affiliated, a highly trained Russian commando unit. It was a very polite, very formal meeting of my mission colleague at our briefing. Being a street cop by nature, it has always been my way of life to size up people I meet from a combative perspective—what I expect from them and how I would go about handling them if I had to in a conflict. I could see and even feel in my bones that this man was many things I was not at this point in my life. I was an outstandingly skilled fighter and as strong as a bull with upper arms bigger than my neck, but I sensed something in this Russian that led me to respect his quiet experience, inner strength, and personal discipline. The thought crossed my mind that I had the greater strength on the outside while my new colleague had the greater strength on the inside. As time progressed and we worked and traveled together performing our assigned tasks of testing on this mission, my wariness ebbed into respect and then curiosity about my colleague who consistently displayed only the most professional of behavior and ethics. I was carefully learning by his example; he was teaching me a great deal by his conduct and resourcefulness. Our nations, our governments, our past histories, and past Cold War conflicts were always on my mind. Was I seeing the face of this person or was I seeing a carefully scripted facade? Perhaps time would furnish the answer.

One evening, after our last, very long day of officer testing (starting at dawn), we decided to celebrate the final day of our successful mission. We walked what seemed like forever and then finally agreed on a small restaurant with a big dirty white stuffed duck out front that had seen better days. The ordering of the food for us was quite simple and most direct. An old man walked over to our table wearing an old suit with his tie stuffed in his shirt pocket and said, "You want eat?" I said, "yes" and my colleague said, "*da*," and the old waiter just turned around and walked off. There are those times when you just have to go with the flow. I was finally starting to get used to the speed of dinner. In the States you walk in, order, eat, pay the bill, and leave. Dinner in other countries is meant to be enjoyed, and that means looking at your dinner and not at the clock on the wall (which doesn't work most of the time anyway). The first bottle of red wine was while we were waiting for dinner and everything just seemed to fall into place with a quiet understanding between us. There was small talk about the testing and the mission. Topics that weren't confrontational dominated the conversation over the first glass of wine. Then it was time for me to stop pretending we were the same, because we sure as hell weren't. We were two different sides of the same United Nations Police Task Force coin working together. I told my colleague that I remembered when I was a young boy in primary school when they would sound the alarm for the practice air raid drill because we were told that the Russian bombers were coming and then we would have to hide under our desks. He said he remembered hiding under his desk during the air raid drills because they were told that the American bombers were coming. He was not a man of useless words or wasted comments. He meant what he said and rarely spoke about anything at a personal level. I saw a slight smile come on his face as we both realized the irony of our childhood air raid drills. He then proposed a toast to a successful mission in the name of world peace. This was a most welcome gesture. It was a pleasure and honor to clink glasses in the name of peace in the world, especially between his country and mine.

This was not a time when I had any interest in politics; my interest was solely in the roast duck making its way to our table. The bottle of wine was done, and a very large and delicious duck dinner had arrived at our small, wooden table. There were platters of sliced dumplings covered with rich brown gravy, and a steaming bowl of buttered, seasoned potatoes, tangy sweet and sour purple cabbage, baked apple twist pastry with frosting and cream, and of course another bottle of red wine. Both of our stomachs roared from the indescribable aroma of the serving platters and we saluted each other with our forks. The old man set down the dishes and uncorked another bottle of red wine and said, "Only red wine here, white wine is shit," and then walked off laughing. We just smiled and slowly spent most of the evening devouring an incredible dinner that cost us a total of $US6.50, and it was worth every cent! Instead of leaving a tip, we took a glass from a nearby table and poured out some red wine for the old man who had been our host for the evening, and invited him to sit for a moment with us. We should have known that the moment would grow into the rest of the evening. It was customary to return the wine gesture. The old man poured us another glass of red "whatever" from the back kitchen area. But this is the way most people are once the protective facade that covers us and stops us from revealing our real self is gone. It didn't matter that we couldn't understand each other; we still laughed, talked, and enjoyed the moment.

As the years and missions went on so did a friendship that was more important to both of us and our wives and families than we could have ever imagined. How could I have ever known, as a young boy tucked up under my desk, taking shelter from the threat of Russian bombers, what the future held in store for me and for those I was to share my war zone life with?

17

The World of Food

INTRODUCTION

Of all of the things that affect your life in a war zone anywhere on the face of this Earth, food has one of the most dynamic effects on you. We all have heard the expression, "eat to live or live to eat," but when you are deployed to a war zone it's more appropriate to say "eat to survive or survive to eat." Of all the billions of people on this troubled little planet of ours we all have one thing in common—food. That, however, is the only part of these stories that is the same because the food itself varies so dramatically. Much can be understood about a nation by understanding or appreciating their cuisine. Just as nations differ greatly in their foods, all the customs and gestures that go on the table or the floor with their fare differ. Countries, regions, zones, cultures ... all these things and more add to the flavor of what is prepared. I would be remiss if I didn't mention that more than once I respectfully declined an invitation to eat something due to the possible health concerns that could follow. Other times it was from a total failure of "courage of the moment."

EGGS AND BREAD

The Cancan Pizza Restaurant in Sarajevo, Bosnia, was a great place to go for food. It was where the locals and the internationals rubbed elbows on a regular basis. It was decorated with the usual array of bullet holes in the walls and motor blast damage on the sidewalks and streets around the building. It was a small place by world standards but by Bosnian

Figure 17.1 If you don't know what's on the plate in front of you, eat cautiously!

standards it was just about perfect in every way. It had all the necessary things to set the proper mood for the lunch crowd it catered to. It had six round wooden tables that were covered with bright red tablecloths and a swinging double door that was constantly banging open and closed from the waiter running in and out carrying pizzas high above his head from the kitchen. Everyone in the place was different and got along or just plain tolerated whoever was sitting at the next table. We all had something else on our mind. The unbelievable aroma always preceded the pizza as it was brought to our table.

The time had come and Balkan-style pizza was proudly placed in front of us, egg and all. Yes, I said egg and all. We were in the Balkans and in this part of the world there is a superstition or tradition about bread and eggs. Why did the chicken cross the road—to get a loaf of bread? (Sorry, I just couldn't resist that joke.) In the Balkans, whenever any bread recipe is prepared it must also include an egg in one form or another. Despite our constant requests to the waiter when we placed our order for our pizza we were always the recipient of a fried egg resting plainly in the center of our pizza when it arrived at our table. We finally gave up and accepted fate. We just gave in to this culinary issue and accepted our "egg" destiny. This tradition has been going on longer than the combined age of all of us sitting at the table and what we wanted or thought of it was not going to change the time-honored tradition of this country. When we finally accepted this tradition we began sliding the egg off our pizza onto a small serving plate and giving it away to locals who were sitting near us. To our pleasant surprise this new gesture was met with big smiles and thanks. The locals interpreted this gesture to mean that we were sharing our good luck with them by giving them our egg. Loaves of bread with a colored egg baked inside were always made for the many holidays that were celebrated in this region. It was believed that whoever got the slice of bread that contained part or all of the holiday egg would enjoy special religious blessings the entire year. The locals could even tell where you purchased your bread that day from the color of the egg that was inside of it. The two biggest bakeries in the area had a friendly competition with each other, with one bakery putting a blue egg inside of their holiday bread and the other bakery putting a red egg inside of theirs. We learned to go with the flow of this cultural river.

As you travel around this wondrous globe of ours you will find that eggs and bread are two of the many food staples that play a critical role in every culture. Most of the bread that is baked in this world doesn't come in a nice wrapper, with food additives that keep it from developing mold in three days or less. You walk into a local store, probably each morning, toss down a very low price, and then someone literally hands you a loaf of bread. This is just the way it's done. The true difficulty comes when you go back home or are deployed to another area of the supposed "civilized" world. You quickly become aware that the bread back there in the war zone actually tasted so much better than the ultraprocessed, ultrawhite, ultrasoft, ultralight, perfectly shaped expensive "stuff" you now hold in your hand. I remember being on patrol in the predawn hours and pulling my vehicle up behind an ancient stone oven bakery to get the day's bread for a few buddies and myself. We had worked out a deal that the one who was assigned to the patrol area that included the bakery was the one who picked up the bread for everyone else on the shift. I would just walk in and hold up the necessary number of fingers and point to the loaves of bread that had just been flipped out of their pans onto a very old wooden table next to the primeval stone ovens. The sound of the men working and shouting and laughing was so loud that yelling to them was useless at best. One of the men walking around with a huge wooden paddle would simply grab and throw the requested number of loaves at me, and may I say that he had a better throwing arm with greater accuracy than most professional ball players. I would just toss the loaves unceremoniously into the back of my patrol unit and drive off. I have to admit that after having been in the bakery with all the unbelievable mouth-watering smells, I would usually spend the next several minutes with a steering wheel in one hand and loaf of still warm bread in the other. As the loaf of bread became smaller and smaller my frame of mind became better and better. (Now don't read this and tell me you would do any different. In fact, I think there is a good chance you're ready to take a break and get something to eat right now.)

Eggs were quite another matter and very different from the bread situation. If the eggs are clean and high-quality then all is fine with the world and you. If the eggs are bad, then how you prepare them will determine whether you will be sick or critically ill. Eggs are a fantastic source of protein and in some areas of the world they are the only source that is affordable. Now is the time to separate the good eggs from the bad eggs. The first trick I learned was to float the eggs I had just purchased in a big bowl of cold water. If the eggs float in the cold water there is a good chance they're bad or close to going bad. Don't ever take the chance of eating anything that may be tainted. It's better to go hungry—believe me—I have been in that situation many times in my war zone life. Another trick I had up my sleeve was to spin the eggs on a flat surface before I even bought them. I learned this trick from a very cleaver, resourceful, brother officer and good friend from Ghana. If the eggs were old or hard boiled they would have the ability to spin like a top, and that means you walk away from that street-side food market and never buy anything there again. That may sound extreme to you but when you consider how sick you could become, it's a matter that leaves you no choice. Bad eggs have even killed people.

When you get to the point of cooking these little white presents from our feathered friends the key word to remember is to *cook*. I remember several times over the years in different war zones where misguided colleagues either made, or ate, restaurant salad dressings from some cuisine that used raw egg yolks in the recipe. These unfortunate people became so severely ill and in outright pain they became an example to all of us of what not to do. You can either put your hand into the flame of the candle to see how hot it really is and get burnt, or you can take my word for it that it's hot. The final choice is always yours as to what you choose to stick in your mouth. That means you should totally and completely cook the entire egg. This may sound like I'm overstating the issue but remember that not only is an egg a great nutritional benefit to your body, it is also a great container for the development and growth of bacteria. Remember that this is why they use eggs in laboratories for the manufacture of vaccines and other medical products and experimentations. Don't be a human lab rat. Cook the eggs you eat!

BURGER OF DOOM

On the bad side of the culinary coin is getting yourself sick. You notice I said getting "yourself" sick and not someone else getting you sick. That's because most of the illness you or a colleague will encounter will be due to your own poor judgment or local food ignorance and not any malicious tricks the locals are playing on you. Follow your country's or organization's guidelines to the letter. If you are coming up short on what to eat and what to avoid, refer to major medical Web sites for some good advice, but remember that advice is only as good as your willingness to follow it. There are some hard and fast rules to follow that will keep you out of most of the pitfalls that trap others in a war zone. Don't be the adventurous connoisseur. If you have the choice of dining in your own military facility do so by all means. Your colon will thank you and you will be reducing the odds of looking at your own green-faced reflection in the toilet. No matter how wonderful the food looks or smells from a roadside stand, a little voice should be screaming in your ear. If you don't listen to that warning you will soon be having a long-term appointment in the bathroom of your choice.

I remember too well that sunny afternoon when I was coming back late from an assignment and my nose and stomach told my brain to pull over at a roadside stand for what I would describe as "a street burger." The stand and the lady behind the window looked very clean and professional but a feeling of doubt and anxiety swept over my body as I paid the one euro price and jumped back in my vehicle to continue on my way. I was in a thoroughly content mood as I drove along chomping away at the soft bread and the tasty mystery meat that would come back to say "Hi" to me repeatedly throughout the night and most of the next morning. It's not the most recommended nighttime experience, sleeping cuddled up to a toilet with your pillow, singing the porcelain serenade. It was much later in the week before I could even consider trying to eat anything solid. When I finally made it to the dining hall I referred to this culinary surprise as a "rainbow burger" when explaining to my friends and colleagues why

I had missed chow for so many days. They looked confused and asked me why I would call my dining entrée such a strange name. I explained it was to describe the colors of my face and not the burger. After the momentous burger moment and the week of hell that followed I made it a habit to carry some candy or one of those cardboard-tasting healthy-type breakfast bars in one of my pockets whenever I went anywhere. This was an experience I was very determined never to repeat.

DRINKING THE WATER

Much can be written about not drinking the local water, but what if you think you are drinking bottled water when you're not? Unfortunately, far too many people in war zones are not getting the bottled water they think they're getting. What a lot of restaurants do as a matter of routine practice is to simply keep refilling the empty water bottles with tap water and replacing the bottle tops from the garbage. They make a nice profit and you are hard pressed to be able to tell the difference between the local tap water and the imported special water you are being charged extra for, especially when the waiter is kind enough to open and pour your water at your table. The solution to this worldwide dilemma is quite simple. Ask for "gas water" to be served to your table unopened. When you ask for gas water you are getting carbonated water, and when you request the bottle be unopened until serving, open the bottle yourself. If your bottle of gas water doesn't hiss or pop then you don't drink it.

The other problem that goes with the water problem most people in war zones overlook is the ice. The ice you request or that is kindly placed at your table is just a tiny cube of frozen little creatures that want no more in their short little life than to spend an evening with you in your digestive track. Stick with the gas water with no ice and you'll be one step closer to an uneventful evening … and a much quieter morning the next day.

ONE TOUGH CHICKEN

It was great to spend time in Africa but the caution that goes with this is that what you see is not always what you get. I was standing at the hotel's reservation desk waiting to check into my room. I was looking across the counter at the smiling face of the young man who was the entire hotel check-in staff. After signing in I received the instructions and cautions regarding my safety and was told to be careful not to wander off the hotel grounds with the snakes and spiders. The young man was courteous and polite but slightly hurried because I was there at shift change. The young man who was finishing his shift took off his white shirt and handed it to the young man who was just starting his shift behind the counter. After the exchange and donning of the "white" shirt the next shift was officially "on duty." The counter that was between us concealed the fact that both of the counter personnel were wearing only a pair of shorts to go with their rotating white shirt. The door behind the counter opened directly into "the bush" or jungle that started almost immediately behind the hotel. In a flash the desk clerk going off shift was running into the jungle and on his way home. If this was how the front reception desk was being run I didn't even want to think about how the kitchen was being run. This is why I always traveled with an ample supply of candy bars in my pockets.

The dining terrace was beautiful beyond description. The plants and flowers were huge and more brightly colored than any artificial flowers sold in shops around the world. The only drawback to this paradise where everything grows to massive proportions is that all of the crawlers, creepers, and sliders also grow to very large proportions. The spiders get so big in this part of the world you can actually see them smile. (Some people say you can put a saddle on them but I think they're exaggerating.) It was far beyond time to eat and I was willing to settle on having anything that had parents on my plate. My colleague was equally hungry so we decided to eat at the hotel instead of looking for a restaurant in an unknown town. The counter attendant ran from the check-in counter to the side of the hotel where the dining terrace was located. We were given a piece of paper that had several dining options scribbled on it but the paper was totally unreadable. I complimented him on the outstanding appearance of the dining terrace and asked if they had chicken or *polo*. The young man, who was now our waiter, yelled something out to the back of the hotel in the local language and shortly thereafter received a laughing reply. With a wide and proud smile on his face our waiter said, "We have too fast boy, he get chicken bird quick." This was good news and bad news. The good news was the chicken, or polo, or bird, at the very least was going to be fresh. The bad news was I had no idea how this bird was going to be prepared and eventually presented to me. When we were given two clean glasses, a bottle of red wine, and two airplane magazines, we realized it was going to be a long wait for whatever dinner was eventually coming our way. Sooner than we had hoped we heard a laughing commotion coming from the back of the building and beheld the much awaited sight of our waiter proudly strutting toward us with two enormous platters held high over his head. I was very hungry and very happy. The aroma was sweet and spicy and, most important, all the food was cooked. Cooked food is always safer than food that's raw and washed in local water. We each had an assortment of fried fish with multicolored fruits and vegetables I had never seen before. But that was just the start. My dinner was very unique and displayed in an extraordinary manner. In the middle of my dinner platter was some unknown species of bird. This unknown bird stood in the center of the platter—head, feet, and all—in proud defiance to the end it had met. It was as tough in death as it was in life, but it still tasted great, and there was no question that what I was dining on that evening was fresh. It's always a good gesture all over the world to ask for an extra glass and when it arrives ask the host to join you for a drink. After much good-natured conversation we were escorted to our rooms with the added bonus of an extra room lizard. I looked over at my colleague as he walked into his adjoining room smiling, stating that he had a bigger lizard than mine. In this part of Africa it's a great advantage to have a couple of lizards in your room due to the appetite they have for the local spiders. I had no problem accepting an extra lizard in my room if it would be an insurance policy against the local spiders! I remember hearing the sound of a scuffle and then a smacking sound several times during the night when we shared our rooms with our little green guests. I just kept saying to myself, *"bon appétit* my friends."

Figure 17.2   All of my new friends were welcome in my room.

PARIS FARE

It was a touch of Paris in Kosovo. I was on staff as an induction trainer at the United Nations International Police Training Center in Pristina, Kosovo, when we all received an invitation to dine with the French contingent. It was their way of saying "thank you" for our efforts in the nine-day program we presented to their officers before they were deployed to different areas of the Kosovo war zone. Culinary skill was an area where the French not only took great pride but, as it was claimed by many, exceeded all others with their national cuisine. The chefs of France take such pride in the men and women of their armed forces that they routinely donate months of their time away from their restaurants to prepare their specialties for the troops in the war zones. The attitude was serious and politely formal as we arrived to dine at the French headquarters facility. We were shown to our tables and advised to remain standing until we had all been assembled. Once we were all standing at our assigned dining place, a toast was made "to all the officers serving in war zones around the world in the name and effort of peace." A loud cheer went up, we sat down, and the formalities relaxed. Before me was a place setting of real silverware and plates and crystal goblets for the different wines that were going to be served with the different courses of food. There was no chow line and tray here. We were to be served, and this state of affairs was very nice to be sure.

We started off with warm bread directly from the ovens and butter, real cow butter that was served with a starting wine selection I can't remember to save my life. The next wine in the selection followed each new course being served; there was the sliced duck, then the escargot with garlic and butter, and then something that was a puff cheese pastry, and of course more bread and cow butter.

It was at this time the master chef from Paris slowly walked past each table to ensure everything was being done up to his standards and instructions. He was dressed from head to toe in a white uniform that actually had metals and patches on it. One of my colleagues politely remarked to the master chef as he passed that the cuisine was wonderful, and the master chef replied without even missing a step, "Of course it is, I prepare this."

By the time the main courses were displayed and served with their selected wines, our stomachs were in heaven and our heads were spinning in the clouds. The final course was assorted custards or flan on sweet dough crusts served with the customary brandy. It was an experience beyond words, and my stomach will be forever indebted to the proud chef from Paris.

HANDFUL OF HOSPITALITY

Amman, Jordan is one of the most impressive cities I have had the opportunity and honor to visit. It embraces the ancient sites of history and still
reveals a major metropolis that is awake and aware of its place in the
world. I was meeting a brother officer from the United Nations Kosovo
mission for dinner. We were invited to dine at the house of his father who
was a greatly respected retired general. To enter the home of an Arab
or Muslim family is to be the beneficiary of unlimited interactive customs. I call them interactive customs because most of your actions will be
received and then acted upon by your host. When you enter the home of a
Muslim family and you remove your shoes, leaving them at the doorway,
you are showing respect for the home. Then, everyone who is in the home
will show you respect by giving and sharing what they have with you. Be
careful what you admire in a Muslim home or what you say looks nice on
a Muslim man. The common response when you admire a ring or ornament or some other item is they will simply give it to you. It will be a gift
from their heart and they mean this with total sincerity. They will ask for
nothing in return from you. If you are in contact with a Muslim woman
or girl it is best to be "overly" respectful and avoid any physical contact
of any kind. Avoid staring at them or looking into their eyes. When I am
asked about a small child I stay out of trouble by saying the standard line,
"*Hom du le la* (thanks be to Allah), for the gift of this child to your family."
When the subject of the dead comes up the gesture of your right hand on
your chest with the quiet saying of *salaam* (peace) will always suffice and
be very appreciated by those present. The hand-on-chest gesture is also
appropriate when meeting the very old—and anyone else that you may
come in contact with. It's a good gesture habit to get into when you're in
that part of the world.

My first Mensa dining experience with my friends in Jordan was great,
and to say the least quite unusual for a "fork and plate" type of person like
me. The Mensa is a very large bowl that's filled with several different types
of food strategically located in different sections of the bowl. This bowl
contains a base of rice and grain that is mixed with a thick type of yogurt.
Then chicken, lamb, and other meats allowed by Muslim religious restrictions are piled on top and the Mensa dinner is complete. This huge, heavy
bowl was brought out from the kitchen by two of the strongest ladies of
the house. The men showed their approval by quietly saying, *Quice quice,
shucran* (good good, thank you). Once the table was arranged to the satisfaction of the eldest lady of the house who was overseeing everything it

244

was time for the men to come to the table and eat. The women would eat by themselves back in the kitchen while the men were eating in the dining area of the house, standing around the table that proudly displayed the Mensa bowl. If we were wearing long sleeve shirts we started rolling up our shirt sleeves for the first handful and with the kind invitation of my host, I reached into the bowl with my open bare hand and grabbed a handful of what I hoped was basically the rice and chicken.

The next step was to squeeze the yogurt and other liquids out of what I was holding in my right hand. It is very important to remember that *only* the right hand is to be used for eating and all social activities. This is because the left hand is used for the other activities that are performed in

Figure 17.3   It was a great new experience in dining with friends.

Figure 17.4   Dining on great food with wonderful hosts.

the bathroom. It is a word to the wise to never mix up the two hands and the functions they are responsible for here in this culture.

   After I had squeezed out the liquid from my first handful from the Mensa bowl, I tried to neatly eat from my hand. My hosts politely smiled and chuckled to themselves. I watched how they performed this maneuver without becoming a total mess but I could never get the knack of eating this way. But compelled by the delicious taste of this new dish I just relegated myself to being a well-fed total mess. My hosts were extremely happy and full of pride that I was obviously enjoying their favorite national dish. When I finished eating after repeated encouragement to eat "just one more handful," one of the ladies appeared from the closed kitchen area with a big warm towel for me so I could wash myself off. After the Mensa and a much needed cleanup by one and all we retired to the main room of the house to sit and talk. We sat in a small circle to provide a closeness for the conversation among us. We all sat with both of our feet flat on the floor. Showing the bottoms of our feet is an insult to others. Never show the bottoms of your feet to your hosts. I was very impressed with how extremely polite everyone was. No one talked in a loud voice and all the conversation was directed to everyone sitting in the circle. If you were in the circle you were part of the conversation whether you were talking or not, and if you didn't want to speak that was fine, too. Most of the men just sat and smoked and nodded their heads respectfully to the comments being made. Out of respect for my presence in the circle my hosts were speaking all the English they could to make me feel welcome. When one of the younger hosts made a comment in Arabic one of the elder males stared at him, and he immediately apologized to the elder host and then to me. Respect and personal values are more than just a custom in Arab countries; they are a way of life. A small cup of coffee was served with a very sweet honey and a small nut cookie. I was thinking of asking for a big cup of their coffee until I tasted it. To say their coffee was strong would be a gross understatement.

I found myself unusually relaxed and content considering I was so far from home and in such a totally foreign environment with customs so different from my own. Perhaps I was feeling the way I was because my hosts were sincere in their hospitality and I was being open with my sincere gratitude and we truly enjoyed being with each other and sharing a part of ourselves with our circle of friends.

THE BANYA EXPERIENCE

To be a guest at a Russian banya is like few experiences you will ever have in your life. The Russian term *banya* refers to a fantastic evening consisting of saunas, cold pools, feasting, and drinking—until the time comes you decide to call it quits or are no longer able to continue celebrating life. The Russian officers who prepared this experience for my partner and me were outstanding hosts in every way. I found their casual and sincere hospitality to be conducive to my having the experience of a lifetime. The festivities were set at a location far away from Moscow, deep in the Russian birch wood forest. One of the major objectives of the banya is to take time to forget about the world and your problems, and just relax with good friends, food, drink, and talk.

Our banya was comprised of three enjoyable stations: the sauna, the pool, and a table covered in food. The plan for the evening was to go from one station to the next stopping only when our hearts, minds, and stomachs were full. Because my colleague and I were guests at this banya we were escorted through every phase of this great evening.

Wearing nothing but an extra big white towel we entered the first station of the banya, the sauna. The sauna was not a unique experience for me because I had been in one before, but drinking beer while in that heated room was a new twist and my colleague was more than interested. No sooner than a big ladle of water was poured over the hot stones my partner and I were offered a very select light beer. The idea of the beer was to replace the lost perspiration with something that would help relax the person enjoying the sauna. (My partner ended up getting very relaxed.) After the light beers we were offered the opportunity to sample some very prized Russian dark lager beer. Being I am not a beer drinker my colleague decided to sacrifice himself for the sake of proper hospitality and imbibe several of the light and dark beers himself.

The next stage of the banya was leaving the sauna for a deep pool of cold water. You will notice I referred to the water as being cold. The water was not supposed to be merely cool. It was supposed to be just out right damn cold, and it was! Theoretically, the physical reaction was to make you feel awake and refreshed, but for me it was closer to the experiences I had in past training as a scuba diver doing ice diving drills. I had heard stories about this part of the banya so I was a little prepared for the effect on my body of going from a hot steaming sauna to an ice cold pool of water. I may have been mentally prepared but I found out just how little I was physically prepared for this experience when my body crashed into that cold water. I came to the surface of the pool to see the smiling faces of my Russian friends and the puzzled look on the face of my colleague as he asked, "How's the water partner?" With all of the control and calmness I could gather in my shocked and shaking body, even though I knew I should tell my colleague the truth, I yelled back at him, "Jump in, the water's warm." Without hesitation my hot sweating, beer-imbibing partner splashed into the pool while I was trying my best to get out of that cold water as fast as I could. When he popped up in the center of the pool his face was red as a beet and neither our Russian hosts nor myself understood what he was yelling at us in his native language. But by the time he reached the side of the pool he had calmed down enough so he was only threatening us that there were going to be beatings, executions, and revenge.

From the steam heat of the sauna to the ice cold water of the deep pool, we now proceeded to the banya table. The table was covered with a very impressive array of meats, cheeses, breads, fruits, and several different kinds of vodka for my colleague to sample as he gathered up his strength for the next round. I decided at the start of this evening I was going to be very conservative with the drink but definitely not with the outstanding display of breads, meats, and cheeses. One of my close Russian friends who I had known from past war zone missions showed us the proper way to consume caviar on bread with vodka. Not wanting to cause an international incident at the banya I thought it best, in the name of peace throughout the world, to participate repeatedly in this endeavor. First my dear friend took a piece of white bread and cleverly spread a thick layer of butter on it. He then spread black or red caviar lightly on the buttered bread. I say cleverly because this is a subtle trick to get the banya guest to consume more vodka than they think they're consuming. When the heavily buttered bread is eaten it coats the throat with the butter so the ice cold vodka is hardly tasted as it goes down the throat. The only sensation is warmth when each shot hits the stomach. As I looked down along the banya table I saw the cow butter strategy was working quite well on my very happy colleague. He was contently moving through the line of different types of red and black caviars that were spread on his heavily buttered bread. Each different caviar had its own unique bottle of vodka with it on the banya table. We were both having a great time and so were our exceptional hosts and friends.

After a little conversation, we were offered the next round of the banya. I totally enjoyed doing about three rounds of sauna, pool, and food but my very happy colleague decided to concentrate most of his attention on food and drink, stating that his first round in the sauna and pool were also his last for that part of the banya. The next day our spirits were still high, riding on a wave of good recollections and appreciation for a great banya night.

GOAT STEW

"The mountains of the Balkans are a truly impressive and magnificent sight. Whether you are viewing them in the summer or the winter, or any other season, they will remain in your heart until the day you are buried at their base." That's what several of my local friends told me when I first arrived in this area of the world, and they could not have been more right about these relatively unknown wonders of the world. As stunningly beautiful as these rolling mountains and hills are with their ancient rivers and lakes scattered in the midst of them, they are also deadly beyond all comprehension. The never-ending war of the Balkans, which has become a tradition of death and misery, has seen to that. Interspersed with the stunning beauty of the countryside are land mines and cluster bombs just waiting for the innocent or careless. As one side of the never-ending conflict was losing ground they would bury land mines to slow down the advancing attack of the opposing side. Then the roles would reverse and the attacking side would become the attacked and lay their land mines in the ground as they retreated. If the dirt could be dug into, there was a land mine in it. Once you see what one of these little monsters can do, you never forget it. I became so preoccupied with this circumstance that even when I went home on leave and at the end of my mission I would be hesitant to walk across the grass. In the Balkans you have no choice but to abide by the rule: Stay on the hard surfaces. This is not a suggestion; it could mean your life or your leg.

There were six of us traveling in two vehicles. All was going well on this beautiful spring day where everything was green except for the snowcapped mountains that looked deceivingly close. There were times when the mountains looked like they were about a 10-minute drive away from where we were, but in truth, we would have been hard pressed to make it there in a full day's journey. Coming on a goat herder we decided this might be the right time to think about our dinner if we wanted to eat tonight. As I looked out in the small scenic valley I noticed how the goat herder was driving his flock ahead of him. This is referred to as "Balkan style" herding because the animals are always sent ahead of the herder due to all of the land mines that litter the ground. Better a goat detonates a land mine and ends up dinner for the village people than the herder gets his leg blown off.

It was a simple negotiation for our dinner. We politely introduced ourselves to the herder and asked if we could have a goat for dinner when we returned at 1800 hours (6 P.M.). The white-haired old man slowly rubbed his grizzly chin thinking about the price. He was dressed in layers of warm clothes and had an old pipe carefully tucked in the corner of his mouth. His prewar shotgun was rusty and looked like it hadn't been fired since the day it was loaded. He told us that his "sheep" were very special and should bring a high price. The time-honored tradition of bartering was now starting. Whatever the price he offered we would counter with half the price and after the usual five minutes of standing around rubbing our faces we would all agree on the deal. Nothing in the Balkan Mountains is done quickly and that's part of the tradition you have to learn to live with. This is the way it's done and that's it. There is no other way to do it. After we agreed on a price we found one goat that looked fatter and healthier than the others. That was going to be dinner so we shot it in the head. That's the best way to insure we were getting what we paid for. We drove off for what turned out to be a happily uneventful tour of the mountain area we were responsible for patrolling.

Upon our return to the valley to collect on our dinner agreement, we were met with the picturesque sight of the sun slowly setting behind a western mountain, casting a peaceful shadow over the village that lay about a kilometer below us. Our vehicles made their way down the only road in or out of the village to the far end of town to meet our new goat herder friend. We drove through a low smoky cloud that just about knocked us out of our vehicles. The aroma of the dinner that was waiting for us was unbelievable and our stomachs told us we were more than ready to eat. We pulled our vehicles up close to the fire so we could use them for cover if we had to and also to keep an eye on them. Trust and carelessness go hand and hand in this part of the world. If you have to think about what the difference is between them you just may find yourself walking instead of riding. It's not just the vehicles you're driving that could be stolen in the blink of an eye but also whatever is in them. Everything that's in a patrol vehicle, from the gas in its tank to the radios and literally everything else that can be removed or carried away will be. Case in point is all the tanks littering the countryside. If you carefully inspect them you will find that they are totally stripped out and gutted. Everything that can be pulled out has been; they are nothing more than rusting shells. Our herder friend had been joined by what we assumed was his happy wife and two obedient teenage boys. These situations of shared hospitality end up being an excellent excuse for the locals to have a little bit of a celebration. As we sat around the fire smelling our wonderful dinner cooking away in two massive covered pots we all shared a small glass of Balkan whisky. This is a custom that is not to be taken lightly. The strength of this homemade white lighting is only matched by its strong odor. The taste and smell are similar to what you would use as a wood sealant on the floor of your home. This whisky is truly nasty stuff! The locals use this potent liquid for everything from toothaches to sleeping medicine, and as a cure-all for every known major illness and disease. It can also be used to get a little extra mileage from the family vehicle when added to the gas tank. As the lids came off the fire-blackened pots our stomachs buckled from the delicious aroma. The lady began serving up our plates to the point where there was no room left. One of the bubbling pots was filled with goat meat and potatoes with onions. The other pot was filled with more goat meat,

251

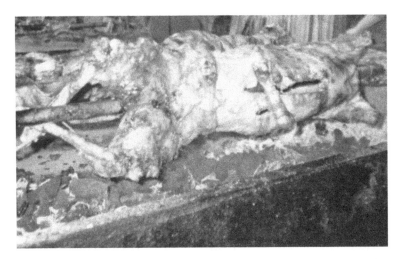

Figure 17.5 Flame-roasting goat is another popular way of eating this abundant food staple.

the organs, and bread that was stuck to the sides of the pot. They would simply pull the bread off the pot and put it on top of each of our overflowing plates. We were more than happy because this evening's feast was far more than we had hoped or bargained for. The lady went around our circle pointing a big wooden spoon at each of us and gesturing to us if we wanted more … and more, and more. When we all were finished and the pipes and cigarettes came out, that was the signal for the lady, the old man, and the boys to have their well-deserved time eating at the fireside. We were more than well fed and it was now time to leave. As was proper, we gave the old man some chocolate and soap for the old lady that had prepared our outstanding dinner. To give anything directly to the lady could be interpreted as disrespectful in this area of the world. We all had a great experience, and because of the way we respectfully came into and left this valley, we ensured that we would always be welcomed if we were to ever return. These people may not have the technology of the rest of the world but they are extremely intelligent and resourceful individuals and will never forget you once you have made an impression on them. We were quite careful to make sure that the impression we left in this valley was positive and that we would be forever welcome with lit pipes and bubbling pots of stew if our vehicles were to ever ramble down this road again.

UNCONTROLLABLE CRAVINGS

Whether you are deployed off base for short term or assigned a long-term mission, you will have to eat local cuisine. In the Balkans this usually means your choices will be either chicken or goat. The chicken can and will take the form of anything from "bone with skin on it" to a plump little loser that didn't run fast enough to save its delicious life. As far as the goat meat is concerned it is usually referred to as "lamb," but if you ever had the chance to actually see this contributor to the evening menu you would see a straggly loser who roamed the hills barely surviving on whatever green it could find to eat.

The methodology of the local food preparation is usually divided into two categories: boil it or burn it. You were expecting something a little more uniquely sophisticated? Until the day Paris is declared a war zone the cuisine will unfortunately simply remain hunger driven and consumption based. Because of the flexibility of a pot full of water this was my favorite way to cook literally everything and anything that was available to me. With the electrical power going on and off constantly any time, day or night, a pot of boiling water was a staple way to cook. Once it was up to heat it was able to cook its contents for quite a while when the power shut off. If it was picked or came out of a can, it went into the pot. If it had parents and was dead, it went into the pot. If it was green, red, white, brown, or anything in-between it was declared a vegetable and it went into the pot. If it was yellow it was declared a banana and that was the only thing that didn't go in the pot.

Finding food, cooking the food, and eating the food were best kept simple. The necessary utensils were more of a tactical consideration than an artistic or decorative display at the table. In Kosovo I cooked with a pot and a spoon, and because I normally dined alone it seemed rather appropriate to utilize this equipment as my tableware. When the random occasion came to clean my kitchen, or if my dinner suddenly contained an unexplained flavor, I found myself relegated to merely scrubbing down one pot and one spoon. My wonderful wife referred to my style of war zone living as being a bear in a cave, or extreme tactical urban camping.

This may be a good time to discuss a serious problem that confronts everyone when they are deployed to a war zone—the "comfort food binge factor." You can't control yourself when confronted by this insidious dilemma; you can only hope to limit its effect. Take heed and beware— the chocolate chip cookies and dried fruit are waiting for you! When you're away from home with the daily stress and all the other unusual things around you, your body will start to build up a hidden craving for whatever it was you ate back home. You won't even be aware of this hidden craving, growing inside you until the time you're confronted by this beast. This time usually comes when you finally get a chance to go to the military PX. I have seen people literally stumble midstride when their eyes glanced on the chocolate chip cookies after having been deployed in a far-out region with no home-style cooking or familiar junk food available to them. What we consider to be junk food at home is pure gold in a war zone. It's food to the mind, body, and soul. It's that touch of home that's so far away. It's the reason for the trembling hands of the person who is grasping that prized package from its place on the sacred shelf of goodies at the PX. You overeat because you actually feel this compulsion you have to give in to because it brings you a little bit closer to the home that is so very far away. I remember seeing one of my colleagues sitting in his room slowly consuming three large boxes of American chocolate chip cookies with a liter of German drinking milk. The cookie wrappers and empty milk cartons were scattered all over his bed. (The transformation to his person was shocking. He could no longer speak in his native language and only emitted a low growling utterance to anyone who dared come too close to the cookies he was guarding with total viciousness.) He would rhythmically "grasp and consume" with one voracious chomp after another. It was a frightening scene that was and is repeated in every war zone the world over.

Not too dissimilar to the chocolate chip syndrome is the critical "chocolate candy bar compulsion." (My personal preference is a Snickers® bar.) This occurs when the victim is able to obtain an entire display box of this mind-numbing and thoroughly awesome candy. Once-strong officers have been known to become reclusive wrecks to the point of becoming like a human cocoon, living entirely on the chocolate bars for their total sustenance until the supply is exhausted.

Another common pitfall in comfort food binging is "the dried fruit dilemma." Back home this delicacy has a positive, nutritious nature but when this delectable delight is consumed in portions that are limited only by the size of the hands grabbing the maximum number of packages off the shelves there will be a problem. Just as the egg of a dragon will hatch to become a horror to the world, so too will the handful upon handful of gorged prunes "hatch" at a later time to wreaking their own unique lower digestive vengeance on their consumer.

For those of us who have returned from the different war zones of the world there are many stories of what we have seen and experienced because of the comfort food binge factor. Thousands of years ago in ancient China, great words of wisdom were spoken by an unnamed ruler. He stated that "food feeds not only the body but more importantly the soul of man." (I think he said that as he was finishing off a huge pepperoni pizza, a kilo of chocolate chip cookies, and a case of cold beer.)

$M^3 - EX = G + B$

There are few words to properly describe the feeling that takes over your body when you come home. From the very first moment you're in your home country it's like you are walking around half drooling with a giant menu in front of your face that only you and the small starving gremlin inside your stomach are able to see. This imaginary menu is all the foods you couldn't get back in the war zone, where you just existed for this moment when you returned back to the land of unlimited munchies. Here in your own country you wake up in the morning to the shocking sight of a gigantic food monster called a refrigerator. This enormous vault of delights and edible fantasies is bigger and better than you remember it to be. Back in the war zone you were doing well if you had a little refrigerator that was big enough to hold a shoebox full of vegetables, a big piece of frozen chicken, and whatever else you got from the local market. Sometimes there was something from the PX that was next to impossible to get to and then they didn't have anything good there. But that was okay because you just thought it was great to have a refrigerator and even better when you had something to put in it, and the best of all was when you actually had some electricity to make that little cooler function. And, now you can behold, touch, and even open the giant refrigerator of your dreams. You stand there in total awe at the little light that goes on and off telling you the electricity is running and the contents of this miracle are actually cold and even frozen. As you stare at this abundant selection you become as frozen solid as the contents of the freezer in front of you and you think, "What do I eat first and can I really demolish everything I see? It's going to take time, but if I just start at the top of the refrigerator I can make my way down to the bottom and consume everything before the sun sets on my broken belt."

Your day starts when you get up and have the breakfast of your dreams. The selection is so endless they actually have a separate menu for just breakfast when you go to a restaurant. Back in the war zone you ate what was there or what you could find as long as someone else didn't find it first, and that was about it. The next meal is brunch and that in itself is such a great idea. An extra meal to eat what wouldn't fit in your stomach at breakfast and a jump-start on all the great stuff you won't be able to eat for lunch. This is just like having a job as a king's taster. Of course, the next big chance to cover the table is the lunch you simply must go out somewhere with friends to consume. Not only do you lose track of the time but also the amount you are putting away. The evening meal now becomes not only your main munch time but also the gateway to a never-ending array of snacks you push into your once-denied mouth until you collapse and fall into a food-induced hibernation for the night. Friends and family know you haven't had some of these delectable morsels so they help by making sure every meal has at least one of "your favorites." And then there are all the times you meet up with an old friend to talk about what you did for the last year and there is always food and drink ... and more food and drink ... and drink.

Reality begins to set in. The first thing you notice is the belt that fit just fine a few days ago is getting a little tight. Perhaps you need to use a different notch? ... let it out a bit ... and then the belt is replaced and the smaller one is retired. (The surrendering of the belt can be a tremendously upsetting and demoralizing moment for any of us who yield to it.)

The next reminder of all the extra eating is the insidious bathroom scale. As the numbers come into view you realize the drastic change in your weight. You can't be this heavy; there is no way that this could be happening. The truth is this is a very normal problem and part of the readjustment to coming home from a war zone. "Over there" if you wanted to go from point A to point B you walked. On an average day you probably walked three or four miles (minimum). Now, the greatest distance you walk is from the television to the refrigerator. There is a very intricate mathematical equation to explain the condition you have become a victim of. It is the equation $M^3 - Ex = G + B$. To explain this to all chunky chow hounds, it breaks down to "Meals times three (daily) minus Exercise equals the size of your Gut and Butt." The main thing to remember is that it's always easier to eat less and stay active doing something you like than it is to lose the weight once you have packed it on. Don't worry—if you start to use a little self-control the day will come when you will be able to reclaim your favorite belt from its retired position on your bedroom chair. You may not be able to buckle it up using the same notch you did before the mission for a little while but if you stay on the "less chow and more exercise" program that day will come.

STRESS AND TASTE

You have just come back from being overseas in some war zone and you are now about to enjoy a wonderful celebration feast with friends and family. Your drink selection will be comprised of room temperature water. Your main course will consist of cardboard with side dishes of paper and other materials that will have no flavor or texture. As ludicrous and totally insane as this dining scenario sounds, there are many returning veterans who have this experience happen to them on a temporary basis. They have lost the ability to taste the very foods they looked forward to eating so much when they were overseas in their assigned war zone. A very common comment from a person who has sustained or endured a high level of stress is that "everything tastes gray." Some of these war zone veterans have been involved in severe conflicts and truly horrible situations while others can't even remember what has impacted them so much as to cause this predicament. This subtle repercussion of war zone stress usually goes unnoticed by not only the victims of this situation but also by the family and friends around them. Even those who interact with them on a day-to-day basis can't tell how bland their culinary world has become.

The loss of taste and its associated repercussions usually takes off in one of two different directions: you either gain a great deal of weight rather quickly or you drop weight like an anchor. You rapidly gain body weight from overeating because you can't taste the food. You eat and eat and eat as you search for the taste you longed for back in the war zone, but since you can't satisfy the taste you just keep eating to fill the void. You can't taste the food so you add spices; more salt and pepper on the cardboard but it still tastes like cardboard.

The other direction of this stress-induced loss of taste is when your appetite unfortunately shuts down because you can't enjoy what you are eating. If it all tastes like cardboard why even bother trying to chew it. The result is that you will start rapidly losing body weight, spiraling down to where you are shedding the pounds you need to maintain good health.

Part of the reason for this "stress and the lack of taste" issue is the situation of being subjected to a severely limited food selection back in the war zone. You were literally eating the same thing for breakfast, lunch, and dinner, day after day, for weeks and even months. Now you have so many choices it actually adds to the stress so by the time you finally decide what it is you want to eat you're no longer hungry. When I came back from my first mission in the war zone of the Balkans, I was treated to what was supposed to be a wonderful dining experience of leg of lamb with all the trimmings. If I would have had this opportunity just a year earlier I would have been more than impressed and willing to consume such a magnificent dinner, but coming from the world of goats this situation was less than desirable for me.

It's important to realize that lack of taste is very normal in any stress situation. As the stress level goes down your sense of taste will slowly start to rise and the heavenly aroma of your favorite food will once again make you hungry instead of nauseous. Talking to others who have served in war zones about how you feel can help. They understand what you are going through and have probably had their share of flavorless meals. Just talking to a sympathetic listener can bring down the stress and help with the adjustment of being home. Remember, you are the best judge of how you feel. There is no shame in getting professional help if it is needed. Just relax and make sure it doesn't add to your stress.

COFFEE AROUND THE WORLD

It's not where you are, but what happens to you while you are there. That saying has proven to be true most of the time for me. I have been in war zones when they were strangely quiet and nothing was happening. I have also been in transit between war zones where I've gotten into some rather serious situations.

I remember sitting in an old street-side café on a cobblestone street where my partner and I were waiting for our coffee to be brought to us. The beauty of that bright, sunny day hid the danger the streets held for me as an American. It was my first time passing through Istanbul and there had been several days of anti-American street riots and demonstrations in this beautiful, ancient city. The feeling in the air was more than tense when we walked past a government building with its display of flags from around the world. All of them were gently waving in the breeze except for the charred remains of the American flag that was barely hanging from its blackened post. My colleague and I were staying off the main streets where all the tourists were being attacked, trying to spend as much time as we could on the back streets. The narrow back streets looked like something out of an old black and white movie that was made in the 1930s about the Middle East. The truth is the streets we were walking on probably haven't changed since they were built much earlier than that. Being rather experienced foreign service officers with the United Nations

International Police Task Force we did the smart thing when out of our environment—we stayed low key and did our best to blend in with the local community.

We were taking a much needed break from our walking and figured a cup of coffee would give us some time to rest. We were sitting with our backs to the stone wall of a Turkish coffeehouse, facing the only door to the café. We were dressed casually in rather drab-colored clothes to blend into the surroundings. I spoke a little German and my colleague stayed with his native language of Russian. Speaking Russian and German in this local coffeehouse would be more than acceptable to any of the locals who might overhear us talking to the waiter while placing our order for coffee and "anything" to eat. Germans and Russians are both a part of the history of this region so hearing either language is common. Somewhere around 1917 many Russians immigrated to this area of the world during the unrest of the Russian Revolution. The Germans and Turks have long-standing trade agreements and the Germans have enjoyed visiting Turkey as one of their favorite holiday choices for decades. This boost to the Turkish economy sits very well with both the government and the local people. There are always reasons why some countries are strange bedfellows and some are not. You just have to look at the history of the nations and their interactions. I tend to explain most of the intrigues of the world with the very old perspective of "my enemy's friend is my enemy, and my enemy's enemy is my friend." This was not only a valid statement thousands of years ago when it was said in China; it is also deadly true today.

Due to my inexperience with the lethal concoction called Turkish coffee, I made a serious mistake when placing my order for this highly concentrated brew. I was using my hand gestures to explain that I wanted *nicht kleine, gross, bitte* (not small, big, please). My colleague was giving me a look that said he thought I had taken leave of my better judgment. When the waiter came to our table he set down a very small cup of coffee in front of my colleague that couldn't have contained any more that about four or five ounces of my favorite brew and food group. Then with a hesitant motion the waiter placed a big cup of coffee in front of me and said *"Sehr gut, mein freund?"* (Very good, my friend?) I got what I had asked for and replied to my kind host, *"Sehr gut, danke schön."* (Very good, thank you.) The waiter placed a large platter of assorted pastries that looked delicious on the old wooden table and took off for the back room kitchen as fast as he could. Without hesitation I took a large gulp of my big cup of coffee. With a red face and all

259

the self-control I could muster in my startled and semigagging state, I leaned over the old wooden table and declared a little bit too loudly, *"Scheiss, was ist das?"* (Shit, what is this?) I suddenly became aware that my comment was overheard by everyone in the café. The repercussion of my remark wasn't a problem; it was just a joke on me that resulted in quiet laughter from all the other customers in the little corner café. My smiling colleague asked in a very calm, quiet, and amused voice, "How is the taste of your big cup of coffee, my friend?" This was *not* coffee to me! This was evil black stuff, comprised of pure caffeine and the blacktop from the street. As we walked out of the café that afternoon I became aware of the fact that I was walking about 3 feet off the ground and had enough nervous energy to run a marathon race backward and forward. Much later that night I found it was hopeless for me to try to sleep, or do anything that required me to remain still. This day would go down in the chronicles of law enforcement as one of the only times I was unable to drink all the coffee served to me. It was just one more time in my international life I was reminded not to foolishly assume any similarities between my country's food and drink and what I was seeing on the international table of the world.

THE PANCAKE QUEST

For some of us the weekend morning ritual of a big pancake breakfast represents one of the most sacred dining moments known to civilization. Being so very far away from home makes whatever you can find that is in any way similar to what you left behind in your home country seem even more important to you. When the rumors of a new restaurant in town spread through the training center where I was deployed in the capital city of Pristina, Kosovo, we all came alive with hungry anticipation. Could it be true that we could actually have a local restaurant on this side of the world that served pancakes? Could it be true that we could actually feast on a delicious reminder of home on this side of the globe? The quest was on! With the efficiency of a tactical team on a mission we assembled in the training room and quickly mapped out our strategy for our "search and discover mission" to find the sacred site of all breakfast-related cuisine. Aggressive but cautious, we separated the possible areas of restaurant location into grid reference areas and committed ourselves to the personal deployment necessary to invade and seize control of these targeted sites. The hunt was on and we were determined to fulfill our mission objective before the next scheduled mealtime. Like a well-oiled machine we searched the streets, secured, and controlled the area. Utilizing all our tactical skills and experience honed in multiple war zones we located and staked out the cherished site of our dreams and desires.

There it was in all its glory—a life-size poster of a giant breakfast in the front window for all those who passed by to see. This was truly a spiritual moment in our quest for the heavenly pancakes. We entered this building with all the reverence of children going to church, and with the appropriate respect sought out our seats at a table. A waiter appeared and gave us the hallowed bill of fare. After a quick glance we requested "everything" listed under "breakfast" on the menu including our soon-to-be-eaten pancakes.

With moments seeming like hours we sat respectfully without even talking as we waited for our platters from paradise to be brought from the kitchen. As our long-awaited platters floated to our table, we were finally at the moment we had longed for. With dining utensils in hand we paused to gaze on the reward of our extensive efforts. The breakfast that had just been placed in front of us was nothing like the poster in the window of the restaurant. Having no firsthand knowledge of what an American breakfast was, the cook simply tried to copy the image from the poster hanging in the window. The long-desired pancakes turned out to be pieces of some unknown kind of dark bread that had the crust removed and were then carefully cut into circles. They were fried with the local salted goat sausage and piled up about four high. The mashed up, strangely lumpy potatoes were also fried in that same unique grease with the distinctive aroma of something I could never identify. The only good news on this platter that had been placed before me was the three duck eggs looked like they might be edible. As far as the distinctive composition, taste, and consistency of the semiwhite gravy, we all decided discretion was the most reasonable and safest path to take.

The kitchen staff and the waiters were all disappointed, and we were disappointed as well. We wanted to just click our boot heels together three times while saying "there's no food like home." But this wasn't just another bad dream we were experiencing. Unfortunately, it was a gastronomic reality. We left a few Euros on the table and left with our hunger and our hopes lost amid our fruitless efforts. The flame of our unfulfilled hunger for back-home food had been extinguished, as surely as if the white mystery gravy had been ladled over it.

261

PANCAKE CREATION

Undaunted by my past failures in my quest for the elusive American pancake, my stomach and I yielded to the growing obsession of creating my own pancake in this foreign land. My mind raced with wild ideas of how and where I could ever come up with all the ingredients I would need to achieve my incredible edible goal. The bulk of my task would be finding the proper batter ingredients or local substitutes that would not alter the flavor of this comfort food. The race was on, and I was sure I was up to this monumental task.

With a pocket full of German candy bars to use as barter or trade, I was off on my quest. The first stop in my search was a neighborhood farm where I had previously spotted some wonderful chickens running around. It didn't matter that they were being chased by a really ugly dog and that their meat was as tough as they were old. I wanted to use chicken eggs and not the usual duck eggs that were so prevalent in that area of the Balkans. With a little bartering and two small chocolate bars I got 10 assorted eggs that I quickly sank in a small tub of cold water right in front of the amazed farmer. He had never seen this test for fresh or safe eggs before in his life. He laughed and I smiled when the eggs didn't float, proving they were truly fresh. I was immediately and enthusiastically on my way in search for the rest of the pancake ingredients.

With the help of a French colleague in my training unit I was able to obtain two kilos of wonderful self-rising flour straight from his French PX. The price for this negotiated treasure was that I had to teach one of his classes for him. It was an easy trade for me because he was teaching a Ukrainian contingent class and they were always a great bunch of colleagues to work with.

I had already decided my pancakes would never (on the pain of death) be tainted with goats' milk so I was off and running to the German PX for some of their sterilized cows' milk. The saint of all pancakes must have been smiling on me because not only did I get a full liter of canned cows' milk and a kilo of cow butter, I also got two kilos of thick-sliced German smoked meat that was excellent for frying up in a pan just like regular American-style bacon. It was a little bit stronger to the taste but this was an acceptable substitution. Now I had everything I needed to create the masterpiece of masterpieces.

The one remaining absolute necessity had just arrived in my APO mail. My wonderful wife, Janet, had just sent two big containers of real maple syrup. I took one from its throne-like resting place in a secured kitchen cabinet in my accommodation and positioned it in a place of honor in the center of the kitchen table. I trembled when I envisioned this final ingredient to my future fantastic breakfast.

When the news spread that I was preparing pancakes with bacon, one and all were soon pouring into my accommodation with their forks and plates in hand. From the biggest to the smallest and the oldest to the youngest, everyone was in a festive mood. It was one of those times when old friends met and new friends were made. I spent the entire morning making pancakes and German bacon and the attitude was great. Many of my colleagues from other countries had heard about American-style pancakes but had never tried them. After that "flap-jack-filled morning" they were all believers in this outstanding culinary experience.

Some of the best times you will ever experience in a war zone are when you share something about yourself or something about your country with someone who has never had that type of experience before in his life. Whatever you chose to share is a window to better understanding between you and your colleague. We try to achieve peace and understanding in many ways, but one of the best ways I have found to be quite effective has been at the end of a fork.

WAR ZONE CUISINE

Janet Rail, United States

Stress can definitely affect your sense of taste. I have absolutely no idea what I ate on the plane the first time I went to see Bob in Bosnia. And with the amount of stress I had, it would not have mattered if it was filet mignon prepared by a famous chef or the cardboard box used to ship the steak. Under stress, everything tastes the same. This is why so many officers have major weight issues when they first arrive in a war zone. They will either eat too much because they can't taste the food or they stop eating because nothing tastes good.

The first thing I actually "tasted" was a fresh beet salad we had on the night I arrived. The landlord and landlady had a special dinner for us. I remember Bob's landlady patiently peeling the beets from her garden and grating them by hand to make the salad. Her hands were covered in the beet juice that was going to stain her weathered hands for days. The salad was beets and onions, a little oil and vinegar—very simple. It wasn't until later I found out from the girl that was Bob's neighbor that this salad was only served for special occasions.

If you like European breads, the Balkans is a great place to visit—golden brown, hard crust, and a creamy white center that just melts in your mouth. Bread is made fresh every day. For Americans who usually buy their bread in presliced packages with a three-week shelf life it can take a little getting used to having the grocer handing you an unwrapped loaf for you to put in your basket.

Coffee in the Balkans is a lot—A LOT! —stronger than American coffee. In both Bosnia and Kosovo coffee is a cross between demitasse and Turkish coffee. You quickly learn to ask for a glass of water with your cup of coffee so you can water down the dark syrup in your cup. In some of the restaurants, there was a thick residue in the bottom of the cup that was almost like a coffee pudding. Even the seasoned coffee drinkers would take a first, small sip from the cup and you could watch shivers go through their bodies as the caffeine rush hit their systems. By the time Bob was in Kosovo, cappuccino was the fashionable way to drink coffee. This was really great for two reasons. First, I do like cappuccino, and second, the coffee itself was not as strong. The best cup of cappuccino I have ever had was at a sidewalk café in downtown Pristina. The sad part of that is I know I will never be able to go back there for another cup of anything. A few months after I went back home someone walked by with a hand grenade and blew the little café into a thousand pieces.

Cold pasteurized and homogenized milk (that's cow's milk, not goat milk!) does not exist in any part of the Balkans I visited. You can buy sterilized or condensed milk in 1-liter cartons or canned milk, but there are no coolers full of gallons of dairy products. Most of the carbonated beverages we were used to in the United States are international brands so it was like finding a "comfort food" when we saw that familiar red and white can.

By the time I went back to visit Bob for a second stay in Sarajevo conditions were fairly stable and Bob had gotten to know the area a lot better. There was a very nice restaurant along the river with a big water wheel and a vine-covered terrace (grape vines full of fruit just waiting to ripen and be used) that was famous for its baked apple dessert. They served a big, red, beautiful apple that had been baked with a walnut, brown sugar filling that spilled out of the top where they had removed the core. I love apples of every kind but really dislike walnuts a lot so when Bob took me out for our romantic dinner we both tried in broken German and English to explain to the waiter how I would like a baked apple but no filling please.

At first the waiter seemed a little confused but all of a sudden he smiled and said, "Yes, yes—just apfel." We both smiled and said "yes," and a few minutes later Bob was served a warm, steaming apple with walnut filling and I was proudly presented a raw apple on a plate with a sharp knife. The waiter was so proud that he had figured out what I wanted I didn't have the heart to tell him he was wrong—the apple was very nice.

18

Bug Out

As casual as the term *bug out* sounds it's actually slang for "Get out now!" It simply means all hell has broken loose in the area of the war zone you are presently in and you are being directed by someone to drop everything and scramble to a prearranged safer area. Hopefully you noted I stated a "safer" area. Remember, when they call a place a war zone that means there are no safe areas. There are bad areas, very bad areas, red zones, green zones, and all kinds of names to describe the zones but they are still in a war zone. I have said it before and I will say it again—It's not where you are but what happens while you are there that matters. It may be reported on the evening news that on a certain quiet day only one bomb was detonated or only one bullet was fired, but as reassuring as that may sound it doesn't matter how quiet it was if you're the one who got blown up by the bomb or shot by the bullet. It doesn't always just happen to the other guy—it can happen to you. Remember: You are in the greatest danger when you start feeling relaxed and not caring about what's going on around you. You can and will become conditioned to the most severe circumstances if you live in that environment for any period of time. But when the "bug out" order comes down, do so!

The best time to plan for a bug out is before it happens when you don't need to gear up and run. When you actually need to get out of wherever you are is the very worst time to think about what you need to do because your thoughts will be clouded by the stress of the moment and you definitely will not be thinking clearly. The best time to do any planning for a bug out is when you can clearly think through the "entire" situation with a map and a cup of coffee on the table and an experienced friend looking over the logistics with you, pointing out the little things you are sure to miss—like, a vehicle? or weapon selection? Or who will be in the exit team and what will be the assigned task of each person on that team? Hopefully everyone on the team is starting from the same point and ending this unique trek at the same destination. Once the final plans have been made it's imperative that they are never considered "final." They need to be reviewed at least monthly with all the team members present. The two most critical and essential points you have to remember are you can never stop until you are at your destination, and you must maintain total flexibility in the commandeering or confiscating anything and everything necessary to complete your ultimate goal of safely reaching your selected destination. This is more than just a useful suggestion. It is the necessary mind-set you will need to survive.

I remember having to plan a bug out from the worst-case situation. I would need to escape from a crowded city environment, travel miles on unprotected open road toward the coastline of another country. I say worst-case situation because I knew I would have to commandeer a vehicle, and that's a nice way of putting it. Hopefully you end up with a running vehicle that has a full tank of fuel, filled with your partners who all have weapons, ammo, water, and candy bars.

Keep all the needed items somewhere in a secured area for a "grab and go" so you can just grab a bag or two and get the hell to where you have planned to be. Do not, I repeat, DO NOT! load up your vehicle with all your bags and needed gear. Remember, you are not the only one who will be looking to commandeer a much needed vehicle to survive and you may have to abandon your original vehicle for a "second choice" anywhere along the route. You are going to be running with your arms full to a vehicle that's long gone and you could very well end up standing there looking at an empty garage or parking space.

Whether you are planning a bug out by land (using a vehicle), or by air (using a helicopter or airplane), or by water (using a boat or major ship), the plan remains the same. Dedicate yourself to the task of planning the operation like your life depends on it, because it does! Plan every small detail with the input of your entire team and never tolerate anyone who skips a meeting without a good excuse (like being shot in the leg). Keep your mode of escape close to you. It does no good to plan on a boat taking you to safety if you can't get to the dock. All team members must be capable of taking over and running the bug out any time the designated leader becomes incapable for whatever reason. Never assume all team members know even the simplest or most minor of details. Rotate the leader of each monthly briefing session to guarantee all members are on the same track. And last but not least, designate a starting point with a head count and a final destination with a head count. I hope the numbers match some place where you have hot water, hot food, and something cold to drink. Be alert and stay supportive of each team member and you will accomplish your goal of a successful bug out to a "safer" place.

19

Lifestyle of Survival

It's the nature of every living creature on this Earth to survive and to live as long as it can even under the most horrific of circumstances. Even the smallest and gentlest of creatures will resist the onslaught of death and all that comes with this final loss. We have all been witness to the sight of a small animal being backed into a corner and then when it realizes it is facing its own demise it will fight for all it's worth to survive for yet another day. Every creature resists the time of its death and the place of its death. All creatures have the instinctive mind-set that the time of their death will be later and not now, and the place of their death will be somewhere else and not here. We are no different than the other creatures we share this Earth with. No matter how badly we thirst, or hunger, or bear our injuries, we still fight to survive for another day and another place to be.

The countryside of the Balkans is full of once beautiful homes and villas that have been destroyed by the recent conflict. It doesn't take much to imagine what it must have looked like in the days before the Balkan Wars that devastated this once beautiful nation. The tragic loss caused by the senselessness of war is almost overwhelming.

A typical Balkan's house would be a two- or three-story stone structure with a red tile roof. The first floor would have a living room or great room where family and guests would gather to celebrate the happy occasions or somber events. The warm welcoming kitchen would always be full of women preparing food to feed the body and soul of everyone who stopped by. Upstairs were the bedrooms and private spaces of the house but this level was filled with the circle of life and events that encompassed a warm and loving home. Now, rooms that once were alive with family

Figure 19.1   Nowhere to hide in this building.

and life are abandoned with only hanging electrical wires and water and gas pipes jutting out from the walls to remind us of happier times.

When you look closer at the shell of what was once a home you notice everything that was constructed of wood has been burned. It may have been used for heat for the family in the last days they lived here or it may be the result of arson. Too many homes were destroyed by fire to prevent the residents from returning to that part of the village. Moving through the doorway with its twisted door hinges sticking out all you can see is desolation. The heavy wooden door that gave the family security but opened wide to invite in guests is missing. Anything that could be stripped out of the house is gone. As you walk into the house the floor is covered with cracked and broken glass. Indentations in the stone walls of all the rooms tell us where and from what directions the bullets were fired. During the conflict the different militia groups would drive up and down the streets shooting into any windows that showed signs of life. If you were foolish enough to leave a light burning after dark it was almost guaranteed the light would be shot. Bullets are not forgiving. They will go through their intended target and anything else that's in their way until they lodge in the cold stone walls of the house. It was an eerie feeling to

Figure 19.2 This apartment complex can't be repaired until the land mines are removed.

have experienced officers tell you what type of gun made which type of hole in a deserted home.

It was easy to tell when a house had been reclaimed because the middle floor would have white sheets hanging over the openings for the windows. The sheets let in enough light so the family could see during the day but it gave privacy and protection for the children playing in that room. Unprotected or exposed children would be shot by the snipers and that was the brutally simple truth.

The middle floor or second floor was the safest area for the family to live. The street level was always subject to the drive-by snipers trying to kill someone—anyone, even a child. If you were lucky enough to have a cow or a few chickens you used the first floor for them. The animals needed some protection and a barn was out of the question. There were too many land mines to have to worry about walking back and forth to the barn, not to mention the risk of being shot as you left your house. The broken glass was swept off the floor, the animals were brought in, and a large bale of straw was rolled in from of the opening where the door once hung. The straw gave the animals both food and protection.

Figure 19.3   This building is already home for two separate families.

Figure 19.4   Land mines and other explosive devices are everywhere!

Figure 19.5   There is no roof, but people are living in this house.

Figure 19.6   A once beautiful villa waits for its owners to return.

Figure 19.7   One of many abandoned homes.

The top floor of the house was also a dangerous place for anyone to live. The official statements may have been that the war had ended but there were still plenty of mortars being fired from the cover of the surrounding hills. Sometimes these mortars would detonate on the roof, sending an avalanche of roofing tiles crashing to the ground. Sometimes they would detonate after they had fallen through the roof into the living area of the third floor. In either case, it was not good.

There were homes that looked like there was little to no damage to the structure but they were totally abandoned. It could have been because there was no one left to claim that property or it could have been because there were too many land mines in the field to the house to make it safe to return home. There were homes with huge gaping holes from mortar shells and thousands of tiny holes from bullets, but the one sheet of wood or carefully placed curtain told the world that the occupants were not going to let this war or any other conflict stop them from living their lives in their homeland.

20

Respect

There I was, standing at parade rest or otherwise called "at ease." My feet were spread approximately 12 inches apart with my hands clasped behind my back. My eyes were looking straight ahead and I was standing very erect and proper ... and sweating profusely under a very hot Balkan sun. Why was I doing this? What was going on? I was there to stand in line-style formation, respectfully waiting for the bodies of the dead German officers to pass by.

It all started as I was hurrying to the German mess hall to get lunch before it closed down. The German military base was a short drive on safe roads and whenever we had a free afternoon a group of us would go there for lunch. It was a secure location and the food was great. The only thing that could be a problem for us was you had to be on time. Lunch was served from 1130 to 1330—not one minute earlier and not one minute later, and that was just how it was. There are countless stories and humorous comments about German strictness. People say when the sun comes up in the morning it hesitates slightly on the horizon to make sure the German troops are already in morning formation on the parade grounds to make sure it's on time. Even German officers joked about their strictness but their dedication, competency, and discipline were never questioned by anyone.

As we rushed toward our lunch we ran into (almost literally) the German Deputy Contingent Commander. He was a tall gentleman with a very large handlebar moustache. His perfectly tailored green uniform was decorated with well-deserved metals and ribbons. The subtle scars by his eyes told us he was a lean and tough veteran who could obviously do everything he asked his troops to do. I remembered the German saying that honor and bravery are more appropriately displayed in scars and not metals. I did feel a little taken back when I glanced down for a split second to see my clean and polished black boots were totally outclassed by the commander's boots. His boots and other leather gear looked like mirrors that were wiped down with black paint. He spoke to us in perfect English, "Would you please honor our contingent by lining up on the street to salute the passing convoy carrying the officers' bodies that died on patrol in the nearby mountains of Sarajevo?" The German contingent was responsible for patrolling the mountains just outside Sarajevo. Sarajevo is in a valley between two sets of mountains so the weather in town can be quite nice while a blizzard is occurring on the mountainside. In the spring the weather can change at any time. Temperatures fluctuate greatly and the snow base becomes very unstable. Avalanches and snow slides become an almost daily event. The German officers had been told there was a chance the snow base was unstable and they could postpone their patrolling until the weather conditions improved. To the man, every officer decided it was their responsibility to patrol and that is what they were going to do. The halftrack made it most of the way up the road before the snow shifted, sending them and tons of snow crashing down the mountainside.

Before thought or any other considerations had time to enter my mind, I answered the commander, "Sir. Yes, Sir. My honor, Sir. My condolences to the German contingent and the families of the troops lost." There was no choice in the matter; respect was due. I walked over to the side of the road and took my place with other officers from many other countries. The respect we showed for the dead was a display to the living of how we felt and the honor we had in serving with them. I remember the West African promise—we all receive at our birth, a time to live and a place to die, and no one will ever know how long they will live or where they will find their end. For the German troops passing by us en route to the airport for their last deployment back to their home country, their promise was met and fulfilled. Their time to live ended yesterday in the service of peace to the world. I remember standing in line with numerous other respectful officers from many nations as the German funeral procession slowly passed by. The somber procession was led by the deceased troops' armored vehicles slowly pulling the deceased's caissons behind them. There were hundreds of officers who were standing on both sides of the roadway in the hot sun that day waiting for the caissons to pass by. None of us were prepared to stand there for the hour it took the funeral procession to go by. There were several officers who became faint from the heat and had to step back for a few moments, but all of them returned to the line without hesitation.

It was out of respect for the ultimate sacrifice these German troops made, out of the entire roadway of assembled officers from over 50 nations, not one officer broke from the formation or complained about the heat of the sun or the dust we were eating, or even looked at their watch. The only thing we were thinking about was that we were paying respect to these fallen colleagues. The final salute was given to the passing deceased as the caissons made their way slowly to the airport. For a brief moment I stood in awe of what was happening in front of me and all the thoughts ran like a river through my mind. As our final salute was done and the brave German troops were off to their final resting place of honor, I just stood there for a moment and stared over the dusty road, over the valley beyond the road, and up into the imposing sight of the snowcapped mountains that were the final site and stage for respect that was earned through courage.

21

The Cargo Net

I was sleeping so soundly I could have appeared to be dead to anyone who saw me hanging there, in the cargo net in the belly of the plane. I was swinging back and forth to the motion of the little (and quite old) two-engine cargo airplane on my way back from a mission. Natives refer to the part of the world I was in as the Middle East, but for me it was the middle of nowhere.

It wasn't the usual air travel most people think of in the civilized and sane world where you actually have seats, a pillow for your head, a blanket, and a snack and drink from the hospitality cart that someone is pushing up and down an aisle between the seats. My usual method of getting from here to there in and out of a war zone was crawling over cargo bags and crates, to find a space between all the mess so I could curl up like a cargo rat for a couple of hours. It might not be as luxurious as first class but there is no waiting in lines for hours and it could be a good way to get some rest.

This was my lucky day! As I was crawling over boxes and squeezing between crates I saw an extraordinary sight. There was a small cargo net hanging from the ceiling that had several boxes marked "fragile" in it. As tired as I was, this decision took no thought. Quick as a rabbit, I threw the boxes out of the cargo net and climbed into my deluxe sleeping arrangement. It was definitely a five-star accommodation. I was hungry and thirsty, and was so exhausted I could have slept standing up. I took a drink of water from my ever-present clean water bottle that was carefully tucked in my back pack and that was the last thing I remember. I woke up to the sound of the cargo plane's hatch door opening and the roar of the plane's idling engines. It was already sitting just off the runway, ready to take on more cargo. I had slept well and was now ready to eat anything and everything that crossed my path. I could continue my quest of getting back to my base by any imaginative means available.

As I sluggishly slid out of the plane's cargo door and dropped down several feet to the runway my stomach became aware of the fantastic aroma of food coming from a small café next to the airport reception and cargo building. Before I could say the words "excuse me," several men and women moved out of my way where they were standing around smoking and talking in the doorway of the restaurant. As I passed by them going through the doorway I stepped over the huge brown dog that was lying in the sun watching each person who passed by or entered. The people all stopped talking and turned away. Everyone avoided making any eye contact with me. My instincts and experience told me something was seriously wrong and I should be alert and on my guard. It's one thing to have people give you a mean look, or even a questioning look, but to look away from you and avoid any eye contact at all was something I wasn't used to and the feeling left me very uneasy to say the least. I did a fast "personal appearance inventory check" of how others might see me. I was fully clothed, appropriately dressed, semiclean. There were no answers from my quick checklist as to why I was being shunned.

As I entered the café I took a seat at a table with my back to the wall and a clear view of the only door in and out, which is my usual survival style. I noticed the couple that was sitting at the table next to me got up and moved across the room to another table. It wasn't that I was being treated badly; it was that I was being isolated for some unknown reason I couldn't comprehend or understand. Now I was more than just concerned. I didn't know if I would have to fight or leave, but I was far too hungry and didn't want to do either.

The next thing that happened was very strange and caught me totally off guard. My mind was trying to decide if I should be defensive or adversarial. I was trying to plan a strategy for either type of confrontation when the old lady wearing a white apron and hat that was taking lunch orders and doing the food service to the tables slowly and cautiously walked over to me with one of the kindest and most sympathetic looks a truly kind person could ever display on their face. She walked up beside me and very slowly and gently placed her hand on my shoulder. She gestured for me to stand up and follow her. With a rush of very mixed emotions I cautiously got up, looked around, and went with the waitress into the kitchen area of the restaurant. There I was seated at a nice little table between the grill and the wall. No sooner had I sat down than I was served a dish with a random selection of a little of everything that could be quickly fried including some kind of meat and potatoes and sliced tomatoes. I ate quickly to stave off my hunger. The food was hot and tasted good. After I finished I guardedly walked into the little bathroom of the kitchen area while everyone in the kitchen just very politely smiled at me and very kindly nodded approval at my actions like I was a small child who was doing the right thing. I made the usual overseas mistake of shutting the bathroom door before I turned on the light and that resulted in my fumbling around looking for any light switch before the old style pull chain switch brushed across my face in the darkness. With a deep sigh of relief I pulled on the switch and turned on the lone bare light bulb in the ceiling. Like a bolt of lightning, in a split second moment of total shock and disbelief, I saw myself in the dirty cracked mirror of the kitchen lavatory and my answer to why I was being treated so strangely by everyone was revealed. There, shouting to me from the mirror was the reflection of a severely grotesque and scarred person with a hideous interweave of disfigurement scars on the left side of his face. I never realized that when I woke up from my hours of deep sleep in the cargo net the pattern of the net had left its temporary but hideous pattern deeply imprinted on the left side of my face.

With a deep sigh of relief I just stood there for a moment, leaning on the sink and thinking about all the different reactions I had received from all the people I had just randomly encountered. The next several minutes were spent rubbing out the unique pattern on my face with the ice cold tap water in the sink. Warm water to the sinks isn't available in most areas of the world so you get used to cold water washing and that's just the way it is. There was quiet knocking on the door and my compassionate friend the waitress was asking, "Man ok? Man ok?" When I opened the bathroom door she and her colleagues in the kitchen were astonished, stunned, and happily surprised. I gestured to everyone that I had rubbed and washed my face. The waitress reached out and touched my face. Then with a big smile on her face she proceeded to give me a very big grandmother-type pinch on my previously "maimed" left cheek. I am not sure what was being said about me in the local language but the mood of everyone within the sound of the waitress's voice relaxed as they breathed sighs of relief. The people started looking me and no one was turning away. The quiet conversation sounded happy and not like hushed whispers of something being wrong. There was also a mute sigh of relief from deep within me.

I left the café by stepping over the same old brown dog that was lying contently in the sun of the doorway, and he gave me the same snort sound as a goodbye that he had given me when I stepped over him to enter the café a short time before. The obvious deformity I displayed when entering the café meant nothing to the dog in the doorway. In the eyes of the dog I was just another person who had come and gone, and what I appeared to be was not as important as who I was. I left the café with gratitude for the kindness of the old waitress lady and respect for the lesson I learned from a dog.

22

The Shared Loss

Wednesday evenings were unique for all of us with the International Police Task Force. We would gather at the house my partner and I were renting in the Sarajevo area for another great night of just relaxing and being together. All our partners from so many different countries would start showing up about 5:30 or 6:00 in the evening. This special time would always be dedicated to absolutely anything anyone wanted to talk about or ask about. There were no rules or imposed restrictions on what was brought into the house, whether it was carried into the house in their hands or carried into the house in their hearts. For these precious few hours our home was a safe haven where fellow officers could unwind and unload whatever had built up in them or had burdened them so heavily it needed to be shared with fellow officers who cared enough to listen. We were all together—we were away from our own countries and our homes and families, but for this evening in the week we shared everything that was on our minds and in our hearts with fellow officers who would understand. We were all in the same situation with insane circumstances and on this night of the week we were truly one big family.

Everyone brought whatever they could to the evening gathering, but if they weren't able to bring something, that was alright as well. The most important thing to all of us was that everyone just took the time to come to our gathering. Everyone was welcomed. Most of the officers of the different countries brought whatever was special from their nation or region in their country. These very special contributions to the night's festivities were brought with the feeling of a special pride for their country and what it had to offer. The French officers would proudly come bearing bottles of first-rate red and white wines from the famous vineyards deep in the French countryside. Most of the time there were minor friendly arguments between the different French officers as to which wines were superior and which region was superior because of the wine it produced. A couple of my colleagues and I would take an "instigating interest" in their wine arguments so we would be involved in the soon-to-be "wine-tasting contest" that would inevitably be the best way to resolve the encouraged arguments. (It was always great to have the opportunity to be an international referee for the red or white wine debate. It was a tough job but someone had to do it.) We also did our best to instigate the same situation between the Germans when they showed up at the house with their sausages. For the weeks and months these wonderful Wednesday nights went on, we rarely ever saw a repeat of the same type of German sausages being proudly displayed and cut up on the table. The old land-lord who didn't speak very much English was one of the few people who knew what was going on with the fun and games of the Wednesday eve-nings. He would just come into our little meeting room and put the out-standing locally baked, still warm breads on the table with all the other contributions for the evening and then tap me on my stomach on his way out as he laughingly would say, "You no talk, just eat." He was so right. The Russians would come with several different types of red and black incredible caviar, and one very cold bottle of vodka. They would then explain the proper method of slicing the bread, then buttering the bread (with cow butter, not goat butter), and finely spreading the caviar over the butter turning ordinary bread and fish eggs into an indescrib-able delight. They would personally demonstrate the proper procedure for eating the bread and then sipping the vodka. When we tried to tempt them into a contest about which caviar was best, the red or the black, they would just tactfully smile and say, "Whatever you enjoy, *moi druk*" (my friend). As much as we shrewdly tried we could never get the Russians into the same contests we did with the French and the Germans. The Russians knew if the bread was heavily buttered it would coat the throat and the vodka wouldn't burn as it went down the throat. It was an easy way to get someone drunk very quickly, if not out cold. It wasn't done to be mean or to cause trouble. The philosophy was if their partner needed "some good rest" they would help. After the friend passed out they would just cover him with a warm thick blanket wherever he was and let him sleep it off for the night. This situation occurred more than once on our Wednesday nights and there were many Thursday mornings where we had a confused and slightly ill guest for breakfast. Sometimes I think with all the fun we were having with the Germans, French, Russians, and other countries, they were having just as much or more fun playing their own games with us. But no one really cared because it wasn't malicious. We were friends, close friends—we were all together and for those few brief hours we could forget where we were and what was going on in the war zone around us.

One unusually warm Sarajevo fall night, one of the Germans started talking about the type of rifle his uncle carried in World War II, and how it was very well machined and crafted, and never malfunctioned like a lot of the mass-produced newer rifles do today. One of the Russians who was sitting on the other side of the room also spoke up about his grandfather and that he too had a very reliable rifle that he prized very much until the day he died in combat. He had served in World War II as well. The German officer then inquired as to where the Russian officer's grandfather was deployed and when it was he died in combat. When the Russian officer said the name of the town we could see the expression on the face of the German officer become coldly amazed. We all sensed something extremely significant had just happened in the room. There were usually two or three conversations going on at the same time but now everybody stopped talking. The German officer very quietly told the Russian officer his uncle had also lost his life in combat in the very same town. Nobody said anything and nobody moved a muscle. We didn't know what was going to happen next. Then, to the total amazement of everyone in the room, the Russian and the German officers both gradually got up and met each other at the food table in the center of the room. They both placed their hands on each other's shoulders and talked in quiet voices, nodding their heads at each other's words. We didn't know what they were saying to each other but we did know it was very personal and confidential. It was their moment and the rest of us didn't need to be involved. We all respectfully let the two of them reach out and touch the past through the shared memories of each other's families. All the other guests in the room slowly restarted their usual Wednesday night conversations while the German and the Russian sat and talked as if they were alone in the room and perhaps alone to the rest of the world.

The combat of the past between two nations was now being shared with understanding and compassion. Both countries suffered loss and all families felt pain. Countries that had once fought each other were now serving together in the name of peace. Two men who could have been enemies were now colleagues and friends. We left them alone to catch up on the 50 years that had just been washed away from between them. For the rest of the night and into the early morning hours they sat in the side of the room, close to each other, and talked. This was a night I never, in my wildest dreams, could have ever thought would occur but it is also a night I will never forget.

23

Two Promises of Death

The dead do not suffer pain, or any of the other burdens of the living, or even the bitter apprehension for what the uncertain future holds for them. For the dead, they have already received the two things that are promised to all of us whether we are rich or poor, powerful or weak. From the moment we are born, we are all promised two things—"a place to die and a time to die." None of us knows how long we have to live on this world and we will never know where we will be ending our existence as we journey through life.

The two promises of death are very different for those of us who are deployed to a war zone and those who are born into that unpredictable environment. For the officers, we know there is conflict, but there is always an "end of mission" and an escape from the war zone. For the local people who survive day by day in a war zone they know their time is severely limited by the threats of their surroundings, and the "where" of their future demise is restricted to the war zone they are constrained to living in. The people who survive moment to moment, clinging to the thin thread of hope that barely sustains any optimism they could have, know full well that their place of death, with great probability, will be where they are, and the time of their death will most likely be sooner than later. I deeply believe the saying that hope is the last thing to die in the heart and mind of any person in this world. I know this because I have seen the look in the eyes of people who thought they were without hope and their eyes were truly as dead looking to me as the eyes of those I have seen who were actually dead. There is no life without hope, and without hope life is without meaning and soon fades.

For those of us who are deployed to a war zone environment, there is one critical and overwhelming factor we all constantly have on our minds that the locals do not have. When our time in this piece of hell on Earth is over we will be going home to the life we left behind. Unfortunately, the locals are already home and their place on Earth is in the hell of a war zone. The officers' time in a war zone ends when their mission deployment time is over; the time spent in a war zone for a local person is over when they are dead. This sounds very blunt and to the point, but that is the rudimentary reality of existence and death in the war zone.

Once death occurs by whatever means or method, the story of that life is finished. Whatever they sought to accomplish has ended as abruptly as their life, and now their legend will be the only comfort found in their death. Just as they lived within a social or cultural system, so too will their memory live on through customs that involve not only their last remains but also the very lives of the people they once touched and embraced. In my travels throughout this Earth I have seen death in countless ways and forms, and have come to the conclusion that many times the way people treat the dead reveals how they themselves wish to be treated, remembered, or revenged when the time comes that they depart this world of ours.

In most of the countries of the Middle East the family of the deceased makes a sincere effort to intern the dearly departed as soon as possible. Because of religious beliefs most are buried the very next day after they die. I have noticed most of the traditions that are practiced today are based on customs from the past that were dictated from both wisdom and necessity. Disease was and still is one of the most telling factors in death rituals that are practiced all over the world. It is very frightening to consider the danger of disease spreading throughout the living because of the dead. Disease from improper handling of the dead is the reason for the majority of the laws and customs on entombment adhered to by the world over to this day. The problem arises when the laws that have been established for the public good are either suspended or totally ignored when the local society is plunged into the conflict of a war zone with all its related problems. When the main focus of the living is based on just staying alive, there is little thought given to the internment of the dead.

In the Kosovo area of the Balkans, the dilemmas of water, burial, and disease came into horrific conflict and are still a severe problem to this day. People living in this region are destined to live with this predicament for generations to come. During the hostilities in this area, the dead were handled with all necessary expediency. Whether they were the remains of the poor or the well to do, they were quickly buried into any available ground. There were so many dead during the conflict and with few or no caskets available, or proper areas open for burial, any type of ground was used to put the dead to rest, ignoring the horrors of their actions on the future. These desperate people were coping with the burden of the dead among them in the only way they knew. When a person died, by whatever means, they were buried with the emphasis on efficiency and swiftness. The bodies were washed and quickly but lovingly placed into their favorite clothing. They were then wrapped into a sheet or blanket because that was all that was available. There was no time or money for a special casket or burial shroud for their last resting place on this Earth. Following all the proper religious customs and cultural traditions the wrapped body was then placed into a hastily dug shallow grave. Typically this burial site was barely one meter (three feet) deep in the rocky ground that would be their final resting place. What the local people did not realize was the deceased had now become a problem for the living. It was far too late when the consequences of their actions were realized. The bodies of hundreds if not thousands of the deceased were buried in shallow graves over the top of the existing water lines. Most of these bodies were in shallow, unmarked graves to prevent grave robbers from digging up the remains to steal anything they could—a small gold band from their finger, or the metal fillings in their teeth, even the very clothes they were buried in. As far as the water lines were concerned, the records of their location were long since lost or burned during the conflict in that region and the problems of seepage were so widespread it would be impossible to trace all of them. There was no way to correct the monumental problem that had been building up unseen in the ground for years. The water systems were old and constantly leaking into the surrounding ground. The water pumps would be turned on and off for routine repair and the pressure would fluctuate drastically. The water in the surrounding soil would leech or seep back into the pipes when the pressure in the pipes was low. As the hastily wrapped bodies rotted in the ground and the rainwater pushed the remains down toward the decade-old piping, the problems of disease and putrefied water became obvious. The putrefaction of the corpse's remains was seeping into the old water lines and then journeying into all the kitchens and bathrooms in all of the houses in the area. Please don't take this as merely a suggestion between you and me; this is an order from me to you whether I have the authority to say it or not! "Do not drink the local piped-in tap water wherever you go in any war zone!" Remember, the problem is not in just drinking the water. It also pertains to using the local water to wash the food you are cooking and eating. Water has to be brought up to a full boil before it can be consumed. Don't just simmer the water when making tea or coffee—better yet use bottled water. Make sure you use bottled water when brushing your teeth. Remember to order gas water and listen carefully as it is opened at your table when eating at a local restaurant.

A very important custom in the Balkans that needs to be understood is the tradition of the empty chair. When a person dies the family will place a chair in front of the residence where the deceased lived, usually by the street or the roadway that runs by the house. They don't run an advertisement in a local paper or make a press release to any local media like is done in many other places in the world. The matter is handled at a very local and personal level. The body of the deceased is usually prepared and interned by family or friends of the family somewhere on the family grounds. This is because some of these families have a tradition of digging up the remains of the deceased after seven years. They clean the bones of their loved one and then place the bones in a final grave site. The empty chair that is placed in front of the house is usually left there for a couple of days to a week or more depending on the wishes of the family of the deceased. If you do see an empty chair outside a residence, don't sit in the chair! I have no idea what the result would be to this mis-gesture because I have never been stupid enough to do it, but I don't think the resulting actions of the bereaved family would be favorable. The best thing to do when you are unsure of a situation is to respectfully stand around for a few minutes to see if someone else will give you a clue to what your action should be—or better yet, just leave the area. If you do choose to stand around you will probably be greeted by a representative for the family who will quite likely invite you into the residence for a cup of tea or a drink of Balkan whisky and a story about the person the empty chair is honoring.

Throughout the world the customs and traditions surrounding the dead are as varied as the countries and people who live in them, but the one part of every tradition that is the same is the respect that is shown for the person who has ended his or her journey.

24

"Courtesy"

We are not talking about a good-looking dog—the kind that when it walks down the street people stop and smile and say something nice about the pooch and want to hold it in their arms or tenderly pet it. This is not a dog people stop and take pictures of. There is no posing with their children and babies. We are not talking about a dog that is the biggest in size, or has long silken flowing hair to attract attention. We're talking about the highly respected pit bull. I will grant you that this is not the most appealing creature to look at or that it doesn't send people with children running in the opposite direction when they meet in public, but it does have its own blunt charm. This is a dog that has its own self-imposed code of conduct to follow, from its birth to its burial under its favorite tree. Strutting down the sidewalk of life, this unique creature seeks only to eat when it is hungry, to sleep when it's tired, and to be ready, willing and extremely able to fight when confronted. Other dogs know all too well not to aggravate a pit bull. I would consider this member of the canine community to be the most deserving of courtesy, if not a good measure of respectful distance.

There are essentially two different kinds of courtesy that are given as a gesture when people meet each other. The first is common courtesy—the random and shallow gestures that are displayed when meeting someone. The other form of courtesy is far more in depth and comes from a far different perspective of the person. It is based on actual knowledge of that person. It can stem from either fear or respect, and in many cases it can be both. What's important to remember is any "attitude" is in the eye of the beholder. If I'm the person who owns the pit bull then I'm comfortable with his presence at my feet, but if the pit bull is yours then I will be courteous and a little bit apprehensive in his presence. Whether it's the English villagers from long ago running from the ocean side when the Viking ships were landing on their beach, or the neighbor quickly crossing the street to get away from an oncoming pit bull strutting toward them, their reputation commands courtesy.

It was a few minutes before 9:00 A.M. and I was quickly walking down the hallway, already covered in sweat. My morning class at the officer's college in Baghdad, Iraq, was teaching interrogation and interview. It was going to be a blistering hot day because it was already miserably hot and it was still early in the morning. I was just hoping that the stupid air conditioner was working for a change. Maybe that was asking just too much for a place like this ... on this side of the world ... in this war zone ... but there was hope. When I turned the corner to walk down the hall toward my classroom, out of nowhere there he was. He was an image like few I had ever seen in my life. His presence conveyed pure power and strength, and he knew just how powerful he really was. Unfortunately so did I. He was, in every sense of the word, a human pit bull. This Iraqi *shorta* (police officer) was about my height but he outweighed me by at least 20 pounds, and that 20 pounds was all muscle and power. I had the advantage of being about 40 years older than he was. This was truly an advantage in this culture because it is very respectful of age and experience. I was introduced to my powerful new pit bull friend by one of my classroom students, and further advised through my student who was acting as an interpreter that this powerful *shorta* had great respect for me. The *shorta* told me of his respect for me as the American Scot who had done all the various hand strength exhibitions for my classes. He said that he also had a modest level of hand strength himself and would be much honored to test his modest level of power against mine, with great respect. I now had no other choice in the matter but to take this little powerhouse on. It was always better to do so with respect and humility, as is their custom in this part of the world. (It is always best to never stop learning about the local culture no matter where it is you have been deployed.) The greater a person's strength or ability in this society the more self-disparaging and overly polite they are. I followed this custom by saying what a great honor it would be for me as an old weak and feeble man to lock hands with such a strong and esteemed *shorta* from such a respected family and tribe. (In Iraq, the family and the tribe a person belongs to are always a matter of great respect and honor.) A growing circle was developing around us as the word of this polite and informal challenge spread throughout the classrooms to most of the school. Two chairs were brought out to us. A chair was placed

Figure 24.1 Iraqi *shorta*. Identity of persons in photo concealed due to death threats.

Figure 24.2 My "courteous" friend. Identity concealed due to death threat.

behind each of us as we were facing each other in a standing position. We then interlaced our fingers with each other's hands. The concept is quite simple. We both try to bend back the other's hands causing the loser to sit down in the chair that has been placed behind him. In the United States this challenge of strength is called "Mercy." The only difference is there are no chairs and the goal is to force your opponent to his knees. In Iraq it is called "Courtesy." You are being courteous by having the other person sit down first and that's exactly what we were going to try to do to each other. We both, very politely, secured a firm grip on each other's hands and then respectfully nodded at each other. I thought it would be a long shot to win or even endure against this pit bull of a man. I knew the far greater exhibition would be displaying respect and comradeship to my brother *shorta* I was about to go full force with. It was important to win this contest but far more important to compete with principle, reverence, and respect. It was important to both of us what our colleagues who were watching would think of us when this test was done. As I waited for the word *yella* (now), I realized my *shorta* friend was slowly applying pressure to his grip. I looked up and there was a discreet smile on his face. I slowly but firmly matched his force and decided not to try to go all out too early in this game. I had to plan a strategy so I didn't burn out too soon. I knew it was too much to hope for but I desperately wanted to see his knees buckle under the force of my hands.

To my amazement, it was starting to look like we were in a dead-lock match. Now the trash talk began; my powerful friend started first. When I say "trash talk" or remarks made during competition, you have to be aware that the Muslim society prides itself on being very formal and respectful. The comments were the opposite of what the rest of the world would expect to hear in our little competition. With a growing smile on his face my *shorta* brother said, "*Afwan yordee, eglis yah ah*" (excuse me please, sit my brother). In the background I could hear the supporters of my *shorta* brother starting a very polite but growing chant of *yordee yajlis* (please sit). My reply to his very kind invitation to sit down was to say, "*La yah ah, entay yordee yajlis yella*" (no thank you, sir, you please sit now). Amid a sea of good-natured respectful involvement and laughing and cheering I could hear chants and comments and repeated invitations for both of us to sit down. Then, to my surprise, in the background I could hear, "*Abyad, abyad, abyad,*" as several of the spectators were pointing and almost touching our locked and shaking hands. At first I was confused because they were saying "white, white, white," and then I saw what they were pointing at. We were both putting so much pressure on each other's hands we squeezed the blood out of our hands and they were turning white. After a couple of times of each of us gaining and then losing the advantage, a strange thing took place. The fellow officers and students who were rooting for us took over the outcome of the match. We were both picked up off of our feet and forcefully pulled apart. This was a great relief to me and to my totally fatigued hands. In this culture we had been honored and cheered on as equals and that made us true brothers. I was relieved and elated with not only the outcome but also with having a new (and may I add formidable) brother.

It turned out this *shorta* was not just a brother in name only. There were many times when we would meet for a cup of hot tea or cool water. Sharing anything with my new brother was an excellent custom. It was always a great moment when we remembered our contest with the appropriate pride and compliments flowing freely to each other. When the time came I was to be deployed home, he was as close to me as a blood brother and tears were shed over a final cup of *chi* (tea). To this day I don't know if this pit bull *shorta* is alive or dead, so in respect to him and to the culture and beliefs of his tribe I will say as I always do when I speak of this man, "May peace be upon him."

It is not how different we are from each other but what we can search out and find between us that we have in common. If we focus on that which is different we will have little trouble finding something to separate us.

25

Returning Back Home

My "brother" is someone you may or may not have ever met in your life. My brother is not a man or a woman who is blood-related to me. He is related to me by his willingness to shed his blood unhesitatingly for me, as I would do for him. I can't explain this bond between all of us that transcends the customary and typical feelings that most casually consider valid in a friend, because I don't understand it all myself. It's not something that you comprehend but more of what you feel and know that the same feeling, without words that are expressed, is within the other person as well. It's like being as one with all of the good and the bad in concert, and words are not even needed to be spoken between us much of the time. It means never having to look behind you to see if you are covered, and covering the back of your partner without being asked or thinking about the consequences to yourself. It's not based on the time we spend together but where that time has been spent, and the desperate conditions or insane circumstances that cemented the bond between all of us. There was no race or gender or religion or politics or other chosen veneer between us. These meaningless layers were burned off very quickly and when there was nothing left to separate us from one another, we became as one with our blood, our laughter, and our pain now being the same because of all we shared. We are like a protective shadow to each other, like a safe harbor of darkness where we can hide from the world and even our own thoughts. We didn't have to look down to know that our shadow was there. At night we knew all the world was our shadow. The shadow is my brother and I am his shadow.

When you have earned every grain of sand in the hourglass of your deployment time and your time is up, and you have filled out enough end-of-mission deployment report forms to wallpaper an entire room, you leave the war zone and finally come home to where you think you belong. With that rush of long-awaited emotions, this is one of the most indescribable and wonderful moments you will ever experience. But now you feel that you are alone because of how you have changed from what you used to be. Alone, because you have left your partners so very far behind and away from where you are now. It's so very great to see and hold all of your loved ones—those you have missed so much and worried about every day you were so far apart from them in the war zone … but they don't understand your constant fear for their safety, and you still feel that you are alone and apart from those you were once with. You want to tell your family so much of all the things that are on your mind but you know they won't understand the world you have just come from or maybe they don't want to understand, so you remain silent about all the coming home conflicts and confusion that are inside of you, and you still feel alone. With shuddering hands you once again taste the incredible food, like steak and ice cream and anything cold to drink, but you still feel like you are alone. You sleep in a bed so comfortable you can't believe it, but you still wake up and find yourself alone. You sit at a table and don't have to eat out of a plastic, military ration bag with food that will taste and look the same today and next year, and are served dinner on a plate and eat with real spoons and forks. But your mind dwells on what your partners back in the war zone are eating or not being able to eat, and you're alone. You can go anywhere and do anything you want to do without paperwork, restrictions, written orders, and passes, but you restlessly walk anywhere and everywhere alone, not even remembering where you have been walking or where you are going. You pace around in total awe when you're at the local supermarket and can't believe all there is on the shelves for you to buy. One aisle of the store you are now in would dwarf the entire PX back in the war zone. There you had to use ration cards, or trade-offs, and wait in lines, and still considered yourself lucky to have even made it into the gate to be there, but you feel alone in this big store that has more than you need, more than you or your former partners could even remember. You go from channel to channel on the television, hearing the stories from the all-knowing "insightful" experts about what it's like to be where you have just come from, but you remember the hard truth and feel like you are the only one at home who knows what's actually going on over there in the war zone and

300

feel so alone because there is no one here you can share your thoughts with that will understand. The politicians and news commentators fly in and out of highly protected "safe areas" that have every comfort and luxury known to man let alone a war zone, and yet they still complain about how tough it was for them to be in an area where you would have considered it a holiday to be there. You hear the manipulated, in-depth, twisted reports, from those who were only there just long enough to get dust on their feet. With their special culled insights obtained, they leave to go back to our country and promote their version of what is going on at the expense of the blood, sweat, and pain of those remaining back where you have just come home from. However, even the bitterly hard fought accomplishments of so many dedicated individuals are relegated to a worldwide interruption on all news programs to report the death of any notable drugged out rock star or other significant socialite or politi-cal event. During those days when society news holds higher priorities, all reporting of the war and sacrifice ends for that media moment. You listen to all of the remarks and opinions and complaining from all of the people who know everything about where you have been and what they think you have done, or should have done. You just take a deep, controlled breath and let the anger and depressions build within you, because there is no place for it all to go, and no partners here—back home—to talk to about everything that is so upsetting for you to think about. You care about some of these people more than the words they say offend and hurt you, so you just let their remarks and conversation flow through the burning embers of your heart and mind. They ask, "Is everything all right?" "Something wrong?" "Thank you for your ser-vice." "Great being back?" But you feel like their words are being asked to some other person who's hiding inside of you. You think now and then about those who will not be coming home or those who have been so badly hurt, and after a deep sigh of relief that you returned home in one piece, there is the thought forever in your mind about the loss that others have suffered.

You feel alone because your war zone partners are back in that place where you have just come from and that's still in your mind every moment. Time does help, and having someone to just talk to during the bad moods and moments means everything in the world. All of the things that hap-pened in the war zone were things and conditions that were dealt with or worked out, no matter how bad it was. It was just handled in some way, and it got done, because we were there together. But here, I am alone in a crowd. Here, I have trouble hearing the music others take pleasure in.

The humor that I see and hear is no longer funny to me. Here, what others touch I can't feel. I know that something is missing or gone that was once within me, but I only feel the emptiness I know is in me here at home. All I know is that something is gone, and I know it was left back there where I have just come from. Back in the war zone I was whole and complete, but here, back with all the people and things I longed to be with for so very long, I realize that not all of me has returned home.

The person who goes off to the war zone is gone forever, and the person who returns is a different person. That person does not even know or fully understand what has happened to him. Time is the great healer and, hopefully, slowly the two become one again, stronger and more secure than either identity ever was by itself.

SWEET DREAMS

Janet Rail, United States

When I was a little girl, I remember watching my father take a nap and in the middle of it he started twitching and moving around in his sleep. I was going to wake him up because I thought something was wrong but my mother stopped me. She said, "Let him sleep. Sometimes it's better not to remember a dream." This happened more than once and the answer was always the same. Mom would always calmly lead me away so my dad could finish his nap undisturbed. When I was older I finally asked my mom what she meant and what my father was dreaming about that was so bad. The simple answer—"The War." Dad served in the U.S. Army during World War II. He was part of the 1st Division (the Big Red 1), and even though he is very proud of his service and what he did he never spoke to me about any of it. I was a child—and a girl—and back then, you just didn't talk about things like that. I knew he drove an ammo truck and spent a lot of time in Germany but while we were children the details were very sketchy. I'm sure my dad was involved in a lot of things that would give anyone nightmares but he never said anything to us. It wasn't until my older brother entered the military that my father talked to us about his time overseas, and even then, most of what I learned was good memories and things that would not be upsetting to anyone. The "nightmares" of the war remained unspoken.

When Bob came home from his first mission in Bosnia there was more than one time he started twitching and moving around in his sleep.

Laying there next to him I started to instinctively reach out to him to wake him up ... but then I heard my mother's voice calmly say, "Let him sleep. Sometimes it's better not to remember a dream." I would lie there, not moving because I didn't want anything to wake him up and I would wait until he would stop moving around. I would gently reassure him that he was home and everything was okay. Sometimes he would wake up and sometimes he would sleep through the whispers but I always noticed his body starting to relax. Most of the time, he would be able to go back to sleeping peacefully. Even after you are thousands of miles away from the fighting, the war can sneak up on you.

After Bob had been home awhile, the nights of rough dreams became fewer and farther apart, but when he returned home from Kosovo and Iraq once again the nightmare of the war came home with him. Talking about things during the day helped make the nights much better. The military calls it debriefing but just "listening" can be very helpful for both the returning soldier and the family that is waiting for them. Most of the time, the thoughts being recalled were random—good things and bad things all mixed together. Stress can do that to your memories and there aren't many more stressful situations than being in a war zone. Sometimes it would be the same story he told me the week before and sometimes it would be all new information. What was important for me to remember was that Bob wasn't trying to hide information from me. He honestly had forgotten about some incident until that moment. There were things that happened in Bosnia that he remembered after he came home from Iraq. Watching the news reports just before going to bed definitely did not help! And it didn't have to be news about the war. It could be something that seemed totally innocent about an event that happened in a small town near home but there could be "something" that reminded him of something that happened "over there" and the floodgates of his memories were opened.

Time is truly the great healer. As the days turn into years the number of nights the war sneaks back into Bob's dreams are less and less and this is good. Sometimes I wonder after all these years if my dad still has nights when the war sneaks back into his bedroom.

26

International Sayings

As my thoughts drift back in time I remember being in the training head-quarters that were located in Sarajevo, Bosnia. I was sitting at my desk, reviewing my notes for teaching my next class of officers and consuming my favorite beverage of coffee when there was a polite but very strong series of three knocks on the frame of my open office door. It was one of my fellow officer instructors from Bulgaria. In a quiet voice he asked, "Robert, very please, help now ok?" He had a look of total frustration on his face and a memo in his hand from a Brazilian officer. It looked like it was going to be just another normal day in the international stew of the United Nations Police Task Force, and I loved every minute of the daily misunderstanding fiasco.

As I read over the memo with my rather huge colleague towering over my shoulder, I babbled out the phrase "this is all Greek to me!" The fate of the timing was perfect. Just as I had made my frustrated remark one of our colleagues from yet another country was walking down the hallway by my open doorway. Overhearing my comment he stopped abruptly and proudly said, "I am Christos, I am from Greece, and I shall translate this problem for you, my friends." It was one of those very rare times that I was caught so off guard that I literally had nothing to say and just handed the paper to Christos. As he read over the form we saw his forehead wrinkle and then watched him as he took a deep breath displaying disappoint-ment. He handed the paper back to my huge Bulgarian colleague and said that the writing was no type of Greek he had ever seen. Was I sure it was Greek? I explained to my colleagues that in the part of America I come from if we do not understand something we say it is "Greek" to us.

305

Christos started to smile and said that in Greece, if you do not understand something they say, "It is all Chinese to me." We all started to laugh and then I announced that I was buying coffee and pie at the restaurant across the street in celebration of this great moment. I think part of their obvious good cheer was more in tune with the free pie and coffee but nevertheless it was a great topic of conversation over the next hour when we decided that we needed to find a colleague from China to see what they say when they don't understand the written words on a page.

This was a moment well worth remembering and was the reason I started collecting any and all of the international sayings I could gather from my colleagues and from my travels over the years to come. Each of the following sayings not only reveals a pearl of wisdom, it also sheds light on the culture of its origin.

Throughout countless hours of extremely personal dialogue with officers from war zones "all over the world," while sharing tea, birch juice, vodka, baoba brew, coffee, beer, grog, fermented milk (not always cow), rockia, sweet yogurt, wine, and some other unknown, really bad tasting drinks, we all sought to understand each other. Through sharing ancient cultural sayings and phrases of wisdom, we discovered how truly the same we all are.

Figure 26.1 Military and police shoulder insignia patches from around the world.

Figure 26.2 Military and police shoulder insignia patches from around the world.

Russia

Eat your breakfast alone.
Share your lunch with a friend.
Give your supper to your enemy.

Senegal

The more I know,
the more I know, I don't know.

Portugal

Not all that shines is pure or gold.

Jordan

Men are measured by their doings.

Bangladesh

That which you do now, you must live with later.

Italy

The hurried cat gives birth to blind kittens.

France

Effort is measured by accomplishment.

Kenya

Better to be a live monkey than to be a dead lion.

Russia

Speak clearly, and briefly.
Ask little, and leave quickly.

Macedonia

We fight whom we hate, but kill whom we fear.

Ghana

The more water, the weaker the tea.
Don't talk too much.

Italy

Who goes slowly,
goes safe and far.

China

The longest journey will start with the first step.

Finland and Kenya

The wounds of weapons will heal.
The wounds of words will always bleed.

Russia

Only the fool is fearless.

Germany

Scars are the signature of courage, not medals.

Spain

A dull wit can never wheel a clever sword.

Finland

Hopelessness is a greater darkness than night.

Austria

Good and bad dwells within us all.
Finding the good in some is a difficult task.

India

The truth does not have friends or enemies.
It stands alone.

Egypt

A gift given gives greatest joy to the giver.

Portugal

Don't leave until tomorrow, what you can do now.

Jordan

All the knowledge of each person is but a small stream going into a great ocean.

Russia

The future is born today.

Spain

Better to be a clever fox than a strong bull.
Foxes are not eaten.

Italy

Who fishes sleeping,
will awaken with hunger.

Norway
Even a small bump in the road can overturn a cart that is too heavy.

Portugal
Whoever wants everything now, loses all later.

Jordan
Eat your breakfast as a king. Eat your lunch as a prince. Eat your supper as a pauper.

Ghana
Better to be a day devil than a night angel.

Russia
Briefness is the sister of talent.

Romania
When the water is not clear, you can catch the biggest fish.

Malaysia
Your good friends will never tell the true bad things about you.

Kenya
He who counts the gifts is a friend to no one.

Italy
Love your friends, respect your enemies.

Russia
We have so many heroes because we have so many fools.

Portugal
Eye for eye, tooth for tooth, will never end.

Bangladesh
Barking dogs seldom bite.

Norway
Behind the clouds, the sky is always blue.

Jordan
You reap what you have planted.

Portugal
For a good understander, half a word is enough.

Russia
We have heroes because they do not know the real danger.

Bangladesh
When many important people work together, nothing gets done.

Portugal
When a donkey speaks, the others put their ears down.

Jordan
It is good to die while learning.

Cameroon
Don't bite more than you can chew.

Russia
Only the hardworking horse is whipped.

Portugal
The son of a fish knows how to swim.

Pakistan
An army of dogs that is led by a lion will defeat an army of lions that is led by a dog.

Russia
Do not be in a hurry to finish your work. You will just receive more work sooner.

Portugal
Who does not cry, does not understand.

Bangladesh
If you learn that there is no end to learning about life, you will learn about all things forever.

France
Cleverness without accomplishment is only waste.

Jordan
Even a small bug can make a lion's eye bleed.

Portugal
Do not buy
what you cannot pay.

Great Britain
When you do good for another, good will come back to you.

Egypt
A dead bull will not pull a plow no matter how hard he is beaten.

Portugal
A thief that steals from a thief will have 100 years of forgiveness.

Sweden
Similar children play the best.

Estonia
When your ego is bigger than your purse, you will soon be poor.

Bangladesh
The young seek to conquer the complex, while the old seek to master the simple.

Jordan
The child of a duck can always swim.

Portugal
Who loves the ugly,
it seems beautiful to him.

Pakistan
Defeat is an orphan while victory has many fathers.

Cameroon
Slow water runs very deep.

Turkey
If you do not touch mud, your hands will never get dirty.

Portugal
There are not three without two.

Bangladesh
They that have nothing
can see the future clearly.

Portugal
He who sees faces
does not see hearts.

Nigeria
When the lion is missing, the monkey becomes king.

Romania
Wherever we come from, and whatever language we speak, our laughing and crying all sound the same.

Portugal
Tell me with whom you are and I will tell you who you are.

Egypt
The skin may be different but the blood is always the same.

Cameroon
When an animal changes its lair, it also changes its prey.

Portugal
In a blind land, he who has but one eye is king.

Bangladesh
Take fruit in morning,
take fruit in afternoon,
take no fruit in evening.

311

Portugal
Who runs for fun
will never become tired.

Turkey
Work as though you are
going to live forever, but
think that you are going to
die tomorrow.

Cameroon
The river has a lot of bends,
because it has no body, it
does not know the course
to take.

Portugal
Between husband and wife,
do not put your spoon.

Ukraine
When you choose to eat
good and choose to sleep
well, God will grant you
health.

Portugal
Who has a skin,
will fear.

Norway
Caught between the wood
and the bark.

Germany
When you feed the ego of
a person who thinks they
have greatness with words
of sugar, it is like throwing
food on the floor for a dog
to eat.
You always know they will
feast.

Kenya
Love is blind but friend-
ship is clairvoyant.

Italy
Instead of tearing down
your house, build a better
house, or else you will
have nowhere to live.

Portugal
Better one bird in your
hand, than two flying.

Norway
Better one bird in your bag,
than two on the roof.

Russia
Hope dies last.

Italy
When you seek revenge,
dig a grave for two.

India
A dull knife and a dull
mind.
Both are dangerous.

Portugal
With the boss away,
holiday is in the house.

Cameroon
The blind also close their
eyes when they go to bed.

Bangladesh
Some who cannot dance
criticize the floor.

Greece
The mother of a killer feels
better than the mother of a
dead man.

Russia
Do not trust anyone, not
even yourself.

Denmark
It is nice to be important,
but it is more important to
be nice.

Portugal
The thief is also the one
that stands at the gate as
the other goes into the
garden.

Kenya
If you look very hard, you
will find.

Cameroon
If a blind man says that he will stone you, know that he is standing on a stone.

China
Blood does not wash out blood.

Spain
We are closer to the God that is above, when we are on our knees.

Greece
Better to be in a courtroom, than in a grave.

Fiji
Who God casts upon my shore, I shall welcome.

Russia
A new broom sweeps in a new way.

Portugal
It is quicker to catch a liar, than a cripple.

Norway
To purchase affection will bankrupt the heart.

Bulgaria
Nations in war run out of money before they run out of blood.

Fiji
Love is a good disease that everyone can catch.

Senegal
Pacifists are parasites that feed upon the courage of others.

Philippines
To learn today is to lead tomorrow.

Kenya
For evil to grow it is enough for good people to do nothing.

India
If he eats until he is full, and still has more food, it is good to give it to one who hungers.

Egypt
If it was not for my tongue my back would not be beaten.

Philippines
When a man throws a stone upon you throw bread back upon him.

Egypt
If we see only the future we blind our eyes for this day.

Norway
Do to others what you would like done back to you.

Jordan
If a man is truly strong then he is gentle to the weak.

Romania
Instead of letting your mother cry, make his mother cry instead.

Bangladesh
A horse that can be forced into the water cannot be forced to drink.

Greece
Rage is blind, courage has sight.

Iceland
When ignorance is banished and hunger is fed only then will there be peace.

Sweden
To give cause to your enemy is to give victory to your enemy.

Zimbabwe
Cowards live with fear every day.

Brazil
When you are loved by those that you love, you are the envy of the king.

Switzerland
We learn by our failures, not by our successes.

Egypt
If you interfere between the onion and the skin, you will only gain a bad smell upon you.

Norway
Empty food cans make the most noise.

Greece
Hope is to smile when sadness is around you.

Bulgaria
If you eat the bird you will never eat the egg.

Jordan
If you escape from the lion do not try to hunt him back.

Egypt
Do not attend the sale of what you have not harvested.

Greece
Hate is a fire that burns the hands of whoever holds it.

Finland
Friends do not keep count.

Zimbabwe
All will have their own black cloud.

Scotland
Storms and tears wash away all dust and pride.

Iceland
Wine and stupidity often fill the same cup.

Kenya
The true eye of love is blind to ugliness.

Egypt
The strength of a woman comes from her knowing her weakness.
The weakness of a man comes from him not knowing his weakness.

Fiji
If we never try, we never fail. Our limits will be unknown.

Egypt
Our life is always dangerous because we could always die.

Norway
As you shout alone in the forest you will only answer yourself.

Brazil
Better to cook and eat one bird than to hunger chasing a flock.

Portugal
The quietest ocean is the deepest.

Ghana
When the ground is too hot you must walk like a cat.

India
It is easy to confuse a weak mind with a twisted fact, or an arrogant person with a false compliment.

Czech Republic
If you live a bad life at least die good.

Russia
Only fools have the same thoughts.

Denmark

Those who succeed seldom complain.

Finland

The fight you run from will never end.

India

Money in the purse is like water poured on the sand, so quickly gone.

Finland

In the world of political correctness, ignorance must be defended.

Denmark

If what has been given has been asked for it cannot be called a gift.

Senegal

When you do not have, you become thankful for what you do have.

When you have all you become thankful for nothing.

Italy

When the cat dies, all the mice rejoice.

Spain

We love from a heart that has no eyes.

Sri Lanka

Gold and love will always shine, while silver and hate will tarnish.

Estonia

Do not be impressed with the words of a fool.

Even a broken watch is correct twice a day.

Philippines

Always look back to your beginnings or you will never reach your destination.

Ghana

That which is politically incorrect is usually true.

Denmark

They who pay choose the music.

Venezuela

When good is quiet evil becomes loud.

Poland

Crime is strong when punishment is weak.

Italy

Criminals are only strong when a country is weak.

Ukraine

Better to be poor in the purse and rich in the heart.

Russia

My God, save me from my friends. I can cope with my enemies myself.

Jordan

A wise enemy is better than an ignorant friend.

Germany

Wounds will stop bleeding but scars will always be there.

Italy

If you want to reveal the real character of a person give them power over others.

Egypt

Who loves us, we love them, and share all that is ours.

Who hates us, we hate them, and cast them from our sight.

Russia

Better is the enemy of good.

Norway
Your enemy will stab your front, while your friend will stab your back.

Jordan
I will sacrifice my eyes for a true friend.

Scotland
The old dog with scars will be respected by some and feared by all others.

Egypt
Shyness in men brings poverty.
Shyness in women brings disgrace.

Philippines
Only the brave man will dare to take risk.
Only the risk taker will survive.

Iceland
If we needed brains to have children then the world would not be so stupid.

Russia
Living is very dangerous, each day you die a little more.

England
The child of a thief knows how to steal.

Senegal
Age gives no gift of wisdom.
Only pain grows into wisdom.

Hungary
Hate is a fire that only burns the hater.

Egypt
The door that a bad wind comes through must be locked and not just closed.

Turkey
The shoemaker's child goes barefoot.
The baker's child goes hungry.
The roofer's house always leaks.

Italy
Never step into clouded water.
You cannot see how deep it truly is.

Scotland
When you serve yourself, your life will never be good enough.
When you serve others, your life will be rewarded.

Nigeria
The sleep of the laborer is the best.

Russia
We were born to die.
What we accomplish before our death is all that matters.

Jordan
No one is so rich that they can let a friend be lost.

Thailand
One should not have 100 dollars.
One should have 100 friends.

Great Britain
Heavy lies the head that wears the crown.

Egypt
The tongue of the gossip will always be bitten.

Italy
Beware when your shadow is not alone.

Jordan
Friendship grows
during the worst of times,
not the best.

Germany
Hypocrisy is in medals,
not in scars.

Turkey
The stone that was thrown,
the word that was said, and
the life that has passed,
never comes back again.

United States
It is not the size of the cat in
the fight but the size of the
fight in the cat.

Italy, Spain, United States
It is easier to get forgiveness than permission.

Romania
Death is a reward for a life
filled with pain.

Senegal
When you are young, you
talk about your victories.
When you are old, you talk
about your losses.

Germany
There are two sides to
every medal.

Canada
If you are not living on the
edge you are taking up too
much space.

United Kingdom
Feast upon your morning
meal as if you were a king.
Dine upon your midday
meal as if you were a
prince.
Pick upon your evening
meal as if you were but a
pauper.

Ghana
When the old die you can
look back.
When the young die
you can only look for-
ward to that which has not
been.

Turkey
The sheep separated from
the flock is eaten by the
wolf.

Turkey
An ember burns where it
falls.

Russia
Pain is life—life is pain.
Without pain there is no
life.

Chile
If you worry about tomor-
row you will miss today.

India
People who ask to make
choices for you will make
those choices in their own
best interest.

Turkey
What flares up fast
extinguishes soon.

Romania
The path to the stars
is only through hardship.

Thailand
You cannot have an argu-
ment when people agree.

Kenya
Kill the head and even the
biggest body will fall.

Bulgaria
It is good to know your
friend.
It is better to know your
enemy.

Turkey
He who gets up in anger
sits down in loss.

Ghana
From the words of a stupid
person you will know
how to avoid other stupid
people in your future.

Switzerland
The oldest rams have the
hardest horns.

Chile
The devil knows more
because he is old, not
because he is wise.

Turkey
The cock that crows at the
wrong time is killed.

Kenya
Fat dogs do not bite.

Sweden
Fat dogs do not hunt.

Scotland
When you work in a large
factory it is best to drink in
a small pub.

Austria
Better a big belly from
drinking than a bad back
from working.

Nigeria
Blood and wine—wine
and blood, one is always
near the other.

Spain
A rich man has friends.
A poor man has only
money.

France
It is best to cry at the misfortune of others, and
laugh at the faults within
ourselves.

Hungary
Advice is best given
when asked for.

Iraq
Cowards cry for them-
selves, while the brave cry
for others.

Sweden
Nothing is so bad
that it cannot get better.

Thailand
The tallest blade of grass
gets cut first.

Turkey
Even the strongest stone
cannot stop hunger.

Russia
If you see an officer running in peace time, this
causes laughter.
If you see an officer running in wartime, this
causes panic.
Officers should not run.

Iceland
A good thought
is a written thought.

Argentina
Not all fingers are the
same but they all make up
the fist.

Sweden
Armies wear uniforms
so they can tell who is
different.

Figure 26.3 What do you see now?

What do you sense now from the same picture you saw at the beginning of this book?

After you have shared the experiences and lessons learned from those who survived the war zone environment, are you the same person with the same perspectives you had before being touched by those who reached out to you with their experiences? For the sake of world peace, we hope you have learned something from what we have shared.

INDEX

For Product Safety Concerns and Information please contact our EU
representative GPSR@taylorandfrancis.com
Taylor & Francis Verlag GmbH, Kaufingerstraße 24, 80331 München, Germany

www.ingramcontent.com/pod-product-compliance
Ingram Content Group UK Ltd.
Pitfield, Milton Keynes, MK11 3LW, UK
UKHW021622240425
457818UK00018B/692